Green, Growth, Globalization and Governance: Challenges and Opportunities

Green, Growth, Globalization and Governance: Challenges and Opportunities

Editors:
Manoj Bhatia, Anupam Saxena, Upasana Singh,
Richa Mishra, Sugandha Shanker

Academic Partners

Cambridge Scientific Publishers

© 2017 Cambridge Scientific Publishers

Printed and bound by CMP Limited, Poole, Dorset.

British Library Cataloguing in Publication Data
A catalogue record for this book has been requested

Library of Congress Cataloguing in Publication Data
A catalogue record has been requested

ISBN 978-1-908106-62-9 (paperback)

Cambridge Scientific Publishers
45 Margett Street
Cottenham
Cambridge CB24 8QY
UK

www.cambridgescientificpublishers.com

Contents

Preface

This edited volume is the outcome of intellectually stimulating deliberations in the 5th edition of our International Conference on "Green, Growth, Globalization and Governance (4G): Challenges and Opportunities". The "4G" theme chosen for the conference was based on intensive discussions on the past editions of the conference that talked about Growth, Globalization and Governance (3G) but had overlooked the connection of these 3Gs with Green.

The incorporation of Green in the 5th edition of the conference was felt to be critical as our planet is undergoing severe environmental challenges, for example: highly polluted cities causing deadly diseases and deaths, natural disasters including floods, droughts, earthquakes and landslides. These environmental challenges are a result of unplanned and unmanaged economic growth devoid of incorporation of good governance and global standards.

All this generated a strong urge and requirement for a platform which could discuss and share experiences of experts from various disciplines regarding the achievement of balance between growth, globalization and governance so that green (environment) can be utilised at an optimum level and maintained for the future. Delegates, speakers and keynote speakers comprising renowned researchers, corporate and academicians from across the globe also suggested making our conference 4G instead of 3G.

This made the conference a combination of various interdisciplinary approaches from multidisciplinary perspectives. The conference also had prestigious national and international partners: St Clouds State University, USA; Cambridge Central Asia Forum, Jesus College, University of Cambridge and Indian Society for Training and Development.

The presence and participation of eminent researchers enriched the theme by broadening our horizons and giving us a new insight and confidence about the role of interdisciplinary researches in maintaining the balance between the 4 G's.

Based on the papers presented by practitioners, academicians and researchers during the two day conference held from February 3–5, 2017 this volume is a collection of selected research papers reflecting upon a new idea about sustainable growth.

Dr. R.L Raina
Vice Chancellor
JK Lakshmipat University

Acknowledgements

The Editors would like to express profound gratitude to Shri Bharat Hari Singhania, honorable Chancellor of JK Lakshmipat University for his inspiration and support in publishing this volume.

We are indebted to Dr. R.L. Raina, Vice Chancellor for his most valuable guidance, inspiration, constructive criticism and ever ready attitude to get along with us in times of desperate needs.

We express our heartfelt thanks to our partners: St. Cloud State University, USA, Cambridge Central Asia Forum, Cambridge, UK, The Indian Society for Training & Development (ISTD), India for their cooperation and support.

We also wish to extend our special thanks to Professor Dave Harris, Dean, Herberger Business School and Professor Ben Baliga, Graduate Director, Engineering Management, St. Cloud State University, USA for their support, sage advice and guidance during the conference.

We express our deepest gratitude to all our sponsors, especially Mr. C. Vasudevan from BSE Limited and Mrs. Smita Singh from UPSIDC for generating sponsorship.

We are thankful to all of the contributing authors without whom this work would have never seen the light of the day.

We would be failing in our duty if we do not acknowledge the cooperation and support extended to us by our faculty colleagues and student volunteers without whom this conference and the volume could not have been possible.

We wish to thank our publisher Cambridge Scientific Publishers, UK for their support in making this volume possible.

Last but not least we would like to thank all our readers whose citations and use of this volume will contribute to their future research and will provide encouragement not only to us but also to our authors.

Editors

Green, Growth, Globalization and Governance (4Gs) Integration and Convergence: The Mantra

Roshan Lal Raina* & Anupam Saxena*

Abstract

India is currently at the stage of implementing several structural reforms aimed at sustainable development. It is in a state of transition to new forms of society-building which are not only growth centric but also sustainable. Despite rich natural resources, youthful human resource base and favourable climatic conditions, the country is facing a number of challenges in dealing with the interface between profit making and sustainable development.

The integration of Green, Growth, Globalization and Governance (4Gs) for achieving optimum output in a sustainable manner, the convergence of 4Gs in planning and implementation issues related to the 4Gs appears as the way forward.

In order to overcome the challenge of sustainable growth, the country is following top-to-bottom approach in its decision-making. This often leaves the public disengaged and detached which in turn, results in ineffective and counterproductive policy outcomes with reference to the original intention. However, if an integrated approach where a feedback mechanism from bottom-up is developed, it will prove highly efficient and offer many options in addressing social, economic, political and environmental issues.

The present work will focus on benchmarking some global best practices applicable in such situations and develop a India specific solution.

Keywords: Sustainability, Policies, Green, Growth, Globalization, Governance, Reforms.

Introduction

India is in a rapid transition from a developing nation to a developed one. Its potential is being recognized by the world. In the past decade, India has witnessed substantial growth in terms of increased GDP and new businesses avenues. The country has grown economically over only a few decades and is expected to become one of the largest economies in the world in the nearest future. Despite this, India has the largest number of people living under the international poverty line, approximately, 224 million people i.e. thirty per cent of the population is living below the poverty line (Business Today, 2016).

---

* JK Lakshmipat University, Jaipur

A study by World Food Programme states that India has a quarter of the world's undernourished people and is home to 194.6 million undernourished people. This is three times the entire population of France and one quarter of all undernourished people on the planet (World Food Programme, 2016). Also, according to another study, India has the largest population of illiterate adults in the world i.e. 287 million people (The Hindu, 2014).

The given statistics paint a contradictory picture, where on one hand India is achieving highest standards of economic growth; while on the other hand, a large portion of its population is suffering from severe poverty, hunger and illiteracy. On top of this, unplanned growth and unmanaged development has resulted in increasing levels of air pollution in Indian cities, some of which are amongst the highest in the world.

Besides air pollution, water, soil, noise and thermal pollution are the root cause of many diseases and the situation is worsening day by day. The ill effects of unmanaged growth can be witnessed in the form of disasters like the Chennai floods in December 2015 and 2016, Alaknanda floods in June 2013, Sikkim Earthquake in 2011, landfall in West Bengal in May'2009 (Seidler & Kamaljit, 2016). These disasters have not only impacted human life but also our businesses to a great extent.

According to Assocham (Associated Chambers of Commerce of India), the automobile industry, small and medium enterprises, engineering, IT (Information Technology) firms, ITeS (Information Technology enabled services) firms, textiles and tourism sectors were badly hit by the Chennai floods of 2015 which alone had an economic impact at Rs 15,000 crore (Sengupta, 2015). This is an estimated loss from one such disaster. Imagine the impact on the businesses if such episodes reoccur due to changing climate and environmental degradation which is devastating our day to day lives and businesses.

The costs of dealing with climate-induced disasters are rising and wiping out the hard-earned gains of development. The increase in record-breaking climate anomalies cannot be explained by natural variability alone and is clearly consistent with that expected from rising temperatures. For the businesses which are dependent on natural resources for their raw material, these changes have brought additional burdens and challenges.

A major cause of environmental degradation is open access to many environmental resources, which are regarded as common property by economic agents. These agents lack incentives to take the full costs of environmental degradation into account. Such costs will tend to increase over time as resources are degraded or depleted and thus become scarcer. This highlights the plight of weak social and policy mechanisms of the country which are also at a transition stage and need time and money to overcome these challenges.

Therefore, this work aims to suggest that the process of making policies can be made more robust through integration of governance and global best practices for growth and environmental conservation. The work consists of a section dealing with challenges for integration of 4G's followed by current trends and a model ending with conclusions and suggestions.

Challenges for integration of 4Gs

The process of integrating governance with growth, globalization and green is a challenging task mainly due to following reasons: lack of awareness, lack of education, lack of adequate infrastructure, poor implementation of CSR & environmental policies, corruption, and caste based politics etc.

These challenges are not confined to India only but are being faced globally. Therefore, in order to deal with these challenges in a planned manner the United Nations in 2015 gave seventeen Sustainable Development Goals (SDGs listed in Appendix: table 1) that set a broad guideline to achieve sustainable development.

Sustainable development in India is perceived in two broad ways: the first one focuses on protection of resources and relies on bureaucracy that often misuses its power against the communities dependent on the resources. The second one focuses on protecting the resource through a holistic approach which focuses on optimal utilization of resources through protection of health, livelihood and integration of other aspects like education, food security etc. (Gadgil, 2016).

The first approach usually leaves the people disengaged and detached with the policies that are formulated for their benefits because the tough bureaucratic system takes a long time to infilterate into the social fabric of a country like India which is extremely diverse and lacks basic infrastructural facilities as reflected in figure 1. Generating awareness, interest and motivation for new policies is a very challenging task especially amongst the rural and urban poor; the majority of whom are uneducated and in some situations lack trust in the government systems. The second approach, however focuses on building an integrated model which should combine the 4Gs.

3

Figure 1: Current Situation of Sustainable Development Policies in India

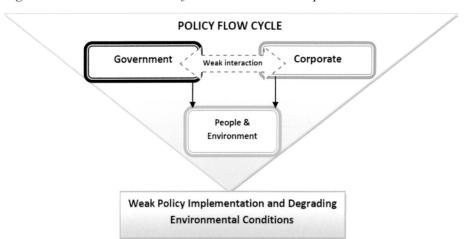

Government mechanisms although extremely useful and valuable cannot address the issues of sustainable development without the cooperation from citizens and corporates. There is a strong need to develop a public private partnership under which oppurtunities can be provided to private entities/businesses to play a major role and are engaged to look at these issues through a holistic viewpoint rather than providing solutions through a piecemeal approach.

Few important trends of sustainability followed by corporates which are globally practiced are illustrated here.These trends have been adopted by various corporates who are taking the second approach and working towards integration of local specific inclusions keeping in mind the changing socio-economic, ecological and cultural dimensions. As of now, only a few such examples exist in India and this work wants to discuss how these globally successful models can help in enhancing the existing Indian models and developing newer ones.

Current Sustainable Business Trends

The past few years have witnessed a tremendous shift of businesses towards sustainability with an approach to integrate green, growth, globalization and governance. In this section, a few of the latest global trends will be discussed where corporates have taken joint initiatives to curb the adverse impact of environmental degradation, the consequences of which have been felt in the form of resource shrinkage leading to lack of raw materials. For example, the total annual turnover risk for publicly listed companies across the globe due to deforestation is estimated to be up to US$906 billion (Simpsom, 2016), in another example, the lack of clean fresh water results in more than $14 billion of costs, including fines, loss of production, new treatment systems and securing water from new sources (Makower, 2017).

Development of SDG Compass
World Business Council for Sustainable Development (WBCSD) which is a CEO-led organization of over 200 leading businesses in collaboration with global compact and Global Reporting Initiative (GRI) has developed SDG compass. This compass has been developed to provide guidance for companies on how to align business strategies with SDGs, they have created a business hub which is a dynamic online platform showcasing businesses insight, emerging tools and resources in the space. Companies across the globe are using these tools to help them approach the SDGs holistically (Makower, 2017). This is an important initiative to achieve sustainability through the integration of businesses. This compass can also be used by the policy makers and corporates in India who are willing to take forward the initiative of sustainable development.

Healthcare Initiative
The second interesting initiative where corporates like GlaxoSmithKline (GSK) have aligned with SDG is on health and is focussed on strengthening healthcare infrastructure fighting malaria, improving access to antiretroviral treatment for HIV, working to help prevent child deaths and tackling non-communicable diseases.

Agri-business Alliance
The third example is the Agri-business Alliance, which is a group of 36 agricultural businesses joined together at Singapore to tackle environmental challenges in farming supply chains and communities around the world. This CEO-led private-sector initiative aims to tackle the SDGs, regarding food security and promote sustainable agriculture.

Champions 12.3
The fourth example is the formulation of Champions 12.3 in Davos, Switzerland on 21st. January, 2016 at the World Economic Forum which is a coalition of 30 leaders. These leaders have taken initiatives to reduce food losses and food waste globally. This coalition's primary objective is to reduce food wastage across the supply chains by 2030. (World Resources Institute, 2016). Thirty leaders from business, government and foundations committed to work together to cut food waste by half over 15 years because food waste and loss is a $940 billion problem in unrealized revenue to farmers and producers. And, because unharvested or uneaten food rots on fields or in landfills, food waste emits enough methane to account for 8 percent of global greenhouse gas emissions (Makower, 2017).

These examples are a few trends which are corporate initiatives and have been adopted not under pressure from government or to meet any other compliance. These initiatives are solely the result of realisation that government alone cannot save this planet earth and business leaders have to take the initiative on their own so that the 4Gs of Green, Growth, Globalization and Governance could be addressed in totality and this is the reason why for this work, we have considered them as our benchmarking initiatives.

These initiatives are good example of a coalition between government, corporates as well as private individuals, however, this coalition is functional only in some areas across the globe (Lipinski, O'Connor, & Hanson, 2016) because there is a lack of commitment of the business community to transform their business models to deliver social and environmental values, and work in partnership with the public sector and civil society.

Proposed Model

The current situation in India is that policy exists, however implementation of policy at grass root levels is low. This happens because India is a vast country with diverse ethnic groups, religions and cultural identities as well as dfferent geographical terrains, languages, making the policy implementation process tough and non – uniform for the government agencies.

Secondly, there is a strong sense of lack of ownership amongst people, corporates and government which makes the tasks of policy implementation even tougher for the government mechanisms alone.

Therefore, this work tends to propose a holistic approach of policy implementation and formulations based on some of the successful models discussed in the previous sections. As those examples suggest the main motivation in developing either the SDG compass and Champions 12.3 or taking an healthcare initiative as well as in agrialliances comes from the corporates who have taken the main lead and facilitated the government mechanisms as well as developed a strong public – private partnership which leads to sustainable profit generation and meets the SDGs as depicted in figure 2.

Figure 2: Proposed Model

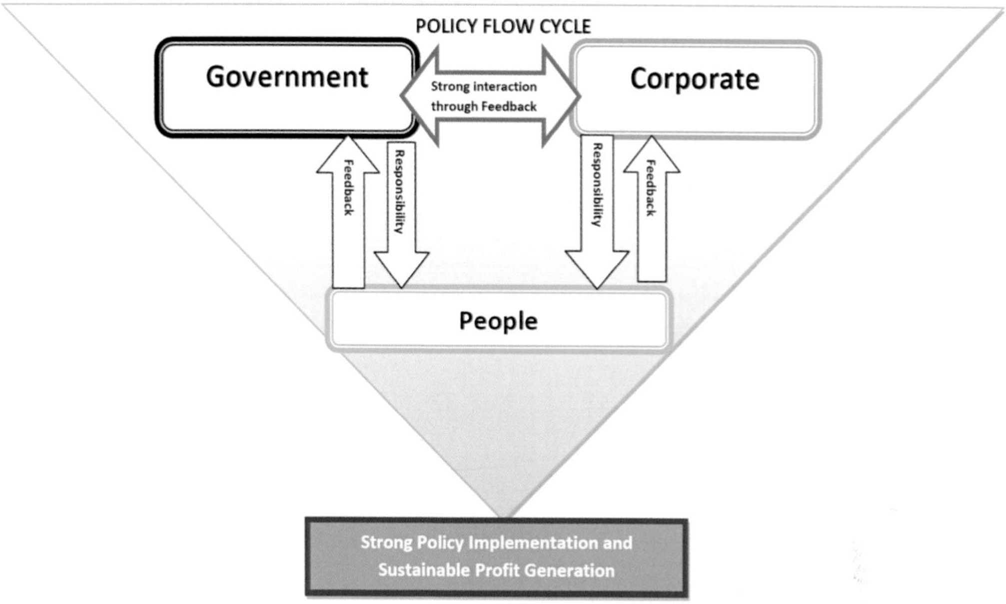

A similar motivation is required by Indian corporates who are beginning to realise the relevance of sustainable development. This can be achieved only if all the three actors i.e. government, corporates and the people share similar responsibilities and collaborate with each other through feedbacks and interaction process.

Conclusion

India is currently in a stage where development has not fully engulfed the environmental notion. Still there is a ray of hope from most parts of the country and different sectors of the business community. small corrective actions if taken through puplic private partnership in the right direction with proper instruments, motivation and strategies can go several miles. This will not only help to protect the existing environment but also help in achieving the SDGs through good governance and sustainable growth.

This goal can be accomplished by aligning government policies with business interests in a sustainable manner as discussed in some examples in previous sections and followed by one of the Indian states Himachal pradesh which has taken an initiative to implement biodiversity act mandatory which will ensure that industries and companies using biological resources of the state have to share their profits with the people (Down to Earth, 2016). This example exhibits a keen interest of government mechanisms in developing policies for sustainable growth and gives us new directions for improvement and incorporation of growth and governance.

Appendix 1: Sustainable Development Goals (SDGs)

Serial No	Sustainable Development Goals
Goal 1	End poverty in all its forms everywhere
Goal 2	End hunger, achieve food security and improved nutrition and promote sustainable agriculture
Goal 3	Ensure healthy lives and promote well-being for all at all ages
Goal 4	Ensure inclusive and equitable quality education and promote lifelong learning opportunities for all
Goal 5	Achieve gender equality and empower all women and girls
Goal 6	Ensure availability and sustainable management of water and sanitation for all
Goal 7	Ensure access to affordable, reliable, sustainable and modern energy for all
Goal 8	Promote sustained, inclusive and sustainable economic growth, full and productive employment and decent work for all
Goal 9	Build resilient infrastructure, promote inclusive and sustainable industrialization and foster innovation
Goal 10	Reduce inequality within and among countries
Goal 11	Make cities and human settlements inclusive, safe, resilient and sustainable
Goal 12	Ensure sustainable consumption and production patterns
Goal 13	Take urgent action to combat climate change and its impacts*
Goal 14	Conserve and sustainably use the oceans, seas and marine resources for sustainable development
Goal 15	Protect, restore and promote sustainable use of terrestrial ecosystems, sustainably manage forests, combat desertification, and halt and reverse land degradation and halt biodiversity loss
Goal 16	Promote peaceful and inclusive societies for sustainable development, provide access to justice for all and build effective, accountable and inclusive institutions at all levels
Goal 17	Strengthen the means of implementation and revitalize the global partnership for sustainable development

References

Business Today. (2016, 10 03). India has highest number of people living below poverty line: World Bank:Retrieved 02,24,2017 from http://www.businesstoday.in/current/economy-politics/india-has-highest-number-of-people-living-below-poverty-line-world-bank/story/238085.html

Gadgil, M. (2016). Today's Environmentalism Time for Constructive Cooperative Action. *Economic & Political Weekly*, 51(46), 57–61.

Jain, R., & Palwa, K. (2015). Air Pollution and Health. Retrieved 03 16, 2017, from http://www.teriin.org/: http://www.teriin.org/projects/teddy/pdf/air-pollution-health-discussion-paper.pdf

Lipinski, B., O'Connor, C., & Hanson, C. (2016). *SDG Target 12.3 on Food Loss and Waste: 2016 Progress Report.*

Makower,J.E. (2017). *Tenth Annual State of Green Business, 2017.*

NitiAyog. (2016, 02 22). Retrieved 03 19, 2017, from Niti Ayog Official website: http://niti.gov.in/content/goal-2-end-hunger-achieve-food-security-and-improved-nutrition-and-promote-sustainable

Seidler, R., & Kamaljit, B. (2016, October). Ancient Risks' Current Challenges in Himalayas. *Economic & Political Weekly*, 51(44), pp. 63–67.

Sengupta, N. (2015, 12 04). *Chennai flood losses pegged at Rs 15,000cr.* Retrieved 03 12, 2017, from http://timesofindia.indiatimes.com/business/india-business/Chennai-flood-losses-pegged-at-Rs-15000cr/articleshow/50036330.cms

Simpsom, P. (2016). *Revenue at risk:why adressing deforestation is critical to business sucess.* CDP: London.

The Hindu. (2014, 01 30). *The Hindu.* Retrieved 02 20, 2017, from thehindu.com: http://www.thehindu.com/news/national/indias-illiterate-population-largest-in-the-world-says-unesco-report/article5631797.ece

World Food Programme. (2016, 07 26). *World Food Programme.* Retrieved 03 02, 2017, from wfp.org: https://www.wfp.org/stories/10-fact-about-food-and-nutrition-india

World Resources Institute. (2016, 01 21). World Resources Institute. Retrieved February 26, 2017, from http://www.wri.org: http://www.wri.org/news/2016/01/release-new-champions-123-coalition-inspire-action-reduce-food-loss-waste

Implementing Cash and In-Kind Transfer in Global and Indian Context

Debdatta Mukherjee*

Abstract

Cash and in-kind transfers in various forms have been used in different countries to target welfare support to the poor and achieve other social objectives. However, empirical evidences suggest that their success is highly dependent on the context and intended objectives. A number of such cash and in-kind transfer schemes exist in India. The Public Distribution System is an important example of in-kind transfer scheme in India that intends to deliver food grains to poor households at subsidized rates. However, this policy has been subject to criticism for a long time on grounds of poor targeting, a leaking delivery system, rising subsidies and inferior quality of grains. Thus, this article aims to discuss the relative efficacy of cash and in-kind transfers and the extent to which their efficacy is context dependent. It also intends to discuss the lessons that the policy makers in India could learn from international experiences with variants of these two types of transfer schemes. Further, this article attempts to make an assessment of the primary causes of the failures of Public Distribution System in India and also discusses the different types of reforms that need to be introduced in order to address these critical shortcomings.

Keywords: Cash and In-kind transfer, Public Distribution System, Targeting, Subsidies.

Introduction

Most of the poor countries in the world suffer from problems such as: growing inequality, poverty and rising levels of food insecurity. Due to increase in the level of vulnerability, social protection has become an integral issue of concern. In order to protect deprived households from suffering these vulnerabilities and to target welfare support to them, social assistance programmes like cash and in-kind transfers have been implemented in many countries.

In fact, in recent times, the scheme of cash transfer has been gaining much support from the economists and policymakers in India. They contend that cash transfer is the best instrument for delivering social security and fighting problems related to chronic poverty, food insecurity, and inequality. This is because cash transfer gives more choices to the people, produce '*multiplier effect*', create lower chances of corruption and is more cost-effective. Moreover, the success stories of this scheme in other parts of the world have made them believe that cash transfer is perhaps the most efficient means to respond to poverty and improve all provisions of social welfare.

*IIM Ahmedabad

However, what they probably do not realize is that this success is highly context and goal specific. This argument is supported by many empirical evidences suggesting that cash transfers might not always be best suited to meet all social objectives. While conditional cash transfer (CCT) programmes like *Bolsa Familia* in Brazil and *Oportunaides* in Mexico have been very successful in improving children enrollment in schools, the impact of such schemes in improving their nutrition levels is scarce.

India hosts a number of such social assistance programmes. One example of such in-kind subsidies in India is the Public Distribution System (PDS) aiming to ensure food security to all. However, despite intentions to help the poor by providing them with low cost food and nutrition, PDS is continuously suffering from several innate and systemic flaws including poor targeting, corruption, rising subsidies, low quality of grains and no dietary diversity. Thus, in order to address these critical shortcomings, different types of reforms need to be introduced.

This paper is divided into three sections. **Section 1** discusses the relative efficacy of cash and in-kind transfers. **Section 2** mentions the lessons learnt by Indian policy makers from international experiences. **Section 3** provides an assessment of the primary causes of failure of PDS in India and suggests reforms to address these failures.

Relative Efficacy of Cash and In-Kind Transfer

This section compares the relative efficacy of cash and in-kind transfers in terms of choice, identification of beneficiaries and corruption.

Choice
One of the main advantages of cash transfer is that it allows expansion of choices for the poor and gives them the flexibility to adequately consume more of other goods that they think satisfy them better. This scheme eradicates the paternalism intrinsic in imposing a set of choices and gives sufficient discretion to poor households to spend the money in ways that they want, particularly in situations of severe cash constraints. For example, if beneficiaries decide to use the cash to pay back to microcredit institutions or usurious moneylenders, they are allowed to do so, which in turn might help them get an easy access to credit the next time. Similarly, if beneficiaries decide to use the additional income to pay for the school fees of their children, they could easily do so without any restrictions.

Many critics argue that poor people would 'waste' the money in buying tobacco and/ or alcohol and prevent their children from deriving any benefit out of the scheme. But there have been more evidences to counter rather than support this argument. For example, the findings from a case study prepared by Devereux, Marshall, MacAskill and Pelham (2005) to review the measures for protecting the rising number of vulnerable children in east and southern Africa suggests that individuals make vigilant and strategic decisions related to the use of this additional income. They do not waste the money but rather use it to meet the best interest of the household members, either in the short term (for example, buying more groceries and food) or in the long term (for example, investing in inputs for farming or meeting the school expenses of children).

On the other hand in-kind transfers are paternalistic in nature and restrict the choices of individuals. Here, the underlying rationale is that people who worry about the dejected conditions of the poor might want to just intervene because sometimes the unrestricted choice made by the poor entail negative externalities for all others who care. For example, poor parents spending less on their children's education do not only curb the progress of the child and the household but would also slow down the growth of the economy as a whole. Moreover, in order to make a choice, one needs to have awareness, access to and adequate understanding of information. In most cases, the poor people lack all of these and so might just fail to make the right choice for themselves. However, this theory has been widely criticized by many because it stands in conflict with the idea that individuals are rational actors, who would always want to maximize their utility. They are the ones who can best judge the situation that they are in and make choices accordingly.

Based on micro-economic theory, the size of the transfer, for example, whether the transfer is an *infra-marginal* or an *extra-marginal* plays a crucial role in determining the choice of transfer (whether cash or in-kind). In case of an infra-marginal transfer, in which the quantity of transfer is less than an individual typically spends on food commodities, an in-kind transfer is equivalent to a cash transfer. For instance, household '*A*' normally consumes 21kg of rice at the rate of Rs 5/kg. He spends Rs. 50 to purchase 10 kg rice. After getting an in-kind subsidy, the price of rice decreases to Rs 2.5/Kg (say). So, now he spends the same amount of money to purchase 20 kg of rice, which is still less than the consumption of the household. This leads to an '*income effect*' because the household could now purchase more of the good by incurring the same cost. Therefore, the family would perhaps prefer to buy rice irrespective of whether the transfer is in the form of cash or in-kind. On the other hand, an extra-marginal transfer, in which the quantity of transfer in cash or kind is more than the individual's normal expenditure on food commodities, results in both '*income effect*' and '*price effect*'. For instance, household '*B*' normally consumes 5 kg of rice at the rate of Rs 5/kg. He spends Rs. 25 to purchase 5 kg rice. After getting an in-kind subsidy, the price of rice decreases to Rs 2.5/Kg (say). So now he spends Rs 12.5 to buy the same 5kg of rice which is half of what '*B*' was spending before. In this case, cash is preferable to in-kind transfer. This is because, under the scheme of in-kind transfer, the household would be compelled to spend the money saved

(Rs. 12.5) on buying another 5 kg of rice, which is perhaps not needed. But cash transfer would allow them to spend the money in whatever way they want.

Targeting
Although the problem of identifying and targeting the potential recipients lies with both the schemes, it is perhaps more difficult to target beneficiaries in case of cash than in-kind transfers. This is because cash transfers incentivize households to identify themselves as poor (Kapur, Mukhopadhyay and Subramanium, 2008; Das et al., 2005 ; Narayanan, 2011). By doing so they intend to use the money to buy goods that they otherwise could have also afforded. Since there is a constraint on the total amount of cash that could be transferred, this kind of an 'elite capture' deprives the poor from receiving the due benefits of the programme. As a result, the rich people continue to enjoy more goods and services, while the poorest fail to meet even the basic needs. One good example to explain this is *Janani Suraksha Yojana (JSY)*, a CCT programme in India that was introduced to support institutional deliveries for pregnant women. This programme had a significant impact on in-facility births and resulted in decreased perinatal death by about 4 and neo-natal death by about 2.4 per 1000. But unfortunately due to the consistent '*elite capture*', the poorest women almost became the least likely to derive the benefits from the scheme.

On the other hand, in-kind subsidies exhibit the property of '*self-targeting*'. If used as an instrument for redistribution, they could by themselves separate out the rich and the poor (Curie and Gahvari, 2007). For example, this could be done by packaging the goods in such a way that a cost is imposed on both the actual and potential recipients. These related costs might be in terms of constraint on quantity of goods and services (for example, housing with low square footage) or on time (for example, standing in a long queue to access the goods) or on quality of the goods (for example, medium to low quality food grains). All of these would automatically lead the rich people to self-select out of the programme. However, the quality of the grains to be consumed by the poor should not also be very low so as to defeat the main purpose of the programme.

Corruption
The social policies in India are often blighted with endemic corruption at various levels. This could be due to many reasons including poor governance, lack of transparency and lower levels of awareness among the poor people. In such situations, social interventions intended to help the poor survive are bound to be corruption prone and so the case with cash and in-kind transfers is no different.

However, it is generally observed that cash transfers are less prone to leakages than in-kind transfers. This is because the process for cash transfer is simple and straightforward requiring fewer steps for completion. The money is directly transferred to the bank account of the actual recipients. This decrease in the number of middle men reduces corruption to a large extent and as a result monitoring only fewer points suffice. Since the amount of transfer is known to all, any case of deduction or non-delivery would be evident and traceable. This increases the transparency of the programme.

On the other hand, in-kind transfers involve numerous middle men making the process complex, decreasing transparency and increasing corruption. Secondly, almost all officials are paid less and so in order to make more money they tend to take bribes, cheat the poor people by giving them less of the goods or services concerned and take more money in return, steal and divert the goods to sell in the open market.

Lessons

The Indian policymakers have a lot to learn from the international experiences on how the various social assistance programmes have impacted the poor people in different parts of the world. It is only when they understand the varied contexts in which these programmes have become successful, that they would be in a position to decide which particular scheme would best suit the need of the situation.

Most of the people typically assume that cash transfer is the best instrument to respond to issues like poverty, inequality, lack of access to food, education and health care facilities. But this assumption is fallacious. Although cash transfer offers several benefits like greater choice and more transparency, it might not be the most appropriate instrument in all situations. In fact, the empirical evidences from different parts of the world suggest that in the context of food and nutrition, in-kind transfers have been more successful than cash transfers. For example, a study on *Programme de Apoyo Alimentario (PAL)*, a food assistance programme for the poor people in Mexico suggests that in-kind transfers have significantly increased the expenses of the poor households on food. In Bangladesh, the Marginal Propensity to Consume Food (MPCf) has been higher for wheat transfers than for cash transfers. Even in India, the *mid-day meal programme*, which is a conditional in-kind transfer, has a positive impact on calorie intake of children in schools.

While in-kind transfers work really well when the intention is to drive the poor towards a particular good, cash transfers work well in situations where household decisions entail positive externalities. For example, *Bolsa Familia,* one of the largest CCT programmes in the world, has increased the monthly expenditure of households on essential items like education, food and clothing by R$ 2.65, R$ 23.18 and R$ 1.34 respectively (Soares, Ribas and Osorio, 2010). The children become almost 3.6 % points less likely to remain absent and 1.6% points less likely to drop out from the school. Similarly, the *Mexican Oportunidades*, a cash transfer programme in Mexico, has led to an upsurge in school attendance and a decline in the drop-out rate. In the area of health care, another CCT programme, the *Colombian Familias en Accion* has been very successful in increasing the probability of vaccinating children up to two years of age and complying with health check-ups for children up to four years of age. The cash transfer programme in Chile has also resulted in an increase in the visit to health centres by children of less than six years of age.

Cash transfers could help in abating poverty and inequality. If individuals decide to invest the cash they receive, more income is generated. Even though the amount of cash transferred is very small and also they intend to help beneficiaries characterized as economically inactive (for example, old people, chronically sick people, etc.) people tend to invest a part of this money in trading, or in purchasing inputs like fertilizers or seeds for farming or in buying assets like livestock. Now, if these investments turn out to be profitable, then their income gets multiplied and they have more disposable income available to buy food and spend on education and health care. The findings from a case study on *National Old Age Pension program* in Lesotho suggest that the money received by old people as pensions were used in small investments, like trading, buying sewing machines for stitching clothes and buying and selling sweets, to earn profit.

The argument that cash transfers reduce poverty and inequality is also supported by other empirical evidences. In Mexico, *Oportunidades* has decreased the poverty headcount ratio by 10%, the poverty gap by 30% and the poverty security index by 45% (Standing, 2012). In Mexico and Brazil, cash transfer programmes have decreased the Gini coefficient, which is a measure of inequality, by about 2.7 points (Soares, 2007). Cash transfers also help in minimizing credit constraints and debts, which in turn reduce the inequity between the poor and the moneylender. A pilot study on the universal cash transfer in Namibia has shown an increase in the income of the poor households. This is mostly because they could buy seeds and sewing machines and also pay back their debts using the cash.

Another reason why cash transfers are largely considered to be more efficient than in-kind transfers is due to their cost-effectiveness. Unlike in-kind transfers, there is no cost involved in storing or transporting the goods in concern. The initial fixed cost is very high but the annual cost is relatively moderate. For example, in the first year when the *Oportunidades* program was just introduced in Mexico, $1.34 for every dollar was spent on cash transfer to the beneficiaries. But in the subsequent years, the amount has dropped to just 5 cents for every dollar that was spent on cash transfers (Kapur, Mukhopadhyay and Subramanium, 2008). On the other hand, in-kind transfers incur high costs and dead weight losses. The per capita benefit from the *Nutribun and milk program* in Jamaica is less than the per capita cost incurred.

Now, although there are very important lessons to be learnt from these experiences, one also needs to pay heed to the wretched infrastructural facilities in India before implementing the same. There are a very small number of schools and colleges in rural India and also among the small numbers that exist, most suffer from problems related to water, sanitation, teacher absenteeism and other essential facilities. The public hospitals lack amenities like electricity, water, beds, medical and paramedical manpower. So even if the households decide to spend their money on child education and health, the quality of service that they get in return is inferior. Therefore, India needs to reduce such kinds of supply side constraints so as to enable the impact of any programme to reach its full potential.

Failure in PDS and Suggested Reforms

The in-kind food assistance programme in India, namely the PDS, intends to provide subsidized food grains to poor households. However, this policy has been subject to critique for a long time due to restricted coverage, a leaking delivery system, rising subsidies and poor quality grains.

Targeting
One of the major challenges associated with implementing PDS in India is identifying and targeting the intended beneficiaries. This system is prone to large inclusion and exclusion errors. While many non-poor households, who can afford to buy the grains otherwise derive undue benefit out of this program, many poor and needy households simply get no access to the PDS grains. In fact, Svedberg (2012) has estimated that 25.7% of all households in India had monthly per capita expenditure below the poverty line in 2004–05. About 9.6 % of these households possessed a BPL or AAY ration card and 16.1 % did not possess the card implying that approximately two-third of the poor families were not even included in the system. This indicates a significant systemic exclusion error. On the other hand, 62% of the non-poor households possessed BPL and AAY cards, indicating a significant systemic inclusion error.

However, these errors could be reduced to a considerable extent by ensuring allocation of aadhaar cards to all eligible households, which in turn would help in identifying the potential beneficiaries in the PDS databases and eliminate the existence of any counterfeit and duplicate recipients from the rolls. Also, if the in-kind subsidy is replaced with cash transfer then systems could be created wherein the aadhaar card number is directly linked to the bank accounts of the individuals.

Diversion
Diversion of grains refers to the actual amount delivered by the Food Corporation of India (FCI) to the state government (off-take) for distribution minus the actual

amount consumed by the households. In other words, diversion refers to the quantity of grains that do not reach households of the beneficiaries. In the current debates around the efficacy of PDS, the large scale diversion of grains has become an integral issue of concern. The estimates by Khera (2011) show that at the all India level, diversion of grains has increased from 24%-54% between 1999–2000 and 2004–2005. However, the overall diversion of grains has come down from 54% to 44% in 2007–2008 (Table 1). This estimates of diversion mostly include leakages due to corruption, spoilage during storage and losses during transportation.

Table 1: Diversion of Food Grains in %

States	2001–02		2004–05		2006–07		2007–08	
	Rice	Wheat	Rice	Wheat	Rice	Wheat	Rice	Wheat
Andra Pradesh	12.3	-210.8	22.3	93	16.1	66.9	19.2	50.3
Assam	69.4	98.1	83.5	100	72.4	98.4	73	97.5
Bihar	77.3	91.6	84.8	92.8	83.6	84.4	92.4	85.1
Chattisgarh	45.8	33.4	45.1	82.6	28.9	65.3	-3.1	57
Gujarat	35.6	27.3	52.7	51.3	66.1	39.6	73	53.3
Haryana	-	94	-	82.7	39.5	29.4	61.8	48.8
Himachal Pradesh	26.0	43.8	7	46.2	11.6	32.4	12.9	14.3
Jammu Kashmir	54.1	79	-8.9	79.4	-36.5	66.4	7.6	59.1
Jharkhand	71.5	83	82.3	87.9	86.4	80.9	83.3	85.2
Karnataka	47	53.7	25.8	41.7	32.6	34.4	42.2	33.4
Kerala	-28.6	66.9	-1.9	78.9	0.8	55.3	3.5	55.6
Madhya Pradesh	50.8	46.4	12.9	56.7	52.8	64	20.8	39.9
Maharashtra	40	53.2	46.5	51	44.6	38.5	40.7	44.1
Orissa	21.4	-	74.1	99	53.4	91.5	46.2	97.1
Punjab	92.5	87.7	100	93.1	71.9	81.1	17.6	18.4
Rajasthan	76.1	75.8	100	93.9	69.8	83.5	75.7	82
Tamil Nadu	-79.2	-	9.4	-86.7	2.4	-105.6	8.7	-186.7
Uttar Pradesh	77.4	67.1	85.4	36.7	72.3	7.8	52.9	-14.5
Uttarakhand	-109.8	-810	44.2	84.8	44.2	88.3	33.3	70.9
West Bengal	42.4	84	70.4	85	72.3	80.4	70.8	77.9
India	18.2	66.8	41.3	70.3	39.6	61.9	37.2	57.7

Source: Khera (2011)

Since households in states like Gujarat and Rajasthan are restricted to consume only rice and wheat, they buy less PDS grains. Since their consumption is always less than the off-take, there is excess grain left behind in the fair price shop (FPS). Thus, the ration shop dealers can always divert these grains into the open market and sell them at a higher price. Despite the growing stocks, the capacity to safely store the grains has also remained largely unchanged. Small scale godowns and the practice of keeping grains in the open result in spoilage. A substantial amount of grain is also lost during transportation from the godowns to the FPS. Since in most cases vans used for transportation are in a state of disrepair, the PDS grains are likely to get damaged in the process.

In order to avoid leakage of PDS grains during transportation, reforms like computerization of PDS, GPS tracking of vehicles transporting the grains and deploying clear marking on these trucks so as to enable monitoring of routes and unloading places, could be introduced. Computerizing PDS would enable the use of ICT tools to capture information and track the PDS grains across the supply chain. This would allow citizens and other stakeholders to get involved in the process and see for themselves how the supply of foodgrains from the FCI to the FPS takes place. All transactions related to PDS in the ration shop could be made online and all information could be uploaded on websites. These portals could contain information such as a list containing the names of all the ration card holders, FPS, minutiae of lifting and sales of PDS supplies by FPS, etc. Such websites are already in place for states like Chattisgarh and Tamil Nadu. *Jan Bhagidari* is the name of the website in place for Chattisgarh, which comprises detailed information related to Chattisgarh PDS. Here, the underlying rationale is to put everything in the public eye so that the officials find no opportunity to cheat them. This would also instill in the officials' a sense of responsibility to provide answers as demanded by the people.

The failure in PDS could be reformed only with the aid of good governance that ensures monitoring at all times and at all levels and increases transparency. In order to ensure more accountability on the part of officials, a grievance redressal system must be put in place. To address the problem of grain diversion at the retail level, digital ration cards should be used in the place of easy-to-forge ration cards. The Aadhaar card could also be used to reduce leakages. Further, the government should find ways to incentivize the dealers and other officials so that they feel motivated to work honestly and not to bribe or cheat others or steal grains.

Rising subsidy
One of the most important causes of the failure of PDS is the constant rise in food subsidies. Food subsidy is quantitatively defined as economic cost (EC) minus central issue price (CIP). EC is equal to the sum of minimum support prices (MSP), which refers to the price paid by the government for the goods they procure from the poor

farmers and the cost of distributing these food grains. CIP is the price at which food grains procured by the central government are transferred to the state government.

Food subsidies have increased from Rs. 2,850 crores in 1991–92 to around Rs. 72,823 crores in 2011–12, an escalation of over 25 times in 21 years (Sharma, 2012). The main reasons for proliferation in food subsidies include an abrupt rise in MSP (Table 2), accretion of fat stocks of grains, mounting economic costs (Table 2), high off-take under TPDS and other welfare schemes and constant central issue prices of food grains (Table 3). Thus, an estimation of rising subsidies for years 2001–02 to 2013–14 is given in table 4 and figure 1.

Table 2: Minimum Support Price and Economic cost of rice and wheat in Rs/quintal

	Rice (Rs/quintal)		Wheat (Rs/quintal)	
Year	MSP	EC	MSP	EC
2001–02	560	1097.96	610	852.94
2002–03	560	1165.03	620	884
2003–04	580	1236.09	620	918.69
2004–05	590	1303.59	630	1019.01
2005–06	600	1339.69	640	1041.85
2006–07	610	1391.18	650	1177.78
2007–08	675	1549.86	750	1311.75
2008–09	880	1740.73	1000	1380.58
2009–10	980	1820.07	1080	1424.61
2010–11	1030	1983.11	1100	1494.35
2011–12	1110	1595.25	1120	2122.94
2012–13		2351.22	1285	1798.96

Source: Food Corporation of India

Table 3: Central Issue Prices

CIP (Rs/quintal)			
	AAY	BPL	APL
Wheat	200	415	610
Rice	300	565	810

Source: Food Corporation of India

Table 4: Trends in consumer subsidy on Rice and Wheat (Rs/quintal)

Years	AAY		BPL		APL	
	Rice	Wheat	Rice	Wheat	Rice	Wheat
2001–2002	797.96	652.94	532.96	437.94	287.96	242.94
2002–2003	865.03	684	600.03	469	355.03	274
2003–2004	936.09	718.69	671.09	503.69	426.09	308.69
2004–2005	1003.59	819.01	738.59	604.01	493.59	409.01
2005–2006	1039.69	841.85	774.69	626.85	529.69	431.85
2006–2007	1091.18	977.78	826.18	762.78	581.18	567.78
2007–2008	1249.86	1111.75	984.86	896.75	739.86	701.75
2008–2009 (P)	1440.73	1180.58	1175.73	965.58	930.73	770.58
2009–2010	1520.07	1224.61	1255.07	1009.61	1010.07	814.61
2010–2011	1683.11	1294.35	1418.11	1079.35	1173.11	884.35
2011–2012 (P)	1295.25	1922.94	1030.25	1707.94	785.25	1512.94
2012–2013 (RE)	2051.22	1598.96	1786.22	1383.96	1541.22	1188.96
2013–2014 (BE)	2343.61	1810.22	2078.61	1595.22	1833.61	1400.22

Source: Food Corporation of India and author's calculation

Figure 1: Increasing Subsidy in Rupees per quintal of rice on BPL Families

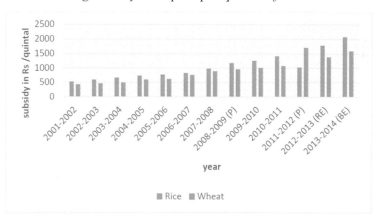

Source: Author's calculation

Since most of these costs are not under the control of FCI, there is very little that FCI could actually do about it. But what FCI could probably do is to reduce administrative charges and storage losses, and to reduce other related costs by introducing appropriate policies on pricing, encourage involvement of more states in procuring and distributing food grains, indulge in public-private partnership to create good storage facilities and improve operational efficiency and make periodic increases in the CIP of food grains.

Nutrition
The quality of PDS grains is generally very low. As a result about 40% of the poor people do not even bother to purchase PDS grains from the FPS but rather prefer to purchase good quality grains from the open market, even if it is at a higher price. For example, in the Pali district in Rajasthan, households have reported that they found 2–3 kg of pebbles out of 25 kg of wheat that they had procured (Khera, 2011).

Moreover, this system provides no dietary diversity and allows only rice and wheat based consumption for the households. Since in states like Rajasthan and Gujarat coarse grains constitute the main staples, the poor people might not want to consume rice and wheat. So even though they get PDS grains at lower prices, they also have to buy their staple grains from the open market at higher prices anyway. Thus, PDS fails to meet its very objective in these states.

However, this problem could be mitigated if farmers are incentivized to produce coarser grains like millets, which are more nutritious than rice and wheat. The poor farmers could sell these millets to the government at MSP. Millets would also provide them with more nutrition when they buy it back as PDS grain at lower prices from the FPS. These millets could also further be sold to wealthy people in the premium market at higher prices.

Conclusion

This article has discussed relative efficacies of social assistance programmes. While in-kind transfers are successful when the state requires the poor people to consume a particular good to ensure their welfare, cash transfers do essentially well when household decisions entail positive externalities. For example, the *Mexican Oportunidades*, a cash transfer programme in Mexico, has resulted in an increase in the school attendance and a decline in the drop-out rate. Similarly, the cash transfer programme in Chile has also increased the number of visit to health centres by children. However, the intention here is not to endorse or undermine the impact of any kind of social assistance programme but rather to argue that their success is absolutely context and goal specific. For example, although the in-kind transfers in Mexico and Bangladesh have significantly increased the food intake of the poor households, PDS in India has been continually suffering from several innate and systemic flaws.

The policy of PDS that was intended to provide low cost food for the poor in India could have been the biggest game changer but has unfortunately failed to do much due to poor implementation. PDS has been widely criticized on the grounds of poor targeting, leakages, rising subsidies and inferior quality of grains. These failures could be addressed by introducing reforms, for example using aadhaar cards for appropriate targeting, computerizing PDS, putting a grievance redressal system in place, uploading of all information on web for greater transparency, including coarse grains to add nutritious value and maintain dietary diversity and also encouraging public-private partnership to improve the operational efficiency of FCI.

Some proponents of cash transfer suggest that replacing food with cash transfer would reduce leakages and corruption to a considerable extent. However, in order to successfully implement the cash transfer programme, the infrastructural facilities need to be upgraded in the country. This includes setting up of banks in remote rural areas so that the poor people could collect the cash from their bank accounts with minimum transaction cost and then use the same to buy food grains; digitizing data of all beneficiaries and linking the Aadhaar card number to bank accounts so as to prevent any cases of fraud.

References

Balani, S. (2013). Functioning of the Public Distribution System. *PRS Report*.

Besley, T. (1988). A simple model for merit good arguments. *Journal of Public economics*, *35*(3), 371–383.

Bhandari, L. (2006). Social infrastructure: urban health and education. *India Infrastructure Report*, 232–257. Castañeda, T. (2000). The design, implementation and impact of Food Stamps Programs in Developing Countries. *Nutrition Toolkit, 6*.

Chaudhuri, A. R., & Somanathan, E. (2011). Impact of biometric identification-based transfers. *Economic and Political Weekly*, *46*(21), 77–80.

Currie, J. M., & Gahvari, F. (2007). Transfers in Cash and in Kind: Theory Meets the Data (Cam bridge, Massachusetts: National Bureau of Economic Research).

Das, J., Do, Q. T., & Özler, B. (2005). Reassessing conditional cash transfer programs. *The World Bank Research Observer*, *20*(1), 57–80.

Devereux, S., Marshall, J., MacAskill, J., & Pelham, L. (2005). Making Cash Count: Lessons from cash transfer schemes in east and southern Africa for supporting the most vulnerable children and households. *London: Save the Children, Help Age International, Institute of Development Studies, University of Sussex.*

Dutta, P., Howes, S., & Murgai, R. (2010). Small but effective: India's targeted unconditional cash transfers. *Economic & Political Weekly, 45*(52), 63–70.

Farrington, J., Harvey, P., & Slater, R. (2006, June). Cash transfers in the context of pro-poor growth. In *Third International Conference on Conditional Cash Transfers, Istanbul Turkey. ODI, London.*

Gentilini, U. (2007). *Cash and food transfers: A primer*. Rome: World Food Programme.

Jha, S., & Ramaswami, B. (2010). How can food subsidies work better? Answers from India and the Philippines.

Kapur, D., Mukhopadhyay, P., & Subramanian, A. (2008). The case for direct cash transfers to the poor. *Economic and Political Weekly*, 37–43.

Kapur, D. (2011). The Shift to Cash Transfers: Running Better But on the Wrong Road?. *Economic and Political Weekly*, 80–85.

Khera, R. (2011). Revival of the public distribution system: evidence and explanations. *Economic and Political Weekly, 46*(44–45), 36–50.

Kotwal, A., Murugkar, M., & Ramaswami, B. (2011). PDS forever?. *Economic and Political Weekly*, 72–76.

Narayanan, S. (2011). A case for reframing the cash transfer debate in India. *Economic and Political Weekly, 46*(21), 41–48.

Shah, M. (2008). Direct cash transfers: no magic bullet. *Economic and Political Weekly*, 77–79. Sharma, V. P. (2012). *Food subsidy in India: trends, causes and policy reform options* (Vol. 8). Working Paper.

Soares, F. V., Ribas, R. P., & Osorio, R. G. (2010). Evaluating the impact of Brazil's Bolsa Familia: Cash transfer programs in comparative perspective. *Latin American Research Review, 45*(2), 173–190.

Soares, S. S. D., & Zepeda, E. (2007). Can all Cash Transfers Reduce Inequality?

Standing, G. (2012). Cash transfers: A review of the issues in India.

Svedberg, P. (2012). Reforming or replacing the public distribution system with cash transfers. *Economic and Political Weekly*, *47*(7), 53–62.

Tabor, S. R. (2002). Assisting the poor with cash: Design and implementation of social transfer programs. *World Bank Social Protection Discussion Paper*, *223*.

Lean Thinking – A Performance Evaluation of Hospital Operations: An Empirical Study.

Deepak Yaduvanshi*, Swapan Kumar Majumdar** & Deepak Gupta***

Abstract

Hospital and healthcare organizations as with any other service operation requires systemic innovation and new thinking to remain competitive, cost efficient and up to date. Lean Thinking provides an effective framework for producing systematic change, controlling cost, improving quality and providing better healthcare. The hospitals over the last few years have faced major issues and challenges, the patients aspire to world class health care quality delivery while state and health insurance companies demand the delivery at the lowest price.

Lean is an integrated system of principles, practices, tools and techniques focused on reducing waste, synchronizing work flows and managing variability in production flows or operations. An essential distinction in lean is between value and non-value added activities. Value added activities contribute to what the customer wants from a product or service everything else is a non-value added activity. The study was undertaken to understand hospital operations and arrive at a composite Lean hospital Index for a tertiary care multi-specialty hospital. The validity of the same was tested at Manipal Hospital. Lean and six sigma which are complementary quality improvement tools can help to achieve these goals however the application of the same is a long term process. An empirical study was conducted at Fortis Hospital Jaipur in year 2014 -16 to arrive at a composite hospital index and to improve the hospital operation activity based on evaluating AS IS SOP to TO BE SOP. The study intends to contribute to better understanding of hospital operations and would lead to informed decision making by the hospital management in a unified way. Their perception and decision making of complex hospital operations would be scientific and predictable so as to deliver world class quality care at affordable price besides unlocking operational efficiency with limited resources.

* Lungkare: Institute of Respiratory and Critical Care, Jaipur
** Presidency University, Bangalore
*** Rajasthan University, Jaipur

The significant contribution of this research is that it provides a path and approach to develop a lean health care management system for specific category of hospitals. The findings of the research provide a vital instrument to assess and measure the quality of the hospital management system termed as Lean Hospital Index (LHI).

Keywords: Lean, six sigma, Lean Hospital Index *(LHI)*, Lean thinking.

Introduction

Managing a hospital is management of complex and multi-disciplinary Healthcare service chains, where failure is fatal, wastage is inefficiency and quality of service is quantified by the subjective judgment of the patients, the receiver of the services. The questions that often concerns senior hospital administrators are how to attain zero defect, zero wastage zero effect and 100% satisfaction while keeping the cost of the service affordable. This research was undertaken to formulate a framework for the attainment of operational goals of 3 zero's at affordable cost.

As the premise of the research is related to the service operation management, the approach that is most appropriate is "Lean Thinking".

Hospital and healthcare organizations, as with any other service operation requires systemic innovation and new thinking to remain competitive, cost efficient and up to date. Lean Thinking provides an effective framework for producing systematic change, controlling cost, improving quality and providing better healthcare. The hospitals over the last few years have faced major issues and challenges, the patients aspire to world class health care quality delivery while state and health insurance companies demand the delivery at the lowest cost.

Lean is an integrated system of principles, practices, tools and techniques focused on reducing waste, synchronizing work flows and managing variability in production flows or operations. An essential distinction in lean is between value and non-value added activities. Value added activities contribute to what the customer wants from a product or service everything else is a non-value added activity. The lean principles have been now successfully applied to the delivery of health care over the last few years. Lean management primarily begins with underlying principle of eliminating waste. In order for lean methodology to be successful and able to enhance the operations the hospital must first work to create an organizational culture that is receptive to lean thinking. The commitment to start lean must start from the top management and the junior staff must be involved. Whether manufacturing a car or delivering health care to a patient, the industry worker or health professional rely on multiple, disorganized, chaotic and complex in built systems and processes to

28

accomplish the goal to deliver value to the customer or patient. It is a widely held dictum that once the lean principles are applied rigorously and throughout an entire organization, they can have a positive impact on productivity, cost, quality, and timely delivery in the resource limited settings of Indian Sub-continent. In the hospital industry the operational efficiency means rapid access to care, minimum waiting time while at the same time delivering defect free quality care at the minimum cost.

While the concepts came to us via Toyota, the term Lean is credited to Jon Krafcif, part of the research team at MIT's International Motor Vehicle Program (Womack et al 1991).

Lean as defined by NIST (2000) is a systematic approach to identifying and eliminating waste through continuous improvement, flowing the product at the pull of the customer in pursuit of perfection.

All over the world the health care industry is facing a major problem of escalating costs more so in a middle income country like India where the out of pocket expenditure is huge together with no regulations and poorly designed care services. At first glance, assessing financial or operational benefit for these programs appeared difficult at best, since most acute care organizations and hospitals rarely share specific financial data also the Lean or lean six sigma is still in its infancy in the country.

The research undertaken has demonstrated that the application of Lean thinking yielded significant operational efficiency benefits for tertiary care hospitals. In addition, the research provided an valuable insight as to where, in tertiary hospitals, these programs appear to be most effective. The study intends to contribute and fill the gap which would lead to better understanding of hospital operations and would lead to informed decision making by the hospital management in a unified way. Their perception and decision making of complex hospital operations would be scientific and predictable so as to deliver world class quality care at affordable price besides unlocking operational efficiency with limited resources.

The significant contribution of this research is that it provides a path and approach for the development of a lean health care management system for the specific category of hospitals. The findings of the research provide a *vital instrument to assess and measure the quality of the hospital Management system termed as Lean Hospital Index (LHI).*

Rationale of the Study & Background:

Hospital and healthcare organizations as with any other service operation requires a systemic innovation and new thinking to remain competitive, cost efficient and up to date. The rationale of the study was that hospital operations and performance all over the world are based on a basic set of parameters bench marked against evidence based guidelines however an Indian version of the composite Hospital Index is lacking.

The study of hospital operations is empirical and exploratory in nature at tertiary level multi-specialty hospitals.

The weights were calculated using Ranking method. Sum of the weights were 1 and lean hospital index was calculated as follows.

Lean Hospital Index = { ($\sum$ Weight × Standardized value) / $\sum$ Weight } × 100

The significant contribution of this research is that it provides a path and approach for the development of a lean health care management system for specific category of hospitals. The findings of the research provide a vital instrument to assess and measure the quality of the hospital Management system termed as Lean Hospital Index (LHI).

Review of Literature

Lean Management is getting the right things to the right place at the right time in the right quantity to achieve perfect work flow, while minimizing waste and being flexible and able to change, Anvari et. al. (2010). Thus lean management is the implementation of the concept that anything that does not create value in the product or service should be eliminated. The hospitals over the last few years have faced major issues and challenges, the patients aspire to world class health care quality delivery while state and health insurance companies demand the delivery at the lowest price, Deepak et.al. (2017).

The most common tool used in the lean method is Value Stream Mapping or VSM (Black, 2008), in which a lean team (process owners and participants and lean practitioners) maps all aspects of a particular process by means of graphical interpretations of process inputs, outputs and through puts, and flow ('Spaghetti Maps').

Many authors Radnor & Boaden (2008), Radnor Z.(2010), Sua´rez-Barraza & Ramis-Pujol (2010), Pedersen & Huniche (2011) and Radnor & Johnston (2013) have also explored Lean applications in different cultural and working-environments in public settings. The findings indicate that the lean approach like VSM, RIE, 5s, Kaizen etc. allowed a process-based view, a focus on value the elimination of waste and employee-driven change leading to improvement in customer satisfaction and efficiency of delivered service.

Authors including LaGanga (2011), Díaz et al. (2012) and Chiarini (2013 managed the patient flow using in hospital using triage and VSM. Al-Hakim & Gong (2012), Díaz et al. (2012) and Meredith et al. (2011) have studied how lean practice of SMED can be applied in OT and surgery to reduce the changeover time. Johnson et al. (2012), Van Leeuwen & Does (2010), Morrow et al. (2012) have discussed how lean nursing can be implemented to reduce the inpatient stay in hospital. Fillingham (2007), Grove et al. (2010), Radnor Z. (2011), Papadopoulos (2011) and Burgess & Radnor(2013) have studied Lean implementation in English hospital trusts to eliminate waste using VSM, Kaizen, RIE, improvement capability and flow, employee development, process capability, continuous improvement and employee development.

Influenced by the work of Womack and Jones (2003), Lean in health care as "an organization's cultural commitment to applying the scientific method to designing, performing, and continuously improving the work delivered by teams of people, leading to measurably better value for patients and other stake holders.".

Mayday Hospital in London UK applied lean thinking to the hospital discharge process. This initiative reduced the length of stay for the average patient by 25%. Mayday was able to close 78 beds and reduce related operation expenses while still maintaining original service levels and capability. By analyzing complexity and length of stay in conjunction with care flow, they created a process that is customized for each medical condition. The results standardized care and discharge procedures across a wide swathe of patients (Mathieson, 2006).

Bay Medical Center (a 413-bed regional acute care hospital in Panama City, Florida) saved $2 million over the course of 18 months by implementing Six-Sigma across the facility. The primary area of improvement was pre-surgical readiness – whereas reductions in cancelled and rescheduled surgeries saved $1.2 million. Reworking the authorization, precertification and pre-operative workflow reduced waste, cancellation and authorization penalties (Hagland, 2006).

Columbus Regional Hospital (a 325-bed facility located in Columbus, Indiana) implemented Lean and Six-Sigma across the hospital. The most notable application, Lean, resulted in reduced lengths of stay in the emergency department. The application of 5S and standardization of care resulting in an LOS reduction by acuity levels, between 26% and 38%~patient leaving without being seen decreased by 75%. The financial impact of this single project was an $800,000 annual increase in revenue (Charles, 2008).

Stanford Medical Center (a 613-bed tertiary/quaternary care hospital located in Palo Alto) engaged GE Medical Systems to implement Six-Sigma process improvement in their diagnostic imaging department. The focus of the project was to increase throughput and decrease outpatient scheduling backlogs. A careful analysis of the schedule and productivity revealed that the center lost at least 35 studies a day due to inefficient operations. In addition, no shows added to lost revenue and contributed to the scheduling backlog. A redesign of the entire scheduling and pre-registration process increased capacity by 75% and created an additional $1.5 million in revenue (Loree, 2003).

Very little research has been carried out relating to the status of lean implementation in the Indian service industry. Díaz et al. (2012) have examined the operations of Arvind Eye Hospital, the largest eye care provider in India. Authors state that the main driver of Arvind's efficiency is an embedded set of lean services practices facilitated by an early triage process and that a better understanding of these can bring improvements in the healthcare sector. By using lean tools for variability reduction, process simplification and optimising inventory less than 80 doctors do 200,000 cataract operations per year and a non-profit hospital is able to treat two thirds of its patient free of charge.

Govindarajan & Ramamurti (2013) have studied 9 hospitals in India to study how these hospitals are providing world-class health care at ultralow cost. They concluded that to deliver it, the Indian hospitals have developed three powerful organizational advantages: a hub-and-spoke configuration of assets (variability reduction or triage), an innovative way of determining who should do what (simplifying and standardizing processes), and a focus on cost-effectiveness rather than just cost cutting (through task shifting, better utilization of resources and skill development of people).

The lack of a precise and holistic approach as a composite model of six sigma and lean methodology for the entire hospital operations is lacking all over the globe and its relevance in the resource limited setting in Indian context is further limited. Our study intends to contribute and fill the gap which would lead to better understanding of hospital operations and would lead to informed decision making by the hospital management in a unified way.

Research Methodology

As India in the next millennium shifts to a care quality culture (as opposed to a fiscally managed care culture of the government), the defects limiting nature of Six-Sigma programs in health will take on more significance. Eliminating defects and inefficiencies by lean application in the delivery of healthcare will eventually lead to a healthier population. We will achieve this at a lower cost with greater consistency, quality and safety. The investments we make in cultural quality transformations, such as Lean and Six-Sigma, will pay significant dividends in the next decade and become second nature. It has happened throughout the industrial continuum. It is now taking hold in the delivery and production of healthcare services by reducing defects, enhancing customer service and generally lowering costs across the board and I want to be torch bearer of the same.

Primary Objective of Study:

To develop a composite Lean hospital index (LHI)

Secondary Objectives:

- To study and analyze the existing hospital operations in various departments.
- To develop and measure the baseline benchmark tools for Hospital Operations.
- To identify gaps, waste in hospital operations.
- To develop a framework for lean management in hospital operations.

Research Methodology:

- Phase 1 : Detailed literature review and analysis of peer-reviewed contents with a meta-analysis of data available to understand the lean concept and practices.
- Phase 2 : Analysis of the existing practices, AS –IS – SOP of various hospital operations and departments
- Phase 3 : Data collection and analysis
- Phase 4 :Application of Lean in hospital operations and services
  - Phase 4a : Critical to Quality (CTQ)
  - Phase 4b : Critical to Process (CTP)
- Phase 5 : Data analysis by statistical methods – Factor analysis/Ranking methods Analytic hierarchy process (AHP)
- Phase 6: Development of new hospital processes, TO –BE –SOP
- Phase 7 : Lean Hospital Index (LHI)
- Phase 8: Validity testing of the LHI

Validity Testing of Index

The LHI subsequently tested at the two comparable multi-specialty hospitals

Decision Making and Implications:

- If index is less than 40 – Poor
- If index is between 40 and 60 – Moderate
- If index is between 60 and 80 – Good
- If index is between 80 and 100 – Excellent

Result and Data Interpretation

The weights were calculated using Ranking method which can be observed from tables enclosed.
Sum of the weights were 1 and lean hospital index was calculated as follows.
Lean Hospital Index = { ($\sum$ Weight × Standardized value) / $\sum$ Weight } × 100
= 56.90 which falls in the MODERATELY performing category of hospital

Discussion:

A composite lean application in a tertiary care hospital would go a long way in our understanding in the resource limited setting of Indian Subcontinent.

The environment in which businesses including healthcare and hospitals today compete is rapidly changing and the rate of change is increasing. Faced with intensive global competition, more demanding customers, rapidly shrinking product life cycles, and shorter responsive time, organizations are now pursuing competitiveness by achieving higher level of product value and accordingly, higher customer satisfaction.

Hospitals face challenges in healthcare operations management in the absence of a mechanism to capture, analyze and present real-time performance about clinical and non clinical processes. Such information is vital to improve the quality of healthcare, for optimal clinical and financial outcomes and real-time performance optimization.

The lack of a precise and holistic approach as a composite model of lean methodology for the entire hospital operations is lacking all over the globe and its relevance in the resource limited setting in Indian context is further limited. We reviewed, studied, analysed the existing literature to contribute and fill the gap which would lead to better understanding of hospital operations and would lead to informed decision making by the hospital management in a unified way. Their perception and decision making of complex hospital operations would be scientific and predictable so as to deliver world class quality care at affordable price besides unlocking operational efficiency with limited resources.

There are now many examples of the positive impact Lean is having in hospitals throughout the world, to summarize Lean methods have resulted in:

1. Reduced turn around time (TAT) for clinical laboratory results by 60% without adding head count or new instrumentation – Alegent Health, Nebraska
2. Reduced instrument decontamination and sterilization cycle time by over 70% – Kingston General Hospital, Ontario
3. Reduced patient deaths related to central-line associated blood stream infections by 95% – Allegbeny Hospital, Pennsylvania
4. Reduced patient waiting time for orthopedic surgery from 14 weeks to 31 hours (from first call to surgery) – Theda CArfe Wisconsin
5. Increased surgical revenue by $8080,000 annually – Ohio Health, Ohio
6. Reduced patient length of stay by 29% and avoided $1.25 million in new emergency department construction – Avera McKennan, South Dakota
7. Saved $7.5 million from Lean Rapid Improvement Events in 2004 and reinvested the saving in patient care – Park Nicollet Health Services, Minnesota.

As in other industries, many in healthcare assume there is an inherent trade off between cost and quality; better quality must cost more. It is true that some methods for improving the quality of patient outcomes might cost more such as new technologies, treatments, or medicines. Hospitals do have many opportunities, however, to improve the quality of health care delivery methods and processes in a way that improves quality and reduces costs.

If you focus on patient quality and safety, you just can't go wrong. If you do the right thing with regard to quality, the costs will take care of themselves."(Graban, et.al 2007). Riverside's laboratory had previously focused primarily on cost, using layoffs and other traditional cost-cutting methods, but the lab's quality of service did not improve. Through a Lean implementation, which focused on reducing errors, improving flow, and getting test results to patients faster, labor costs also came down. The lab found that good quality, through reducing rework and waste in the process, can cost less.

The extensive work has not tried to incorporate the strategy of the meta- analysis as the reports or publications being considered here are not sufficient to cover the entire range of efforts being contributed. Recently, private enterprises and groups are putting lot of health models for the development of the lean philosophy especially in resource limited settings in the developing and emerging economies.

With the recent enthusiasm of various hospital management boards, policy makers, funding agencies and grants, the need is now to innovate, improve and redefine better tools to design and implement Lean Six Sigma to achieve operational efficacy. The next logical step is to develop a composite healthy hospital index (HHI) and suggest strategies for increasing the operational efficiency and benefit the hospital administrators in fine tuning the management practices.

In the next millennium, as India shifts to a care quality culture (as opposed to a fiscally managed care culture of the government), the defect limiting nature of Six-Sigma programs in health and hospital will acquire more significance. Eliminating defects and inefficiencies in the delivery of healthcare will eventually lead to a healthier population. We will achieve such at a lower cost with greater consistency, quality and safety. The investments we make in cultural quality transformations, such as Lean and Six-Sigma, will pay significant dividends in the next decade. It has happened throughout the industrial continuum. It is now taking hold in the delivery and production of healthcare services. by reducing defects, enhancing customer service and generally lowering costs across the board and achieving nirvana for operational efficiency in hospitals. (Deepak et.al, 2017)

The Conclusions

The findings of the present study were analyzed. This helped to prove that the findings were true and the use of lean application greatly enhanced the hospital operations. This study also was an eye opener for the routine hospital operations in various departments and standardization and wastes could be identified and eliminated. Thus the revised Lean Hospital Index as well as development of standard operating procedures will uplift the quality standards of a unit of a hospital. This provides a framework and approach to lean thinking in hospitals.

To summarize the lean principles have been now successfully applied to the delivery of health care over the last few years. Lean management primarily begins with underlying principle of eliminating waste. In order for lean methodology to be successful and able to enhance the operations the hospital must first work to create an organizational culture that is receptive to lean thinking. The commitment to start lean must start from the top management and the junior staff must be involved. Whether manufacturing a car or delivering health care to a patient, the industry worker or health professional rely on multiple, disorganized, chaotic and complex in built system and processes to accomplish the goal to deliver value to the customer or patient. It is an widely held dictum that once the lean principles are applied rigorously and throughout an entire organization, they can have a positive impact on productivity, cost, quality, and timely delivery in a resource limited settings of Indian Sub-continent.

The significant contribution of this research is that it provides a path and approach for the developing a lean health care management system for specific category of hospitals. The findings of the research provide a *vital instrument to assess and measure the quality of the hospital Management system termed as Lean Hospital Index (LHI).*

On the basis of the findings of the study the following recommendations have been made.

- The Lean Hospital Index (LHI) is a vital instrument to assess and measure the quality of the hospital Management system.
- The composite LHI approach can be applied on real time basis to monitor hospital systems on a wide scale.
- The model developed encompasses hospital operation systems as whole and the data analytics is a predictive model for a healthy hospital in terms of not only financial health but also structurally as measured by the grade of quality of hospital.
- A study on a wider scale should be conducted at multiple hospitals and sectors to validate the Lean hospital Index both in Private and Government sector.
- The lean hospital index can be used as a template to derive operational efficiency and standardization of the processes which are critical as many processes have evolved over the years and have become redundant with time.

References

Albright, B. (2008). Lean and mean: In addition to strengthening the bottom line, process improvement methodologies are improving patient care. *Healthcare Informatics: the Business Magazine for Information and Communication Systems,* 25(6), 40A, 42A, 44A passim.

American Society for Quality. (2009). *The ASQ Hospital Study: Hospitals see benefits of Lean and Six-Sigma.* Retrieved from http://www.asq.org/ mediaroom/ press-releases /2009/20090318-hospitals-see-benefits-lss.html

Arnold LA, Faurote FL. Ford Methods and the Ford Shops. New York :The Engineering Magazine Company ; 1915.

Atkins, P. (2006). Six-Sigma projects add efficiency to discharge process. *Hospital Case Management, 16(2),* 23–5.

Baczewski, R. (2005). Four methods for improving performance: A comparison. *Healthcare Financial Management, 59(7),* 101–102.

Bahensky, J., Roe, J., & Bolton, R. (2005). Lean sigma—will it work for healthcare? *Journal of Healthcare Information Management, 19(1),* 39–44.

Black, J. (2008). *The Toyota way to healthcare excellence: Increase efficiency and improve quality with Lean.* Chicago, IL: Health Administration Press.

Bowen, D., & Youngdahl, W. (1998). "Lean" service: in defense of a production-line approach. *Int. Journal of Service Industry Management, Vol.9 No. 3,,* 207–225.

Burgess, N., & Radnor, Z. (2013). Evaluating Lean in healthcare. *International Journal of Health Care Quality Assurance,Vol. 26 No. 3,* 220–235.

Caldwell, C. (2006). Lean-Six-Sigma: tools for rapid cycle cost reduction. *Healthcare Financial Management,* 60(10), 96–8.

Caldwell, C, & Stuenkel, K. (2008). Moving from good to best in healthcare: Embracing accounting in improvements. *Healthcare Executive, 23(3),* 10,12,14–15.

Chadha, R., Singh, A., & Kalra, J. (2012). Lean and queuing integration for the transformation of health care processes: A lean health care model. *Clinical Governance: An International Journal, 17* (3), 191–199.

Dahlgaard, J., & Ostergaard, P. (2000). TQM and lean thinking in higher education. In *The Best on Quality,Vol.11,.* Quality Press c/o American Society for Quality, USA.

Damrath, F. (2012). *Increasing competitiveness of service companies: developing conceptual models for implementing Lean Management in service companies.* Thesis at Politecnico di Milano.

Das, B. (2011). Validation Protocol: First Step of a Lean-TQM Principle in a New Laboratory Set-up in a Tertiary Care Hospital in India. *Ind J Clin Biochem, 26* (3), 235–243.

Deepak Yaduvanshi, Ashu Sharma. Lean Six Sigma in Health Operations: Challenges and Opportunities- Nirvana for operational Efficiency in Hospitals in a resource limited settings. *Journal of Health Management*. April 27,2017, DOI:10.1177/0972063417699665.http://jhm.sagepub.com.

De Feo, J., & Barnard, W. (2005). *JURAN Institute's Six-Sigma Breakthrough and Beyond – Quality Performance Breakthrough Methods*. New York, NY: McGraw-Hill Professional.

Fairbanks, C. (2007). Using Six-Sigma and Lean methodologies to improve O throughput. *AORN Journal, 86(1),* 73–82.

Fillingham, D. (2007). Can lean save lives? *Leadership in Health Services*, 20(4), 231–241.

Ford, Henry, and Samuel Crowther, *MyLife and Work (Garden City, NY: Doubleday, Page & Company, 1922*), 219.

Fosdick, G., & Uphoff., M. (2007). Adopting cross-industry best practices for measurable results. *Healthcare Executive, 22(3),* 14–6, 18–20.

Govindarajan, V., & Ramamurti, R. (2013). Delivering World-Class Health Care, Affordably. *Harvard Business Review, Nov.*

Gottfredson, M., & Aspinall, K. (2005). Innovation versus complexity: What is too much of a good thing? *Harvard Business Review, 83(1*1), 62–71, 164.

Hanna, J. (2007). Bringing 'Lean' Principles to Service Industries. *HBS.*

Hagland, M. (2006). Six-Sigma practices: A strategy based on data is perfect fit for healthcare. *Healthcare Informatics,* 23(1), 27–8, 30.

Juran, J. (2004). *Architect of Quality: The Autobiography of Dr. Joseph M. Juran*(First Edition), New York, NY: McGraw-Hill.

Kim, C, Spahlinger, D., Kin, J., & Billi, J. (2006). Lean health care: What can hospitals learn from a world-class automaker? *Journal of Hospital Medicine,1(3),* 191–9.

Kohn, L., Corrigan, J., & Donaldson, M. (2000). *To Err is Human: Building a Safer Health System.* Washington, DC: National Academy Press

Kollberg, B., Dahlgaard, J. J., & Brehmer, P.-O. (2007). Measuring lean initiatives in health care services: issues and findings. *International Journal of Productivity and Performance Management, 56* (1), 7–24.

Liker JK. The Toyota Way. Madison, Wisc: McGraw-Hill; 2004.

NIST. (2000). *Principles of Lean Manufacturing with Live Simulation.* Gaithersburg, MD.: Manufacturing Extension Partnership, National Institute of Standards and Technology.

Noguchi, J. (1995). The Legacy of W. Edwards Deming. *Quality Progress, 28(12):* 35–38.

Services Sector. (2013). Retrieved March 2014, from India Budget: http://indiabudget.nic.in/echap-10.pdf

Shah, R., & Ward, P. (2003). Lean manufacturing: context, practice bundles, and performance. *Journal of Operations Management, 21*, 129 -149.

Shingo, S., & Dillon, A. (1989). *A study of the Toyota production system from an industrial engineering viewpoint.* Portland, OR: Productivity Press.

Staats, B., Brunner, J. B., & Upton, D. (2011). Lean principles, learning, and knowledge work : Evidence from a software services. *Journal of Operations Management, 29(5)*, 376–390.

Swank, C. K. (2003). The lean service machine. *Harvard business review,81(10)*, 123–130.

Taiichi, O. (1988). Toyota Production System: Beyond large scale production. Portland, OR: Productivity Press.

Van den Heuvel, J., Does, R., Bogers, A., & Berg, M. (2006). Implementing Six-Sigma in The Netherlands. *Joint Commission Journal on Quality and PatientSafety, 32(1),* 393–9.

Varkey, P., Reller, M., & Resar, R. (2007). Basics of quality improvement in health care. *Mayo Clinic Proceedings. Mayo Clinic, 82(6),* 735–9.

Walston, S., & Bogue, R. (1999). The effects of reengineering: Fad or competitivefactor? *Journal of Healthcare Management, 44* (6), 456.

Womack, J.P.Jones, D T and Roos, D (1990). T*he Machine that changed the world:*

the story of Lean Production. New York: Rawson Associates.

Womack, J. & Jones, D. (2003). *Lean Thinking: Banish Waste and Create Wealth in Your Corporation,* Revised & Updated, New York, NY: HarperBusiness.

Zidel, T. (2006). A Lean Toolbox—Using Lean principles and techniques in healthcare. *Journal of Healthcare Quality, 28(1),* W1–7.

Annexure A: Definitions – Metric

Sr. No.	Asset	Metric	Definition	Targets
1	OPD	%Patients waiting beyond 15 mins of appointment	% pateints waiting in OPD beyond 15 min of appt time to see the consultant. The entering time in to OPD chamber wil the taken as the patient seen time	<5%
2	PHC	% PHCs completed within 4:30 hrs	% PHCs completed within 4:30 hrs (including final consultation). It starts from the billing time till the patients final consult is over	90%
3	ER	%Pts with Length of Stay more than 4 hrs in triage	Length of stay of patients in ER (Observation/Triage). The patient must be admitted/discharged and moved out of the ER within 4 hours of his/her arrival at the ER.	5%
4	ER	% of Ambulance calls responsed outside 10 mins of receiving the call	Total time taken by our ambulance to leave the hospital after receiving an emergency call.	5%
5	Wards	% Discharges before 11 am	Physical movement of patient from the room before 11 am.	75%
6	OT	% of Procedures/ Surgeries starting within 30 mins of scheduled time	All planned procedures/surgeries must start within 30 mins of allocated time	90%

7	Lab Med	% of Short lead time tests completed within 1:30 hours	Total time taken in processing the defined short lead tests. These tests are machine based investigations – Bio Chem, Hem, COAG, SER	90%
8	ER	% Ambulance calls turned back	Any ambulance call refused due to any reason	5%
9	IPD	% of Patients denied Admission	Any patient refused for a bed under any circumstance.	0%
10	ICU	% step downs planned	% of planned step downs that are communicated to bed manager an evening in advance out of total step downs that actually happen from ICUs	80%
11	Wards	% discharges planned	Discharges that are planned and communicated an evening in advance to the Bed Manager and stakeholders divided by the total discharges that actually happened.	80%
12	Wards	Length of discharge process	Total time taken from the doctors intimation for discharge till the patient physically leaves the room. Doctor's intimation can be telephonic or physical round.	120 min
13	House-keeping	TAT for Room cleaning post discharge	Total time taken to clean the discharge room to make it ready for next admission.	30

Annexure B: Value Stream Mapping (VSM) – Spaghetti Maps

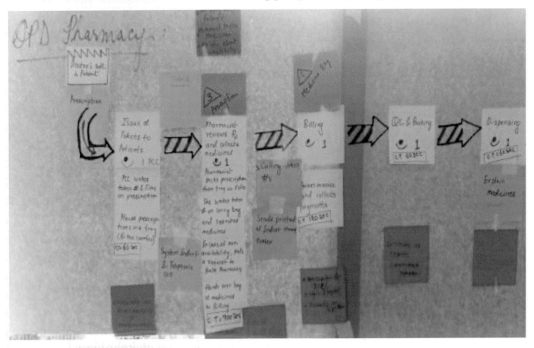

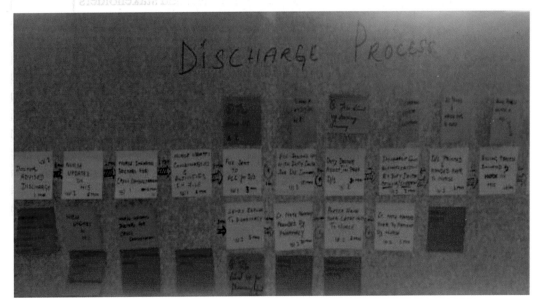

Financial Inclusion in Digital Economy

Priyanka Jain*, Ankur Roy** & Vishal Vyas***

Abstract

The present study explores the nexus between financial inclusion and the digital economy in India. The objective of the study concludes the level of influence caused by antecedents of digital economy on financial inclusion. Data was collected through survey method, using random sample of educated adults in the state of Rajasthan (India). The structural equation modelling was used to study the series of dependence relationships among involved latent constructs. The results indicate that among involved latent constructs, Consumer/User Value Proposition significantly influences financial inclusion. The study is useful for Government and Non- government agencies to spread awareness for derived benefits associated with digital transactions and feasible economy.

Keywords: Financial Inclusion, Digital Economy, Structural Equation Modelling.

Introduction

The digital economy is swiftly developing as the fundamental driver of innovation, growth and competition across the globe. The speed of technological change in the digital economy is often mentioned as "sharing economy". A sharing economy largely brings together the wide spectrum of people, process, corporations, governments, and policy makers for sharing resources and information. It generates a network effect that increases access and value for all involved.

No industry is impervious to this digital transformation. The financial services industry, situated at the heart of the global economy, figure prominently in this equation. An important aspect of digital economy is the creation of a financial system that leverages technology and ingenuity to provide access for those who need it. The responsibility of inclusive digital financial services is to offer and evolve such market-technology led-self-sustaining alternatives that can interact more easily and adapt to the financial needs of a diverse set of customers.

* Mody University, Laxmangarh
** Management Development Institute, Gurgaon.
*** ABV-Indian Institute of Information Technology & Management, Gwalior

Financial inclusion is broadly understood as access to formal financial sector for marginalised and deprived sections of society. Policymakers all over the world are exploring ways and means to ensure greater inclusion of the financially excluded segments of society. However, available evidence from most developing economies shows that access to banking and other formal financial services is limited largely due to factors which can either be attributed to the demand-side (access and usage) or supply-side (capacity of formal financial service providers) (Sun & Siagian, 2015).

The contemporary philosophy at the global level has also had its echo in India. Policymakers at various levels are undertaking a wide range of measures to include the excluded or the under-served within the umbrella of formal finance. Accordingly, the Government and the Reserve Bank of India has undertaken a whole host of innovative and dedicated measures to drive forward the financial inclusion agenda.

As a result over the last decade, India's financial inclusion agenda has seen a paradigm shift from an emphasis on credit to a more comprehensive approach toward financial services and products. This new approach demands a change in the financial architecture of India's economy. Henceforth, a comprehensive blueprint for the architecture of financial inclusion was created by the Mor Committee (2014). It accentuates the adoption and reliance on technology to cut costs and improve service delivery, such that by 2021 over 90 % of the hitherto underserved sections of society will become active stakeholders in economic progress empowered by formal finance. The new architecture of inclusion reflects the failure of the traditional formal sector (brick- motor system) and the need to adopt modern methods.

Literature Review

The world has undergone a transition from a traditional economy (agricultural or industrial) to a digital economy (Economist Intelligence Unit (EIU), 2010). This transformation has a manifold impact which can be acknowledged in terms of changed business models, renovated government policies and practices and day to day activities of common people (Weill and Woerner, 2013). Acknowledging the role of digitalization for growth and inclusiveness, worldwide governments have been developing national digital economy strategies. This progression of digitalization puts a strong emphasis on the promotion of information technology and induced its use for improving business processes and in service delivery by government entities (Nograšek and Vintar, 2014). The adoption and success of technology acceptance models (TAM) depends on their perceived usefulness, perceived ease of use and self-efficacy (Hung et al., 2013; Alomari et al., 2012). However, these TAM models are required to be integrated into a broader context (organisational, social, and national) and include variables related to both human and social change processes (Bélanger and Carter, 2012).

With the prospect of reaching billions of new customers, banks and nonbanks have begun to offer financial services through digital platform for financially excluded and underserved populations. These services should be suited to the customers' needs and delivered responsibly, at affordable cost (Gangopadhayay, 2009) to customers and sustainable for providers (Rajan and Zingales, 1998). Dabholkar (1996) determined the intention for using technology-based self-service option constructed on expected service quality and found that it is influenced by speed of delivery, ease of use, reliability, enjoyment and control. Moreover, customers are attracted to electronic banking technologies because of convenience, ease of use and cost savings (Anguelov et al. 2004).

"Fintech" is a catchall used for advanced, mostly internet-based technologies in the financial sector. The term describes modern technologies for enabling or providing financial services, in the e-commerce field, mobile payments or early-stage crowd-based financing of start-ups.

The Fintech movement is being buoyed by the accelerating pace of developments in mobile devices, big data analysis, cloud computing, and the growing convergence of information and communication technologies (ICT). This technological induction perhaps requires more consumer involvement, as it demands regular interaction with additional technology (Kolodinsky et al., 2004).

Mobile banking models leverage off the enormous success of mobile phone uptake in developing countries by using the phone as a key channel to reach new and underserved customers (Pickens et al., 2009). Mobile banking models rely generally on a large range of non-traditional agents such as retailers to provide cash-in and cash-out functions, while keeping service costs low. It addresses confidentiality and trust in service providers (Liao, et al., 2011) and behavioural trade-offs that individuals undertake when conducting economic transactions (DellaVigna, 2009). KPMG (2009, 2010) conducted a survey on consumers and digital technology and found high level of concern regarding privacy.

Infrastructure has been identified as another major antecedent of implementation of digital economy in the quest for financial inclusion (Gheysari et al., 2012). Literacies are therefore required that allow participants to engage in self-directed learning by supporting participation and collaborative knowledge construction within the digital environment.

New hybrid models (mixes technological and economic features) don't restrict the financial services within specific boundaries. It extends the reach of banking services and financial transactions to everyplace where internet facility could be found (Khan & Craig-Lees, 2009). To aid higher levels of inclusion, entry thresholds that have excluded socially vulnerable customers such as affordability, eligibility, and geographical barriers are being addressed through these hybrid models.

EFInA (2013) found a positive correlation between financial inclusion and the proportion of electronic transactions in a society (Solo, 2008). However, emerging evidences from literature has indicated that attainment of high levels of financial inclusion requires aggressive policies that promote digital economy (Ebiringa, 2010).

Conceptual Framework, Hypothetical Model and Hypothesis

The digital economy is multidimensional in nature (Tapscott, 1996). It is too dynamic and wide to be described synthetically and precisely by a single definition. It is interpreted as information technology, e-commerce (Moulton, 2000) and human intelligence networking. It is defined as the "proliferation of the use of internet", "connectivity among multiple heterogeneous ideas and actors" (Carlsson, 2004). Therefore, the challenge is how to define and measure the digital economy, as it is multidimensional and constantly evolving.

To address the aforesaid issue authors identified four variables as enablers of digital economy from literature review. These four inclusive enablers acknowledge the characteristics of digital economy and are supported by the measures developed and tested by the Economist Intelligence Unit (EIU) (2010) (Figure 1).

Figure1: Proposed Measures of Digital Economy

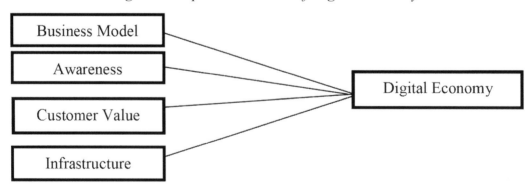

Source: Authors own representation

The Indian financial services landscape is undergoing a technology driven shift. The steps taken by RBI on financial inclusion needed support of digital infrastructure to reach the unbanked population. This shift from Brick and motor business to digital platforms will subsequently increase digital financial access at a low cost. Digital India coupled with payments infrastructure, is building the platform for digital economy, based upon the increasing willingness of people using the internet, and the rising data traffic in the country. The National Payments Corporation (NPCI) is putting across the country a digital network which will eventually enable a lot of payments to be made on the digital platform.

Following the foregoing discussion, it can be concluded that the digital environment may act as a stimulator in promoting increase financial access across the country and is seen as one of the preconditions for comprehensive financial inclusion. Consequently, in this context the present study proposed the hypothetical model (Figure 2) and has employed structural equation modelling to explore the influence of enablers of digital economy on financial inclusion.

Figure 2:- Proposed Model

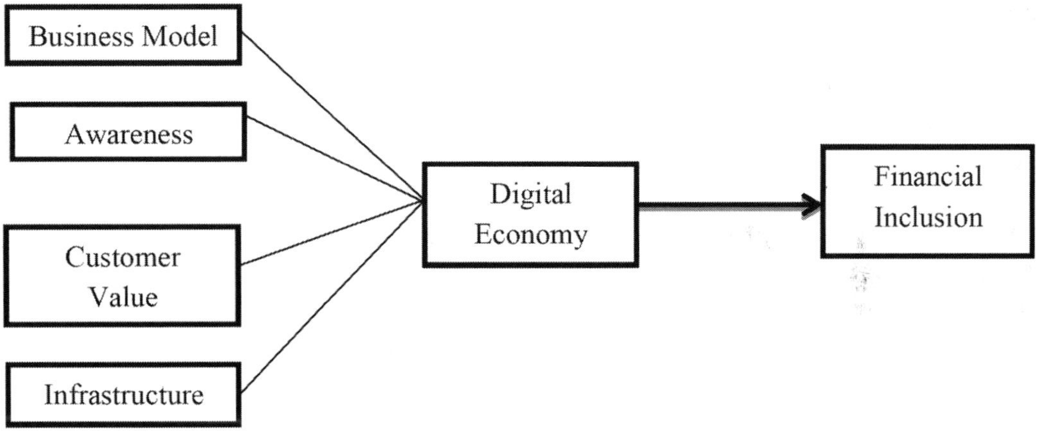

Source: Authors own representation

The study proposes the following hypothesis:

H_1:- Digital economy has significant effect on financial inclusion

Research Objectives

The study attempts to explore how the enablers (based on selected factors) of digital economy influence financial inclusion in India, (with specific reference to Rajasthan). Therefore, the specific objectives are:

- ➤ To examine the effects of change in business models of financial service providers on financial inclusion.
- ➤ To examine the effects of awareness of electronic channels on financial inclusion.
- ➤ To assess the effects of using enhanced formal financial services on financial inclusion.
- ➤ To examine the effects of accessibility of payments infrastructure on financial inclusion.

Research Methodology

The present study has characteristics of both exploratory and descriptive research designs. To develop an understanding regarding the subject matter, knowledge and its applicability in the context of Rajasthan state an experience survey as a part of exploratory research design has been used. Moreover, for conceptual understanding and for development of hypothetical model and hypothesis an extensive literature review has done. The study is descriptive in nature too because it intends to find out who is involved, and the size of the group etc. From the population of more than 38,275,282[1] educated adults in the state, a large sample was chosen.

Population and Sampling Frame

The educated adults (males and females) residing in different districts of Rajasthan constituted the population as per the Census survey conducted in year 2011. Based on convenience an appropriate sampling frame is prepared from the records available with the "Directorate of Literacy & Continuing Education" an undertaking of Rajasthan government.

Sample Size and Sampling

The data would be analysed with multivariate data analysis technique, therefore a large sample size is required to justify the number of variables included in the study. The total population which formed part of the sample frame is 10,804,263 from various districts of Rajasthan having high literacy rate as per census, 2011 as shown in the following table (1). In total, a sample of 400 should be selected from a targeted population of 10,804,263. To resolve the problem of missing data, biases arising out of outliers, non- responses, a sample of 450 educated adults is considered to precede further (Hair et al. 2006). Proportionate stratification sampling technique a type of stratified random sampling is employed for creating proportionate stratums (table 1).

---

[1] http://www.rajliteracy.rajasthan.gov.in/literacy-scenario.htm

Table 1: Sampling Procedure

Rajasthan State				
District	**Literacy rate (as per census 2011)**	**Population**	**Calculation**	**Proportionate Sample**
Kota	76.56 %	1298345	1298345/10,804,263*450	54
Jaipur	75.51 %	4300965	4300965/10,804,263*450	179
Jhunjhunu	74.13 %	1370360	1370360/10,804,263*450	57
Sikar	71.91 %	1652117	1652117/10,804,263*450	69
Alwar	70.72 %	2182476	2182476/10,804,263*450	91
Total		**10,804,263**		**450**

Source: Authors own representation

Sample and Data Collection Method

Information is collected from both primary and secondary sources. The relevant secondary data related to educated adults is collected from the report on literacy scenario of various districts of Rajasthan as per Census 2011 published by the Directorate of Literacy and Continuing Education, Government of Rajasthan. For primary data, bank intercept survey technique is found to be appropriate as responses are required from relatively large number of respondents. A detailed structured questionnaire containing 29 questions covering all the aspects of digital economy and financial inclusion measures are administered to the selected sample. The scale used is adapted from previous researches in this domain (Bello & Bayero, 2015) and each item has been measured using a Likert scale of five points, ranging from "Strongly Disagree" to "Strongly Agree". Out of 450 distributed questionnaires 399 questionnaires were found to be useful for the analysis purpose depicting the 89% response rate. Demographic characteristics of the sample are as follows (table 2).

Table 2: Demographic Characteristics of the Sample

Demographic Variables	Frequency	Percentage
Annual Income		
Between Rs 1–5 Lakhs	113	28.3 %
Between Rs 5 to Rs 10 Lakhs	150	37.5 %
Between Rs 10 to Rs 15 Lakhs	92	23.05 %
Between Rs 15 to Rs 20 Lakhs	44	11.02 %

Demographic Variables	Frequency	Percentage
Occupation		
Government Servant	123	30.8%
Private Sector Employee	109	27.3%
Businessman/Woman	79	19.7%
Self employed	88	22%
Education Level		
Secondary	57	14.2 %
Senior Secondary	54	13.5%
Graduation	113	28.3%
Post-Graduation	106	26.5%
Professional/others	69	17.2%
Age Group		
Under 30	75	18.79%
Between 30 to 45	159	39.84%
Between 45 to 55	113	28.3%
Above 55	52	13%
Gender		
Male	243	60.9%
Female	156	39%

Source: Authors own representation

Research Tool

A two-step structural equation modelling (SEM) is employed for estimating parameters (Anderson & Gerbing 1988). The measurement model is a confirmatory factor analysis (CFA) used to specify the relationship between observed variables and latent variables. To provide a more parsimonious account for the correlations among the lower-order factors second-order CFA has been used. To explore the kind of relationship between multiple dependent and independent variables (Smith, 2004) SEM is employed.

Results of Data Analysis Measurement Model

IBM AMOS 19 software was used to perform CFA. The analysis focused on one second order latent variable i.e. Digital Economy (DE); four first order latent variables viz. Business Model (BM), Awareness (AW), Customer Value (CV), Infrastructure (IN), Financial Inclusion(FI) and 29 observed variables. CFA provides an assessment of reliability and validity of the observed variables for each latent (first and second-order) variable (Joreskog and Sorbom, 1989). The constructs under consideration (DE and FI) are jointly analysed in measurement model.

In measurement model, degree of variance is measured by squared factor loadings. Observed variables are considered to have higher explanatory power when the squared factor loading for each one is more than 0.50 (Holmes-Smith, 2001).

The model fit was assessed using CMIN/DF, goodness-of-fit index (GFI; Joreskog and Sorbom, 1989), the comparative fit index (CFI; Bentler, 1990), root mean square error of approximation (RMSEA; Browne and Cudeck, 1993), Tucker-Lewis coefficient (TLI; Bollen, 1989), adjusted goodness of fit index (AGFI) and root mean square residual (RMR). The threshold for CMIN/DF should be less than 3.0 (Hu and Bentler, 1999) or less than 2.0 in a more restrictive sense (Byrne, 1989). However, CMIN is affected by sample size and normality of the data (Tabachnick and Fidell, 2001; Schumacker and Lomax, 2004). Therefore, the CMIN test should be used in combination with other indices. Values of GFI, AGFI, TLI and CFI should be over 0.90. Moreover RMSEA should be lower than 0.05 to indicate a close fit of the model in relation to the degree of freedom.

The proposed measurement model showed that all regression weights are significant ($p < 0.001$). The absolute fit statistics showed a chi-square of 410.124 with 297(df) is significant ($p = .000$) [CMIN/DF = 1.381] with RMSEA = .031, RMR = 0.106, CFI = 0.978, and TLI = 0.976. This suggested that the model fitted adequately to the data and is acceptable, moreover other fit indices viz. GFI = 0.929, and AGFI = 0.916, are also supportive.

All items factor loadings are statistically significant and are greater than 0.60, which confirmed the convergent validity of the model. Moreover, covariance among the factors (DE and FI) are significant ($p < 0.001$). As model fitted the data adequately respecification is not required. However, composite reliability (CR) and average variance extracted (AVE) is calculated to test the convergent validity. AVE should be either greater than or equal to 0.50 and CR should be greater than or equal to 0.60 (Bagozzi and Yi, 1988). The CR and AVE calculated for the second-order construct is satisfying the minimum cut off set in theory. Hence it could be concluded that the measures used within this research are within the acceptable levels supporting the reliability of constructs. Additionally, construct's factor loadings are statistically significant. Hence convergent validity of the constructs is established. After evaluating the reliability, unidimensionality, constructs validity and convergent validity of the measurement model, the next stage is to perform the analysis of the structural model. To establish discriminant validity, the variance shared between a construct and any other construct in the model need to be assessed (Fornell et al. 1982). The values in table (3) suggested that discriminant validity is present at the construct level in the measurement model. Table (4) displays the summary results of CFA.

Table 3: Discriminant Validity for the Measurement Model

	FI	DE
FI	(0.773)	
DE	0.477	(0.556)

Source: Authors own representation

Table 4: Summary of Confirmatory Analysis

Variable Label	Final Standardised Loadings	Squared Multiple Correlation	AVE	CR
BM1	0.796	0.645	0.576	0.814
BM2	0.681	0.47		
BM3	0.723	0.527		
BM4	0.803	0.647		
BM5	0.772	0.602		
BM6	0.771	0.601		
AW1	0.828	0.659	0.535	0.727
AW2	0.804	0.634		
AW3	0.793	0.618		
AW4	0.804	0.634		
AW5	0.257	0.06		
CV1	0.575	0.575	0.578	0.836
CV2	0.593	0.593		
CV3	0.593	0.593		
CV4	0.624	0.624		
CV5	0.758	0.577		
CV6	0.720	0.52		

IN1	0.802	0.657	0.593	0.800
IN2	0.788	0.627		
IN3	0.761	0.586		
IN4	0.752	0.573		
IN5	0.747	0.565		
FI3	0.769	0.593	0.598	0.746
FI4	0.831	0.691		
FI5	0.757	0.573		
FI6	0.732	0.535		
BM	0.541	0.293	0.309	0.616
AW	0.524	0.274		
CV	0.595	0.354		
IN	0.534	0.285		

Model Fit: Chi Square = 410.124 (df = 279), p = .000, RMSEA = 0.031, AGFI = 0.916, RMR = 0.106, GFI = 0.929, TLI = 0.976, and CFI = 0.978

Source: Authors own representation

Structural Model

SEM, a multivariate technique is employed to study the relationship between DE and FI. Goodness-of-fit indices are analysed to evaluate the fitness of hypothesized structural model. As the assumptions underlying structural equation modelling are met, overall model fit indices along with the various coefficient parameters are estimated to test the relationship between the two latent constructs (DE and FI). The indices for goodness-of-fit demonstrate that model fits the data adequately (Chi-square = 410.124, df = 297, p = .000). The GFI = 0.929, AGFI = .916, RMSEA = .031, CFI = .978, TLI = .976, RMR = .106 and CMIN/DF = 1.381. The R^2 for the model came to 0.23 (Table 5). The structural model is depicted in figure 2.

The result indicates that the independent variables succeeded in explaining 23 % of the variance in the dependent variable. The $R^2 = 0.23$ is reasonable and substantial considering the nature of the study (Cohen, 1998). The relationship is statistically significant (at 0.001 probability level) and in the hypothesized direction. However, investigation of independent variables in the explanation of the dependent variable (FI) revealed that Business Model (0.29), Awareness (0.27), Enhancing Consumer/User Value Proposition (0.35), and Infrastructure (0.29) have significant contribution.

Table 5: Structural Equation Result: Direct Relationship

	R²
DE Financial Inclusion	0.23

*p=0.001

Figure 2: Structural Model

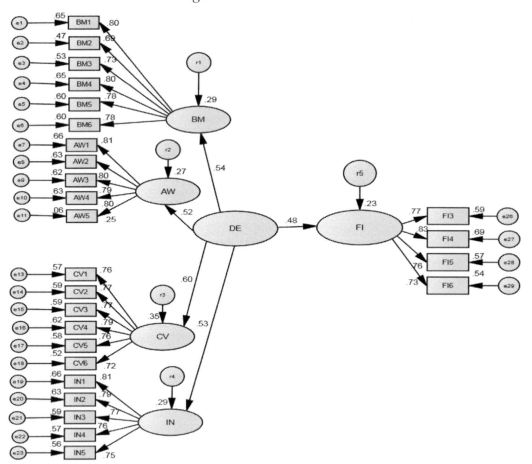

Managerial Implications

The inferences revealed allow the policy makers (Government) and other agencies to know about the influence of business models of financial service providers, awareness of electronic platforms, customer value proposition and infrastructure as facilitators of digital economy on financial inclusion. Being the policy makers they have to understand that evolution of digital economy however unlocks new business models, yet at the same time, there is an imbalance in demand and supply of financial services. Supply side enablers are acutely constrained by lack of viable and sustainable business models. For their part they are required to build market-led self-sustaining alternatives supported by rapid technological innovations. It would extend banking and other financial services to the excluded along with the establishment of dispute settlement mechanism to take care of errors in transactions. For encountering the demand side business models must be easily accessible, simple to comprehend and priced according to consumer perceived value. It must offer a variety of savings options with security features and must establish consumer trust. Offering right product mix certainly holds promise for a viable business model by meeting consumer needs and aspirations.

Another important facet of the digital economy that contributes to financial inclusion is awareness or more precisely the digital literacy. It can be defined as "user's knowledge about the technological capabilities, features, potential use, cost and benefits, i.e., it relates to awareness-knowledge. Most of the rural consumers in India are still lacking familiarity with digital technology. They often experience difficulties and are averse in their attitude towards its adoption and are less keen in learning. To resolve this issue policy makers must assign or involve educated agents, social groups, mass and media to make the people sensitive towards this matter. They must be committed to promote, together with their proximity and such teaching learning relationship with clients may generate significant impact on the demand generated.

Enhancement of the customer value proposition is the most crucial pillar of digital economy that contributes significantly in financial inclusion. Therefore, policy makers must increase their focus on customer centricity. To accomplish this agenda they are required to develop a wide range of products offering true advantage in terms of cost and utility. Introduce a customer-centric model that normalizes dialogue with customers to better inform product design, processes and rules. Partnership with organizations that serve customers who are situated at the base-of-the-pyramid would help formal financial service providers to focus on customer-centricity. It will help them to understand the consumer demand for digital financial services and it will lead to sustainable digital ecosystems.

Robust and trusted infrastructure is another artefact that contributes to financial inclusion. Henceforth, policy makers are required to invest in such infrastructure that enables open, interconnected systems. It encourages shifting from cash to digital payments with minimal behavioural change on account of customers. The usefulness of transaction accounts is augmented by a broad network of access points. A variety of interoperable access channels would help in achieving wide geographical coverage. In a country like India with diversified culture there is a requirement of infrastructure which supports multi-lingual, voice based interactions, that can simplify the service offerings. From a financial inclusion perspective, payments are the primary daily need of unbanked individuals that can be satisfied by formal financial service providers. Therefore, efforts to offer efficient, safe, widely accessible and customer-friendly payment services infrastructure play a key role in promoting financial inclusion.

Conclusion

The digital economic environment necessitates inclusive-financial access. An effective financial inclusion requires a lot of resources, efforts and a belief in the concept of all-inclusive financial access. Lack of one of these variables will dilute the agenda of universal access to formal financial services. The results of the study show that the model of the study is significant and customer value proposition, infrastructure, business models and awareness, have significant statistical association with financial inclusion. Hence it can be concluded that if digital power is harnessed in financial services then this could prove transformative for developing economies.

Limitations and Directions for Future Research

Few recommendations for future studies to take care of the limitations are:

- ➢ Due to time and financial constraints a generalized impact of digital economy policy on financial inclusion is presented. Factors like gender, age, marital status, literacy level, and occupation were considered as control variables.
- ➢ Secondly the scope of model in explaining the impact of digital economy on financial inclusion is quite narrow. Henceforth, future studies must incorporate other factors that may have significant effects on aforesaid variable.
- ➢ Moreover, mediating and moderating roles of other variables like digital literacy, financial literacy, cultural values and income level can be incorporated in the existing model to study their impact on this relationship.

References

Alomari, M., Woods, P., & Sandhu, K. (2012). Predictors for e-government adoption in Jordan: Deployment of an empirical evaluation based on a citizen-centric approach. *Information Technology & People, 25*(2), 207–234.

Anderson, J. C., & Gerbing, D. (1988). Structural Equation Modelling in Practice: A Review and Recommended Two-Step Approach *Psychological Bulletin, 103*(3), 411–423.

Anguelov, C., E., A.Hilgert., M., & M.Hogarth., J. (2004). U.S. Consumers and Electronic Banking, 1995–2003. *Federal Reserve Bulletin, 90*(Winter), 1–18.

Bagozzi, R. P., & Yi, Y. (1988). On the evaluation of structural equation models. *Journal of the Academy of Marketing Science, 16*(1), 74–94.

Bélanger, F., & Carter, L. (2012). Digitizing government interactions with constituents:an historical review of e-government research in information systems. *Journal of the Association for Information Systems, 13*(5), 363–394.

Bello, B., Garba., & Bayero, A., Musa. (2015). Perceived Effects of Cashless Policy on Financial Inclusion in Nigeria: A Study of Kano Metropolis. *Abuja Journal of Business and Management, 1*(4), 158–167.

Bentler, P. M. (1990). Comparitive Fit Indexes in Structural Models. *Psychological Bulletin, 107*(2), 238–246.

Bollen, K. A. (1989). *Structural Equations with Latent Variables*. New York: Wiley.

Browne, M. W., & Cudeck, R. (1993). *Alternative Ways of Assessing Model Fit*. Newbury Park: Sage.

Byrne, B. M. (1989). *A primer of LISREL: Basic applications and programming for confirmatory factor analytic models*. New York: Springer-Verlag.

Carlsson, B. (2004). The digital economy: what is new and what is not? *Structural Change and Economic Dynamics, 15*(3), 245–264.

Cohen, J. R., Pant, L. W., & Sharp, D. J. (1988). *The Effect of Gender and Academic Discipline Diversity on the Ethical Evaluations, Ethical Intentions, and Ethical Orientation of Potential Public Accounting Recruits* (Vol. 12).

Dabholkar, P. (1996). Consumer evaluations of new technology-based self-service options: An Investigation of alternative models of service quality. *International Journal of Research Marketing, 13*(1), 29–51.

DellaVigna, S. (2009). Psychology and economics: Evidence from the field. *Journal of Economic Literature, 47*, 315–372.

Ebiringa, O. T. (2010). Automated Teller Machine and Electronic Payment System in Nigeria: A synthesis of the critical success factors. *Journal of Sustainable Development in Africa, 1*(12), 71–86.

EFInA. (2013). What does the CBN's Cash-less policy mean for financial inclusion in Nigeria? Retrieved from www.EFInA.or.ng

Fornell, C., Tellis, G. J., & Zinkhan, G. M. (1982). *Validity Assessment: A Structural Equations Approach Using Partial Least Squares, Proceedings.* Paper presented at the American Marketing Association Educators' Conference.

Gangopadhayay, S. (2009). How can Technology Facilitatate Financial Inclusion in India?A discussion paper. *Review of Market Integration, 1*(2), 223–256.

Gheysari, H., Rasli, A., Roghanian, P., & Jebur, H. (2012). The Role of Information Technology Infrastructure Capability (ITIC) in Management. *International Journal of Fundemental Psychology and Social Sciences, 2*(2), 36–40.

Hair, J., Black, W., Babin, B., Anderson, R., & Tatham, R. (2006). *Multivariate data analysis* (6th ed.). Uppersaddle River, New Jersy: Pearson Prentice Hall.

Holmes, S. P. (2001). *Introduction to Structural Equation Modelling using LISREAL.* Perth.

Hu, L., & Bentler, P. (1999). Cutoff Criteria for Fit Indices in Covariance Structure Analysis: Conventional Criteria versus New Alternatives Structural Equation Modelling. *6*(1), 1–55.

Hung, S. Y., Chang, C. M., & Kuo, S. R. (2013). User acceptance of mobile e-government services: an empirical study. *Government Information Quarterly, 30*(1), 33–44.

Jöreskog, K. G., & Sörbom, D. (1989). *LISREL7, A Guide to the Program and Applications* Chicago: SPSS Publications.

Khan, J., & Craig-Lees, M. (2009). Cashless Transactions: Perception of Money in Mobile Payments. *International Busness and Economic Review, 1*(1), 23–32.

Kolodinsky, J. M., Hogarth, J. M., & Hilgert, M. A. (2004). The adoption of electronic banking technologies by US consumers. *International Journal of Bank Marketing, 22*(4), 233–241.

Liao, C., Liu, C.-C., & Chen, K. (2011). Examining the impact of privacy, trust and risk perceptions beyond monetary transactions: An integrated model. *Electronic Commerce Research and Applications, 10*(6), 702–715.

Moulton, B. R. (2000). *GDP and the Digital Economy: Keeping Up With The Changes. Understanding the Digital Economy: Data, Tools, and Research.* Cambridge and London.

Nograšek, J., & Vintar, M. (2014). E-government and organisational transformation of government: Black box revisited? *Government Information Quarterly, 31*(1), 108–118.

Pickens, M. (2009). *Window on the unbanked: Mobile money in the Philippines.* Washington, DC: CGAP.

Rajan, R., & Zingales, L. (1998). Financial Dependence and Growth. *American Economic Review, 88*(3), 559–587.

Schumacker, R., & Lomax, R. (2004). *A Beginners Guide to Structural Equation Modelling* New York: Lawrence Erlbaum.

Smith, D. (2004). Structural Equation Modelling in Management Accounting Research: Critical Analysis and Opportunities. *Journal of Accounting Research 23*, 49–86.

Solo, T. M. (2008). Financial exclusion in Latin America – or the social costs of not banking the urban poor. *Environment and Urbanization, 20*(1), 47–66.

Sun, Y., & Siagian, P. (2015). Financial Inclusion in Indonesia and Its Challenges. *Pertanika Journal of Social Sciences and Humanities, 23*(S), 85–96.

Tabachnick, B., & Fidell, L. (2007). *Using Multivariate Statistics* (5th ed.). New York: Allyn & Bacon.

Tapscott, D. (1996). *The Digital Economy: Promise and Peril In The Age of Networked Intelligence* (Vol. 1). New York, NY: McGraw-Hill.

Weill, P., & Woerner, S. L. (2013). The future of the CIO in a digital economy. *MIS Quarterly Executive, 12*(2), 65–75.

Influence of Perceived Organizational Climate on Turnover Tendency of Premium Hotel Employees

Amit Datta & *Amit Jain**

Abstract

The turnover of hotel employees is an interminable HR issue. The hotel industry is a service oriented industry and depends heavily on employee's work attitude for its sustainability. The most essential thing that directs the attitude of the employees is their own perception about the working condition of the organization, i.e. organizational climate. The purpose of this study was to investigate the influence of organizational climate and its dimensions on turnover tendency of hotel employees. Data of 163 respondents of selected premium hotels in India was collected through a structured questionnaire. The organizational climate was measured by 59 item THOCS by Davidson,et.al,(2001) consisting of seven dimensions and the turnover tendency was measured by 3 item scale by Camman, et.al (1979). The data analysis revealed that there is significant negative correlation among the dimensions of organizational climate and turnover tendency. Regression analysis found that the seven climate dimensions explain 27.1% of the variation in turnover tendency, of which 'Professional & Organizational Esprit' and 'Regulation, Organization & Pressure' were found to have significant unique contributions to prediction. ANOVA analysis revealed a significant difference in turnover tendency across 04 operation departments of the hotels and the mean plot suggests that the housekeeping department records the highest turnover tendency amongst other operation departments. The probable reasons were analyzed and suggestions pertaining to the improvement in working condition of the hotel that reflect organizational climate are given. The climate need to be such that it suits the characteristic and meets the expectations of the concerned employees. The study suggests suitable measures to create healthy working environment to increase retention.

Keywords: Organizational Climate, Turnover Tendency, Hotel, Hotel Management, Employee.

Introduction

The study on 'Organizational Climate' (OC) can be traced back to the work of Lewin, et.al (1939), and has persistently been the emphasis of many empirical

* Manipal University, Jaipur

research studies (Cornell, 1955). OC as a word was possibly outlined by Cornell, (1955) and expressed as a "delicate blending of interpretations or perceptions by persons in the organization of their jobs or roles in relationship to others and their interpretation of the roles of others in the organization". In the study Litwin & Stringer, (1968) stated that "climate is a set of measurable properties of the work environment, based on the collective perceptions of the people who work in the environment and demonstrated to influence their motivation and behaviour". The study by Pritchard & Karasick, (1973) integrated several explanations given by earlier researchers and collectively presented OC as a constant quality of an organization's internal environment, different from other organizations, which are significances of the behaviour of the organization's members, which are perceived and interpreted by the members and regulate the consequences of the behaviour of the members.

The concept culture and climate have constantly been either confused or used interchangeably. Through an extensive study on both climate and culture literature, Denison, (1996) acknowledged many dissimilarities between OC and culture. The author concluded that organizational culture represents the essential structure of an organization, rooted in the values, beliefs, and assumptions of organizational members. Whereas OC is devulged in the practices and actions, that are deceptive at the surface of the organization. OC is emphasized to be temporary, subject to direct control and restricted to characteristics that are perceived by the employees.

From a research point of view, therefore, OC is a very interesting phenomenon. It can be influenced easily, and changes in OC can be observed over a short time span (Putter, 2010) and reflected in the behavioural outcomes of its members and in turn influences organizational performances (Manning, et.al, 2004, 2012; Johnston & Spinks, 2013; Johnston, et.al, 2013).

Theoretical Framework

In the research Denison, (1996) discusses that evolving a universal set of dimensions was often the fundamental issue of the climate researchers so that relative studies could be made possible in different organizational settings. This approach was compared to that of culture research that used a post-modern perspective which examined the qualitative features of individual social contexts where each culture that was observed was seen as unique and was not expected to have generalizable qualities which had become crucial to the OC research.

Based on past studies Jones & James, (1979) developed Psychological Climate Questionnaire (PCQ) consisting of 35 'a priori concept' (potential dimensions) which was further modified and used by Ryder & Southey, (1990). The study conducted by Davidson, et.al, (2001) in fourteen 4/5 star hotels in Australia used the further modified version of the same instrument. This scale was called the Tourism & Hospitality Organizational Climate Scale (THOCS) and is widely acknowledged and the framework has been used by researchers in different tourism & hospitality settings to measure climate (Manning, et.al, 2004, 2012; Johnston & Spinks, 2013; Johnston, et.al, 2013).

Lewin, (1951) submitted that the behavioral outcome of an individual within an organization is a function of the individual and the organizational environment as represented by the principle of environmental influences on an individual's behavior. Past researches had indicated that OC perceptions are allied with a diversity of significant consequences for an individual, work group and organization as a whole (Davidson, et.al, 2001; Manning, et.al, 2004, 2012; Subramanian & Shin, 2013).

The hotel as an organization is highly diversified, the 04 operation departments of the hotel such as Culinary, Food & Beverage Service (F&B Service), Housekeeping and Front Office are unique by the nature of the job and may not be generalized with other departments. The employees working in these departments are of hotel management background (Andrews, 2009) and they undergoes maximum turnover than other supportive departments (Gangai, 2013). Studies of OC has established the fact that different departments of an organization would perceive the climate differently and which in turn would have dissimilar impact on turnover (Jones & James, 1979; Zhang & Liu, 2010; Subramanian & Shin, 2013). Since actual turnover is difficult to measure, the constant study of Turnover Tendency (TT) in hospitality industry is essential (Griffeth, Hom, & Gaertner, 2000).

Research Methodology

The objective of this study was primarily to investigate the relationship between OC and TT of hotel employees. Qualitative research was implemented and was based on secondary data. Secondary research was initially undertaken and a vast range of literature was reviewed, based on which the research objective was identified and research design was framed. The empirical research was based on primary data.

The respondents considered as sample have the following characteristic:

- Employees working in the premium hotels (4/5-star) located in India
- All were hotel management graduates and working in any one of the 4 major

operation departments of the hotel, i.e. Culinary, F&B Service, Housekeeping and Front Office.

- Employees working in the Entry level, Supervisory level and Managerial level within 35 years were included as samples

Convenience sampling method was adopted to choose the hotels. The questionnaire was delivered to the Training Manager of the 10 selected hotels in India. They were briefed about the purpose, criteria of the respondents and were assured that the confidentiality of the employee and the hotel would be maintained. Each hotel's representative was asked to return the filled data within a month. 169 questionnaire was returned, out of which 06 were found to be incomplete. Responses of 163 hotel employees were loaded in SPSS-21 software for analysis.

Hypotheses

H_{o1}: There is no association between overall OC and TT in premium category hotels in India.

H_{o2}: There is no association between 'Leaders Facilitation & Support' dimension of OC and TT in premium category hotels in India.

H_{o3}: There is no association between 'Professional & Organizational Esprit' dimension of OC and TT in premium category hotels in India.

H_{o4}: There is no association between 'Conflict & Ambiguity' dimensions of OC and TT in premium category hotels in India.

H_{o5}: There is no association between 'Regulation, Organization & Pressure' dimension of OC and TT in premium category hotels in India.

H_{o6}: There is no association between 'Job Variety, Challenge & Autonomy' dimension of OC and TT in premium category hotels in India.

H_{o7}: There is no association between 'Work Group, Cooperation & Friendliness' dimensions of OC and TT in premium category hotels in India.

H_{o8}: There is no association between 'Job Standards' dimension of OC and TT in premium category hotels in India.

H_{o9}: TT of the employees of premium category hotel is not significantly influenced by the dimensions of OC.

H_{o10}: There is no significant difference in perception of overall OC amongst employees of 04 operation departments of the hotel.

H_{o11}: There is no significant difference of TT amongst employees of 04 operation departments of the hotel.

Data Processing, Validity and Reliability

The 59 item THOCS developed by Davidson, et.al, (2001) & the 3 item TT scale developed by Camman, et.al, (1979) was used to measure the responses of 163 employees working in 04 operational areas of the selected hotels. Later the questionnaire was used in various researches and considered to be highly valid (Manning, et.al, 2004; Liu, 2005).

The data of the respondents was uploaded in the SPSS-21 software. Recoding of the reverse coded 08 items of OC and 01 item of TT was carried out. The reliability of the two variables was checked by Cronbach's Alpha statistic and was found highly acceptable (Table 01).

Table 01: Reliability Statistic

Variables	No. of Items	Cronbach's Alpha Score	George & Mallery, 2003
Organizational Climate	59	0.923	Excellent
Turnover Tendency	03	0.856	Good

Data Analysis and Interpretation

Descriptive statistic of each item and composite scores of the dimension and overall mean and standard deviation of the two variables of the instrument were calculated (Table 02).

Table 02: Descriptive Statistics of the variables of 163 samples.

Dimension Name	Item	Mean (M)	Standard Deviation (sd)	Overall Mean	Overall Sd
LEADER FACILIATION & SUPPORT	Overall I think my immediate supervisor is doing a good job.	4.01	1.012	4.033	0.586
	My supervisor is friendly and easy to approach	3.96	1.143		
	My supervisor is attentive to what I say.	4.0	0.994		
	My supervisor offers new ideas for job and related problems.	3.81	1.097		
	My supervisor sets an example by working hard himself/herself.	4.01	1.066		
	My immediate supervisor is successful in dealing with higher levels of management.	4.23	0.772		
	My supervisor provides the help I need to schedule my work ahead of time.	4.09	0.878		
	My supervisor encourages the people who work for him or her to exchange ideas and opinions.	4.08	1.012		
	My supervisor encourages the people who work for him/her to work as a team.	4.15	0.897		
	Staff members generally trust their supervisors.	3.92	0.875		
	The ideas and suggestions of staff members are paid attention to.	3.99	0.93		
	Supervisors generally know what is going on in their work groups.	4.02	0.926		
	My superior emphasizes high standards of performance.	4.2	0.961		
	My manager is successful in dealing with higher levels of management.	4.12	0.932		
	Staff members generally trust their managers.	3.93	0.924		
	I have good information on where I stand and how my performance is evaluated.	4.06	0.848		
	I am aware of how well my work group is meeting our objectives.	4.01	0.953		

PROFESSIONAL & ORGANIZATIONAL ESPRIT	The hotel strives to do a better job than other hotels of the same type.	4.02	0.952		
	The hotel emphasizes personal growth and development.	3.93	0.95		
	The objectives of the hotel are clearly defined.	4.09	0.99		
	The hotel has a good image to outsiders.	4.36	0.837		
	It is possible to get accurate information on the policies and objectives of this hotel.	3.92	0.882		
	Under most circumstances I would recommend this hotel to a prospective staff member.	3.88	0.901	3.982	0.553
	This hotel is concerned with assisting the local community.	3.6	1.114		
	Working in this hotel is beneficial to my career.	4.09	0.83		
	Managers keep well informed about the needs and problems of employees.	3.99	0.916		
	Discipline in this hotel is maintained consistently.	3.95	0.974		

CONFLICT & AMBIGUITY	Procedures are designed so that resources are used efficiently.	3.98	0.899		
	I have opportunities to complete the work I start.	4.22	0.916		
	My job responsibilities are clearly defined.	4.14	0.915		
	I am able to get the money, supplies, equipment, etc. my work group needs to do its work well.	3.98	0.929		
	I am given advanced information about changes (policies & procedures) which might affect me.	3.85	1.016	4.080	0.521
	The hotel's policies are consistently applied to all staff members.	4.15	0.865		
	The methods of my work are kept up to date.	4.14	0.838		
	Staff members gets on-the-job training they need.	4.15	0.848		
	Responsibility is assigned so that individuals have authority within their own area.	4.12	0.856		
REGULATION, ORGANIZATION & PRESSURE	Excessive rules and regulations interfere with how well I am able to do my job.*	2.74	1.191		
	The way my work group is organized hinders the efficient conduct of work.*	2.48	1.102		
	In this hotel things are planned so that everyone is getting in each other's way.*	2.74	1.158		
	Things in this hotel seem to happen contrary to rules and regulations.*	2.82	1.228		
	Communication is hindered by following chain of command rules*.	2.54	1.056	2.833	0.620
	In this hotel the only source of information on important matters is the grapevine. (rumors)*	3.17	1.395		
	Compared with other work groups, my work group is under much less pressure to produce.	3.32	1.158		
	People act as though everyone must be watched or they will slacken off.*	2.86	1.211		

JOB VARIETY, CHALLENGE & AUTONOMY	There is variety in my job.	3.85	1.172	3.946	0.623
	I have the opportunity to do a number of different things in my job.	4.03	0.878		
	I have opportunities to learn worthwhile skills and knowledge in my job.	4.19	0.798		
	I have opportunities to make full use of my knowledge and skills in my job.	4.08	0.923		
	Most of the personnel in my department would not want to change to another department.	3.63	1.123		
	Opportunity for independent thought and action exists in my job.	3.9	0.957		
WORK GROUP COOPERATION, FRIENDLINESS	Members of my work group trust each other.	4.13	0.879	3.850	0.549
	A friendly atmosphere prevails among most of the members of my workgroup.	4.05	0.888		
	There is friction in my workgroup.*	3.08	1.202		
	A spirit of cooperation exists in my workgroup.	4.02	0.902		
	Most members of my work group take pride in their jobs.	3.96	0.867		
JOB STANDARDS	My job requires a high level of skill and training.	4.17	0.914	4.205	0.552
	I am required to meet rigid standards of quality in my work.	4.03	0.984		
	My job demands perfection.	4.24	0.784		
	My work is important.	4.38	0.897		
OVERALL ORGANIZATIONAL CLIMATE				3.847	0.403
TURNOVER TENDENCY	I often think of leaving this hotel.	2.86	1.457	2.916	1.144
	It is very possible that I will look for a new job next year.	3.25	1.321		
	If I could, I would continue to work for the current hotel.*	2.64	1.093		

*Reverse Coding

The relationship between OC and TT was investigated in two ways. Firstly the correlation coefficients (R) were calculated between TT and overall OC and its 07 dimensions (Table 03) and then followed by Multiple Linear Regression (MLR) to predict hotel's employee TT (Table 05). The analysis described above are in accord with the study of Manning,et.al, (2004).

Table 03: Correlation between TT and overall OC and its 07 dimensions

		Pearson Correlation of Turnover Tendency (R)	Significance (2 tail)
Overall Organizational Climate		-0.428	0.000
Seven Dimensions of Organizational Climate	Leaders, Facilitation & Support	-0.210	0.007
	Professional and Organizational Esprit	-0.358	0.000
	Conflict & Ambiguity	-0.306	0.000
	Regulation, Organization & Pressure	-0.356	0.000
	Job Variety, Challenge & Autonomy	-0.307	0.000
	Work Group, Cooperation & Friendliness	-0.380	0.000
	Job Standards	-0.190	0.015

Table 03 presents the significant correlation (Significant at 0.01 level for 2 tail test) that was found between overall OC and its dimensions with TT. Pearson Correlation of overall OC was found (R= – 0.428) which disprove the null hypothesis (H_{o1}) and accept that there is a significantly strong association (negative) between the overall OC & TT. Simultaneously Pearson correlation of the seven dimensions of OC and TT like Leaders, Facilitation & Support (R= -0.210), Professional & Organizational Esprit (R= -0.358), Conflict & Ambiguity (R= -0.306), Regulation, Organization & Pressure (R= -0.356), Job Variety, Challenge & Autonomy (R= -0.307), Work Group, Cooperation & Friendliness (R= -0.380) and Job Standards (R= -0.190) was found not to accept the null hypotheses ($H_{o2}, H_{o3}, H_{o4}, H_{o5}, H_{o6}, H_{o7}$ & H_{o8}) and to accept that there is a significant association with the seven dimension of OC and TT, as interpreted by Davidson, et.al, (2001).

Table 04: Regression Model Summary

R	R²	Adjusted R Square	Std. Error of the Estimate	Change Statistics				
				R Square Change	F Change	df1	df2	Sig. F Change
.520	.271	.238	.999	.271	8.217	7	155	.000

Table 04 presents the regression model which indicated a significant link between the set of predictor variable of OC and employee's TT ($F_{(7, 155)} = 8.217$, $p<0.001$). The link was reflected by a relatively strong multiple correlation coefficient (R= 0.520). This result means that the 27.1% ($R^2= 0.271$) of the variance in employee's TT may be explained by the 07 organizational climate dimension.

Table 05: Regression coefficients and associated probabilities of MLR using OC dimension to predict perception of hotel employee's TT.

Model	Unstandardized Coefficients		Standardized Coefficients	t	Sig. (p)	Correlations Part (SR²)
	B	Std. Error	Beta			
(Constant)	8.002	.813		9.84	.000	
Leaders, Facilitation & Support	.215	.206	.110	1.04	.300	.071
Professional & Organizational Esprit	-.505	.220	-.244	-2.29	**.023**	-.157
Conflict & Ambiguity	-.153	.252	-.070	-0.60	.546	-.042
Regulation, Organization & Pressure	-.585	.138	-.317	-4.24	**.000**	-.291
Job Variety, Challenge & Autonomy	-.170	.206	-.092	-0.82	.412	-.056
Work Group, Cooperation & Friendliness	-.226	.209	-.109	-1.08	.281	-.074
Job Standards	-.029	.168	-.014	-0.17	.863	-.012

The MLR model presented in Table 05, thus interprets that the null hypothesis (H_{09}) is not accepted and agrees that TT of the employees of premium category of hotel is significantly influenced by the dimensions of OC. Significant unique contributions to prediction were found for dimensions, which are 'Professional & Organizational Esprit' ($SR^2= -0.157$, $t= -2.29$, $p<0.05$) and 'Regulation, Organization & Pressure' ($SR^2 = -0.291$, $t= -4.24$, $p<0.05$).

The data percentage of the 04 operation departments shows Culinary (35.6%), F&B Service (28.2%), Housekeeping (17.8%) and Front Office (18.4%). The calculated means and standard deviations of the OC & TT are presented in Table 06.

Table 06: Descriptive statistic of employees of operation department with OC & TT

Department	Frequency	Percent	Organizational Climate		Turnover Tendency	
			Mean	**Standard Deviation**	**Mean**	**Standard Deviation**
Culinary	58	35.6	3.845	0.367	3.063	1.101
F&B Service	46	28.2	3.895	0.396	2.644	1.199
Housekeeping	29	17.8	3.692	0.450	3.310	0.950
Front Office	30	18.4	3.934	0.409	2.666	1.203
Total	163	100.0	3.847	0.403	2.916	1.144

For testing the hypotheses it is required to compare the means of the samples or groups in order to make inferences about the population means. The Analysis of Variance (ANOVA) is the suitable procedure for comparing the means and to understand whether population means are equal.

Table 07: ANOVA results 'between the groups of' department of hotel

Variable	Sum of Square	Degree of Freedom	Mean Square	F-Value	Sig α	Result at 95% confidence level
Overall Organizational Climate	1.009	3	0.336	2.110	0.101	Insignificant
Turnover Tendency	11.012	3	3.671	2.899	0.037	Significant

Table 07 presents the ANOVA statistic of department for overall OC (F= 2.110, α= 0.101) and for TT (F= 2.899, α= 0.037) which interprets that null hypothesis (H_{o10}) is accepted and (H_{o11}) is not accepted in the given condition. Thus significant differences were found in between the 04 groups of operation department of the hotel with TT only.

Since the significance value from the ANOVA test, does not explain exactly in which condition the employees perception of TT means are different for operational department of premium hotels, Post Hoc Test was carried (Table 08).

Table 08: Post Hoc LSD Test of variable TT across operation department

Department(I)	Department(J)	Mean Difference(I-J)	Standard Error	Significance α
Culinary	F&B Service	0.418	.222	.062
	Housekeeping	-0.247	.255	.336
	Front Office	0.396	.253	.119
F&B Service	Culinary	-0.418	.222	.062
	Housekeeping	-0.665	.266	**.014**
	Front Office	-0.021	.264	.934
Housekeeping	Culinary	0.247	.255	.336
	F&B Service	0.665	.266	**.014**
	Front Office	0.643	.293	**.029**
Front Office	Culinary	-0.396	.253	.119
	F&B Service	0.021	.264	.934
	Housekeeping	-0.643	.293	**.029**

Significant differences were established between Housekeeping & Front Office (α = 0.029) and F&B Service & Housekeeping (α = 0.014) at 95% confidence level which interprets that housekeeping department to be the major contributor of differences in TT.

Figure 01: Mean Plot of TT of employees of different departments of premium hotels

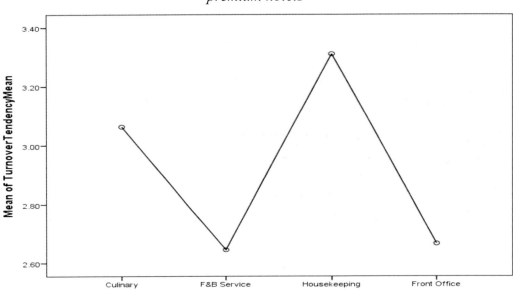

Mean plot of different departments (Figure 01) shows that employees of Housekeeping department perceive highest TT (M= 3.310) followed by Culinary (M= 3.063). F&B Service (M= 2.644) and Front Office (M= 2.666) shows least affinity towards turnover in the given condition.

Result Discussion

The purpose of this research was to determine the relationship between OC and TT of employees working in four operation departments of premium hotels in India through 59 items of THOCS.

The bivariate correlation reveals that there is significant negative correlation between overall OC and TT (R= -0.428). This means that with improved perception of the employees about their working condition would reduce attrition.

Similarly, significant negative correlation was found between the seven dimensions of OC and TT which means that the improved perception of the hotel employees for dimensions 'Leaders, Facilitation & Support' (R= -0.210), 'Professional & Organizational Esprit' (R= -0.358), 'Conflict & Ambiguity' (R= -0.306), 'Regulation, Organization & Pressure' (R= -0.356), 'Job Variety, Challenge & Autonomy' (R= -0.307), 'Work Group, Cooperation & Friendliness' (R = -0.380) and 'Job Standards'

(R= -0.190) would reduce TT. The result is in accordance to the work of Manning, et.al, (2004).

The regression model predicted that the 27.1% of the variance in employee's TT may be explained by the 07 OC dimension. The TT of the employees of premium category of hotel is significantly influenced by the dimensions mainly by the 'Professional & Organizational Esprit' (SR^2= -0.157) and 'Regulation, Organization & Pressure' (SR^2= -0.291). The may be because the employees prefer that the policies and characteristic of the organization and its subsystem should be clearly defined and it should be consistently and fairly applied across all members without any ambiguity. Further there should not be any conflict towards the employee's role and job characteristic. The results justifies the research findings of (NAS Recruitment Communications, 2006; Shaw & Fairhurst, 2008; Solnet & Hood, 2008) about the characteristic and expectation of the Y generation employees.

The operation department showed significant differences with TT (α= 0.037) which is in accordance to the findings of Gangai, (2013). The TT mean suggested that Housekeeping perceive maximum turnover (M= 3.31), followed by Culinary (M= 3.06). F&B Service (M= 2.64) and Front Office (M= 2.66) shows the least affinity towards turnover. This is contrary to the findings of Gangai, (2013) which suggested F&B (Service & Culinary) to have highest attrition than the Rooms Division (Housekeeping & Front Office). Repetitious and not exciting work may be one of the factors which results in highest TT among the present generation Housekeepers'. Also another interesting thing which is revealed is that operation departments have no significant differences in perceived OC, but it has differences in TT. This may be due to the fact that, employees may go for job change irrespective of their perception towards OC. OC might be a contributory factor but not the only factor contributing to turnover. Easy job availability, easiness of job hunt through internet & mobile apps and general perception of the Y generation that faster career growth may be achieved by switching job (NAS Recruitment Communications, 2006) could be factors influencing TT. Based on the analysis the climate needs to be such that it suits the characteristic and meets the expectations of the concerned employees. The other factors mentioned above are not in organizations control.

Limitations and Future Research

The present study is based on samples of selected employees working in premium hotels in India. The findings presented here may not be generalizable to other settings owing to limitations of sample characteristics and size. Further studies with more detailed and comprehensive OC scale with larger sample size and different organizational characteristic are suggested for better understanding of the concept in Indian hospitality.

References

Andrews, S. (2009). *Introduction to Tourism & Hospitality Industry.* New Delhi: Tata McGraw-Hill Education Private Limited.

Cammann, C., Fichman, M., Jenkins, D., & Klesh, J. (1979). The Michigan Organisational Assessment Questionnaire. *University of Michigan.*

Cornell, F. (1955). Socially perceptive administration. *Phi Delta Kappa, 36*(6), 219–223.

Davidson, M., Manning, M., Timo, N., & Ryder, P. (2001). The dimensions of organizational climate on four-star and five-star Australian hotels. *Journal of Hospitality & Tourism Research, 25*(4), 444–461.

Denison, D. R. (1996). What is the difference between Organizational Culture and Organizational Climate? A native's point of view on a decade of paradigm wars. *Academy of Management review, 21*(3), 619–654.

Gangai, K. N. (2013). Attrition at Work Place: How and Why In Hotel Industry. *IOSR Journal of Humanities and Social Science, 11*(2), 38–49.

George, D., & Mallery, P. (2003). SPSS for Windows step by step: A simple guide and reference 11.0 update (4th ed.). Boston: Allyn & Bacon

Griffeth, R. W., Hom, P. W., & Gaertner, S. (2000). A meta-analysis of antecedents and correlates of employee turnover: update, moderator tests, and research implications for the next millennium. *Journal of Management, 26*(3), 463–488.

Johnston, N., & Spinks, W. (2013). Organisational Climate and Employee Turnover Intention within a Franchise System. *Journal of New Business Ideas & Trends, 11*(1), 20–41. Retrieved from http://www.jnbit.org

Johnston, N., Sharma, B., & Spinks, W. (2013). Organizational Climate, service climate and customer satisfaction: An investigation of their relationships in franchised hospitality enterprise. *Social & Behavioural Research in Business, 4*(2), 34–51. Retrieved from http://www.ejsbrb.org

Jones, A. P., & James, L. R. (1979). Psychological Climate: Dimensions and Relationships of Individual and Aggregated Work Environment Perceptions. *Organizational Behaviour and Human Performance, 23*, 201–250.

Lewin, K. (1951). Field theory in social science. New York: Harper.

Lewin, K., Lippit, r., & White, R.K. (1939). Patterns of aggressive behavior in experimentally created "social climates". *Journal of Social Psychology*, 10:271–299.

Litwin, G. H., & Stringer, R. A. (1968). *Motivation and organizational climate.* Boston: Mass: Harvard University Press.

Liu, Y. (2005). Investigating turnover intention among emergency communication specialists. *Graduate Theses and Dissertations.* Retrieved from http://scholarcommons.usf.edu/etd/744

Manning, M. L., Davidson, M. C., & Manning, R. L. (2004). Towards a Shortened Measure of Organizational Climate in Tourism and Hospitality. *Journal of Hospitality and Tourism Research, 28*, 444–462. doi: 10.1177/1096348004267516

Manning, M., Shacklock, A., Bell, N., & Manning, R. (2012). Organizational Climate and Service Climate in Tourism and Hospitality: A review. *Journal of New Business Ideas & Trends, 10*(2), 1–18. Retrieved from http://www.jnbit.org

NAS Recruitment Communications. (2006). *Generation Y: The Millennials Ready or Not here they come.* Retrieved June 19, 2012, from NAS Insights: http://www.nasrecruitment.com/docs/white_papers/Generation-Y.pdf

Pritchard, R. D., & Karasick, B. W. (1973). The effect of organizational climate on managerial job performance and satisfaction. *Organizational Behaviour and Human Performance, 9*, 126–146.

Putter, L. (2010, March). The relation between organizational climate and performance and an investigation of the antecedents of organizational climate. *TuDelft*, 1–66.

Ryder, P. A., & Southey, G. N. (1990, August). An Exploratory Study of the Jones and James Organizational Climate Scales. *Asia Pacific Human Resources Management*, 45–52.

Shaw, S., & Fairhurst, D. (2008). Engaging a new generation of graduates. *Education + Training, 50*(5), 366–378.

Solnet, D., & Hood, A. (2008). Generation Y as hospitality employees: Framing a research agenda. *Journal of Hospitality and Tourism Management, 15*, 59–68. DOI 10.1375/jhtm.15.59.

Subramanian, I. D., & Shin, Y. N. (2013). Perceived Organizational Climate and Turnover Intention of Employees in the Hotel Industry. *World Applied Sciences Journal, 22*(12), 1751–1759.

Zhang, J., & Liu, Y. (2010). Organizational Climate and its Effects on Organizational Variables: An Empirical Study. *International Journal of Psychological Studies, 2*(2), 189–201.

Assessment of Service Parameters for Jaipur Urban Transportation System

Pankaj Sharma*

Abstract

Since the beginning of 21ˢᵗ century, most nations are involved with serious issues and challenges related to urbanization. Urbanization is due to increased prosperity, most of which goes in fulfilling the needs of increased mobility. People travel daily for different physical, psychological and economic needs, for example – work, shopping, leisure, recreational, etc. A collective outcome of increased population, high percentage of urbanization rate and rapid growth of private vehicles combined with increasing needs for mobility is a matter of great concern.

Predominantly, with the arrival of personalized mode of transport, people are more oriented against the use of public transport. So in order to make them shift to public transport, a decent standard of service quality should be provided to them.

The aim is to find extent of quality of service of the bus transportation system in Jaipur by recognizing five important factors from similar studies done in India and abroad: Tangibility, Reliability, Responsiveness, Assurance and Empathy. The results can be used by urban planners, municipal authorities, transport authorities, etc., for improving the level of service.

The data set was explored in two stages. Firstly, passengers' satisfaction levels related to each service parameter were compared using means, median and mode. Thereafter, principal component analysis with Varimax orthogonal rotation method was implemented to define the fundamental parameter. Factors were extracted by following condition: an eigenvalue > 1 and factor loadings greater than 0.3. A reliability analysis through Cronbach's alpha was done to evaluate the association between variables of each recognized factor.

Keywords: Public transportation, Urban Transportation, Service quality, passenger satisfaction level.

Introduction

At the start of the 21ˢᵗ century, most countries are facing critical issues and challenges related to urbanization. India is the second most populated nation in the world having

---

* Amity University, Jaipur

more than one billion people residing in it. As per 2011 census, India is resident to 1210.2 million with around 31.2 percent or 377.1 million people living in cities and it is likely that in the next 15 years around two-fifth of the population would be residing in cities (Mishra R. and Parida M., 2012). Transportation plays a very crucial part in socio-economic and sustainable growth of any nation. As the cities grow, a concurrent expansion of transportation requirements also happens but at a much faster pace.

People are using their individualized motorized transport modes more frequently to fulfill their ever-changing mobility demand (Cirillo et al., 2011). In todays' setup, major Indian cities have high percentage of vehicles ownership and specifically private ownership. This collective outcome of increased population, high percentage of urbanization rate and rapid growth of private vehicles combined with increasing needs for mobility is a matter of great concern (Kenworthy, 2008).

Literature Review

Public Transportation System and its Transit Quality

Service quality is being demonstrated towards a constructive outcome on commuters' behavioral intention (Lai and Chen, 2011). Providing a good quality of service to meet commuters' requirements is crucial to hold the current passengers along with attracting new ones who currently use some other modes of transport. Parasuraman et al. 1988 described service-quality as a gap analysis amongst passengers' expectancy and his observation of that service. Generally services comprise five distinctive measurements namely *tangibles* (observable parameters, and look of the bus driver and conductor), *consistency* (capacity to provide the service as promised), *receptiveness* (readiness to assist passengers and give speedy facility), *assertion* (information and politeness of employees and their skill to stimulate faith and self-reliance), and *compassion* (considerate, personalized consideration to passengers).

Public transportation is one of the crucial services most citizens need in their day-to-day lives. Today, transit providers have limited resources which should be used to best use for most benefit to their passengers (Eboli and Mazzulla, 2008). A satisfactory level of service quality in public transportation is still an intangible objective for most of the Indian cities and its commuters. Apart from the modernization of public transportation, it is significant to take care of the quality aspects during service delivery. If the service delivery is not as per the passengers' satisfaction levels and also not well executed, it develops an adverse sensitivity and dissatisfaction towards that service (Karen and Peter, 2007).

Tools for Measuring Service Quality

Review of literature shows that many theories were developed aimed at measuring different aspects of quality parameters for public transport service in the recent past. The subject of assessing quality related attributes in bus service through diverse areas are being discovered by various scientists like Parasuraman et al., 1985. The traditional SERVQUAL measures (RATER i.e., R-reliability, A-assurance, T-Tangibles, E-Empathy, R-Responsiveness) may not be meaningful in all situations and contexts.

SERVQUAL scale needs to be altered to adjust to a specific research condition (Akan, 1995). Service quality parameters of transport services includes five important parameters, specifically, is consistency, well-being, provisions, safety and affordability, commonly denoted as RECSA which is an amendment to Parasuraman et al.'s (1988) RATER model. The proposed research is to explore commuters' perceptions of the public transport facilities is in terms of parameters (Table 1) related to service quality perception of the users specifically, Reliability, Comfort, extent of service, Security; and Affordability (RECSA). McKnight et al. (1986) specified that it is a challenge for the public transport service providers to measure the service quality factors as it is quite a tedious task due to its subjective nature.

Table 1: Measures for the Mass Transit Service Quality

S. No.	Parameters	S. No.	Parameters
1	Service Punctuality	13	Service availability on Holidays
2	Time-table availability	14	Service availability at late-hours
3	Timely arrival at Destination	15	Behaviour of Drivers
4	Adherence to Routes	16	Accident Rates
5	Seat Availability	17	Injuries due to accidents
6	Smoothness of Service	18	Driving skills of drivers
7	Availability of Air Conditioner	19	Condition of vehicles
8	Ride Comfort	20	Driver obeying the traffic rules
9	Condition of Bus shelters	21	Fare Affordability
10	Exact location-destination	22	Value for Money Service
11	Service availability on Weekends	23	Reliability of the Service
12	Service availability on Weekdays		

Source: Parasuraman et al. (1988); McKnight et al. (1986)

Reliability Analysis through Cronbach's Alpha Tool

Reliability is the degree where a series of scale objects might give outcomes which are consistent if repetition of collected records takes place. It is to be evaluated by defining the amount of organized distinction in a particular measure of scale. Computing the Cronbach Alpha number of a scale measurement is a more frequently skillful indicator of internal reliability. The perfect Cronbach Alpha co-efficient should be over 0.7. A value less than 0.7 indicate unacceptable internal consistency. Cronbach's Alpha is used in this research to measure the internal reliability of scale items of the questionnaire.

Case Study Area – Jaipur City

Modal Share

Jaipur is one of the best planned cities in India. It has beautiful architectural features; planned economic growth and has a multicultural attractiveness which gives it an exclusivity in India's metropolitan background.

Figure 1: Mode Share for Jaipur City (Source: Trip Information (Updated DPR of JMRC Phase II))

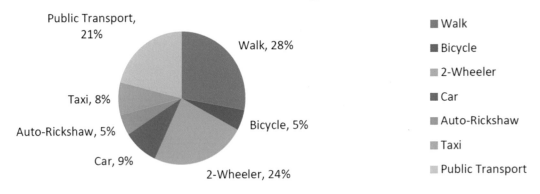

Result and Discussion

Before analyzing the data, all the service quality aspects and features were reorganized and tabulated. Further, each of these parameters was given a representation to make it easier to comprehend, investigated in SPSS with the uses of Cronbach's Alpha, and Exploratory Principal Component Analysis and the results were presented in the study report.

Reliability test

The most extensively used technique of testing the reliability of an instrument is by Cronbach's Alpha, where its value varies from 0.0 to 1.0. A value greater than 0.70 was usually considered satisfactory. A value nearer to 1.0 specifies strong reliability of the parameter, ultimately signifying consistency and steadiness of the questionnaire. As shown in Table 2, the present instrument resulted in a considerably high Cronbach's Alpha of 0.881. Since this value is greater than the required 0.7 Cronbach's Alpha, the items used have an acceptable internal consistency and can be considered as consistent and reliable statistically.

Table 2: Reliability Analysis for the Parameters

Reliability Statistics		
Cronbach's Alpha	**Cronbach's Alpha Based on Standardized Items**	**N of Items**
.869	.881	37

5.2 Communalities for the Parameters

Factors loadings can take values as positive or negative. The greater the loading the more significant is the factor. But if factor loading is above 0.44, then that factor could be taken as prominent. As loading increases, that particular factor will become more vibrant in defining the factor. All the loadings in this particular study are positive.

The following Communality table explains Variances of decision making scales for user's perception. (Extraction Method: Principal Component Analysis) (Table 3)

Table 3: Communalities for the Parameters

Parameters	Initial	Extraction
ease of connection with other modes of transport	1.000	.367
break down of busses on road is rare	1.000	.512
bus arrival on time	1.000	.478
journey time satisfactory for distance travelled	1.000	.454
ease of purchasing of ticket	1.000	.477
passenger request are satisfied	1.000	**.603**
frequency of service	1.000	.400
finding info(routes, stops, timetables) is easy	1.000	.424
availability of next stop information on bus	1.000	**.651**
printed time table info at bus stops	1.000	**.704**

arrival of busses at scheduled time	1.000	.544
maintaining journey time	1.000	.583
total hours of service is sufficient	1.000	.549
services of weekends and public holidays available	1.000	.539
services on weekdays is available	1.000	**.642**
waiting time at bus stops is less	1.000	.577
visibility of route names and number on buses	1.000	**.609**
announcement of arrival at stops	1.000	.601
timely and efficient services	1.000	.441
cleanliness in bus and bus stops satisfactory	1.000	.593
staff attire neat and clean	1.000	**.644**
bus condition satisfactory	1.000	.492
getting in and out of bus is easy	1.000	.559
spacious seats in busses	1.000	.541
legroom and foot space sufficient	1.000	.527
seat available during peak hours	1.000	**.710**
level of crowding in buses is high	1.000	**.620**
damage to seats, fittings and windows	1.000	.527
comfort at bus stops	1.000	.580
accessible grab handles and poles	1.000	.553
safety at bus stops	1.000	.579
safety inside buses	1.000	**.641**
drivers and conductors behaviour	1.000	.524
drive safely and smoothly	1.000	.466
convenient operational hours	1.000	.458
bus routes as per needs	1.000	.548
fares are affordable	1.000	.542

From the Table 3 it is found that the passenger's perception varies from 36.7% to 71%. It means that the extracted factors that are not able to explain much variance in that variable, such variable may be dropped from the analysis.

On the basis of econometric models, established in this study, the most significant satisfaction factor while using bus transport was frequency, reducing over-crowding, comfort, safety, trailed by the delivery of service information.

The assessment of the reliability of factor analysis and the acquired principal components is caused via Cronbach's alpha whose values range between 0 and 1. The greater the value of coefficient signifies that components from factor analysis are more consistent and objective. It is observed that coefficient values greater than 0.70 guarantees the reliability of factor analysis. In our study, for all aspects the Cronbach's alpha has values > 0.75. The primary aim is to recognize the service quality parameters in light of perceptible attributes (cleanliness/comfort) towards bus transit system in Jaipur. As per the result obtained from the study, it is clear that these tangible aspects affect the service quality delivery of the public transportation system currently available to citizens of Jaipur city.

Recommendations

On the basis of study undertaken and interpretation of results, the following recommendations are made:

1. There is a need for assimilation for all the public transportation systems.
2. Public transport services should cater to new areas so that more commuters can use the services.
3. Planners should try to focus on increasing modal share by providing better service to existing and future demand.
4. Also, study of effect of mixed land use on the mode choice and urban form and structures can also be taken in future.

References

Mishra, R. K., Parida M. and Rangnekar S. (2012). Urban Transport System: An Environmentally Sustainable Approach. *Journal of Environmental Research and Development*, 6 (3), 500–506.

Cirillo, C., Eboli, L., Mazzulla, G. (2011). On the Asymmetric User Perception of Transit Service Quality. *International Journal of Sustainable Transportation*, 5 (4), 216–232.

Kenworthy, J. R. (2008). Energy Use and CO_2 Production in the Urban Passenger Transport Systems of 84 International Cities: Findings and Policy Implications. Droege, P. (ed) Urban Energy Transitions. Chapter 9, 211–236. Elsevier.

Lai, W., Chen, C. (2010). Behavioral intentions of public transit passengers—The roles of service quality, perceived value, satisfaction and involvement. *Transport Policy*, 18 (2), 318–325.

Parasuraman, A., Zeithaml, V.A. and Berry, L.L. (1988). SERVQUAL: A Multiple Item Scale for Measuring Consumer Perceptions of Service Quality. *Journal of Retailing*, 64 (1), 14–40.

Eboli, L., Mazzulla, G. (2008). An SP Experiment for Measuring Service Quality in Public Transport. *Transportation Planning and Technology*, 31 (5), 509–523.

Karen, T., Peter, S. (2007). An investigation of the relationship between public transport performance and destination satisfaction. *Journal of Transport Geography*, 15(2), 136–144.

Parasuraman, A., Zeithaml, V. and Berry, L.L. (1985). A conceptual model of service quality and its implications for future research, *Journal of Marketing*, 49, Autumn, 41–50.

Akan, P. (1995). Dimensions of service quality: A study in Istanbul. *Managing Service Quality*, 5 (6), 39–43.

McKnight, C.E., Pagano, A.N., and Paaswell, R.E. (1986). Using Quality to Predict Demand for Special Transportation in Behavioural Research for Transport Policy. *International Conference on Travel Behaviour*, Noordwijk, The Netherlands, Utrecht: VNU Science Press.

Exploring places, Creating Unique Tourism Experiences – Case of Incredible Indian Moments Private Limited

Kavaldeep Dixit*, Tanjul Saxena** & Sandeep Vyas*

Abstract

The case details the start-up and growth of Incredible Indian Moments Private Limited branded as Indian Moments an Indian online travel company providing comprehensive information about travel and tours to India. Incorporated on 18 June 1999 and headquartered in Jaipur the company provided services including flight tickets, domestic and international holiday packages, hotel reservations, rail and bus tickets. We utilized corporate presentations, stakeholder's reviews and founder's view, to highlight the operational dimensions of effectively running the portal with focus on travel and tourism. The focus had been on the differing marketing-mix strategies adopted by the company for enhanced customer experience.

Keywords: Tourism industry, Handicrafts, Indian Moments.

"Exploring places, Creating unique tourism experiences" – Case of Incredible Indian Moments Private Limited

'One of the most richly rewarding places to visit in the world, India can turn out to be a treasure rediscovered for some, and a place belying all expectations in the same breath, for others. It is a place where old meets new as if they were never ever distinct. We started Indian Moments to help customers discover India with customized tour packages. Our expertise and understanding about India as a destination has been appreciated by all. Most of them were simply amazed how each and every of their specifications about their tours used to be accommodated and executed by our team-members so effortlessly.'

Pankaj Sharma, Founder and Chief Executive Officer

Incredible Indian Moments Private Limited

Increased number of tourists planned their itineraries online (including their tickets, accommodation, travel insurance and other related services) which led to an augmentation in the number of offerings made by the e-Travel portals in the country. Online travel portals evolved from being separate entity to a "one stop shop" for all the travel

---

* International School of Informatics and Management, Jaipur

**IIHMR University, Jaipur

needs of a traveler. Foreseeing the opportunity Incredible Indian Moments Private Limited branded as *Indian Moments (IM)* an Indian online travel company providing comprehensive information about travel and tours to India was founded by three enterprising entrepreneurs Nirmla, Pankaj and Neeraj on 18 June 1999. Based in the heart of colourful state of India, Rajasthan the company provided services including flight tickets, domestic and international holiday packages, hotel reservations, rail, bus and flight tickets. From designing customized package holiday tours of a destination, to contacting airlines, hotels and ground transport services, *Indian Moments* offered assorted services. They prepared itineraries for travelers with just a few clicks of mouse, and arranged the trip in a manner that the tourists could enjoy the best India had to offer.

Committed to the idea of showcasing India's rich cultural heritage their offerings covered special interests of tourists like Indian fine art and culture, local culinary experiences, beaches, ayurveda, forts/palaces, yoga/meditation, temples, shopping, Buddhist monasteries, visit to Himalayas or river Ganga. The company also arranged tours to exotic destinations like, Dungarpur, Hampi, Tanjore, Namdapha, Kutchh, Karwar, Kaziranga, etc.

Awarded runner-up for Best Value Tour Operator for 2010 by *Sunday Times Travel* magazine, UK the company's unique selling proposition had been creating customized touring experiences with the assistance of widely travelled and culturally sensitive employees. In its eighteen years of existence the company found great success in combining comfort with adventure, offering luxury desert accommodation, desert safari, rural tourism, ecotourism and wildlife tourism. Company maintained its web presence through www.indianmoments.com and www.pushkarcamelfair.com.

CEO File

Born on 26th April 1974 to an RBI officer in a middle class family, Mr. Pankaj was the youngest child in the family with three elder sisters. He completed his schooling from Maheshwari Public School in 1992 in Jaipur. Thereafter, he graduated in Arts from University Rajasthan College, Jaipur in 1995.

It was in his college days, Mr. Pankaj developed a bend of mind towards tourism. He was always thrilled by the rich cultural heritage of India. He enjoyed visiting places across India and exploring new destinations was his passion. In frequent deliberations with his friends, he used to share his knowledge on tourism which he had acquired by virtue of his inherent interest and curiosity in the subject. After completing graduation Pankaj attended the Indian Institute of Tourism and Travel Management, Gwalior to pursue higher studies in tourism. After completion of his two year Diploma, in 1997 he went to Mumbai and started working with an organization named *Tour Club Express* where after working for a short while, he returned to his home town and joined *Network Travels*. Employed with them he suggested a number of strategies to augment their tourism business. One of his recommendations at that point of time was to develop a website for the company to make its services easily accessible to the client world over. In late 1990's internet-based services and office automation in tourism industry in the city was a far cry from present. Implementation of Pankaj idea brought positive growth for *Network Travels*. Having learnt the intricacies of tourism industry Pankaj left the company in March 2000 and decided to venture out on his own. In May 2000, together with two of his family members he laid the foundation of Incredible Indian Moments Private Limited and started operations under the flagship brand 'Indian Moments'. He started the company on strong ethical values with customer-focused philosophy.

Tourism industry in those days lacked service quality and client centric approach. Moreover, the industry also lacked infrastructure to cater to the tourists from abroad. Pankaj was strong-willed to turn the challenges into opportunity so he decided to showcase the rich and colourful culture of Rajasthan in a unique way. He purchased a Haveli in the Shekhawati belt of Rajasthan, renovated it and made it a part of his tour package as accommodation to give an awesome experience to those foreign tourists who were interested in exploring the rural culture of the state. By owning more properties in the region, Pankaj managed forward integration of the business by not merely providing tour packages, but also differentiated, hygienic and quality accommodation at reasonable price. Under his leadership Indian Moments offerings were designed to cover a wide range of tour packages ranging from premium to economy tours thus catering to a wide range of clients.

In his own words, *"Our ways of working have remained unpretentious. Not much to say except being very ethical, highly passionate and very customer friendly. When we started, we began by taking personalization of services to each customer to a new level. We called this- hitting the Big players where they are the weakest. We are carrying the same philosophy till date through our company – Indian Moments. We still explore places, interact with our customers and create unique tourism experiences."*

Indian Travel and Tourism Industry Environment

The travel and tourism sector holds tactical importance in the Indian economy extending varied socio economic benefits. Generation of income and foreign exchange, employment development or extension of other industries such as agriculture, construction, handicrafts etc. are some of the significant economic benefits provided by the tourism sector. Tourism in India had appreciable potential considering the prosperous cultural and historical heritage, diversity in ecology, places and terrains of natural beauty spread across the nation. The World Travel & Tourism Council estimated that tourism in India in 2015 provided ₹8.31 lakh crore (US$120 billion) or 6.3% of the nation's GDP and sustained 37.315 million jobs, 8.7% of its total employment. By 2025 the sector is envisaged to grow at an average annual rate of 7.5% to ₹18.36 lakh crore (US$270 billion) contributing to7.2% of GDP.

The travel market in the country is marked by fascinating opportunities and absorbing challenges (Table 1):

Table 1: Opportunities and Challenges of Indian Travel Market

	Opportunities	Challenges
Domestic market	• The current population of India is 1.3 billion, out of which 1/6th of the population is online i.e. 278 million. India has the third largest internet population in the world, according to Google India 2017 will witness 500 million internet users in India. • E-channels for ticketing being used by almost all airlines. • An increase of 16.5% from 2011 in domestic tourist visits numbered 1,036.35 million in 2012. • In 2014, Tamil Nadu, Maharashtra and Uttar Pradesh were the most popular states for tourists. • Mobile internet is being used by 76% (213 million) online users in India	• Other online travel services providers with comparable offerings and sizeable funding support create a major challenge. • Competition bound to rise and varied ranging from the tour operators, travel agents and the suppliers.
Visitor exports	• Compared to 80.27 lakh (8.027 million) in 2015 about 88.90 lakh (8.89 million) foreign tourists arrived in India in 2016 recording a growth of 10.7%. • Foreign tourists during the year 2015 had visited Jaipur, Delhi, Mumbai, Chennai and Agra the most.	• Number of external factors impact India's potential as a travel destination, the most crucial being terrorism threat. • Security issues and crime, specifically against women, continues to be a major challenge that tainted the reputation of Indian tourism industry in recent years.

External Factors	• India ranks 52nd out of 141 countries overall as per The *Travel & Tourism Competitiveness Report 2015* while in price competitiveness the country ranks 8th out of 141 countries in tourism sector. • The same report ranks India 35th in terms of good air transport and 50th in context of reasonable ground transport infrastructure. It also scored 12th rank on natural and cultural resources. • During 2012 India's receipts from tourism ranked 16th in the world and 7th among Asian and Pacific countries as per the World Tourism Organization report. • Indian Government to advance tourism decided to implement a new visa policy, permitting visitors to acquire a visa on arrival at 16 designated international airports by obtaining an Electronic Travel Authorisation online before arrival without the requirement to visit an Indian consulate or visa centre. As an outcome of this, 56,477 tourist arrived on e-Tourist Visa during the month of October, 2015, vis-a-vis 2,705 during the month of October, 2014.	• Customers expect removal of travel agents from the ambit of service tax as it culminates in higher travel costs, limiting demand in the tourism sector. Travel agents also assist in hotel reservations and taxi services and charging service tax is resulting in increase of the average cost of holiday and travel. • Tourism infrastructure remains insufficient and underdeveloped. • Low ATM penetration and few hotel rooms per capita by international comparison in India was crippling the sector.
Segment Traits	• Younger generation in the country had higher disposable income with interest in travelling. • There has been a positive shift amongst the middle-aged (45–58) customer who is willing to spend on travel and vacations.	• The Indian traveler has specific desires which call for modulated travel choices. • There has been considerable internet penetration but still not enough to reach out to the massive Indian population.

Segment Traits	• Use of credit cards as a mode of payment was emerging as an accepted alternative. • Ease of use and expediency were also expediting Net penetration in India. • The Indian consumer at heart is a value conscious deal seekers.	• Indian customer is a deal hunter but is hesitant to transact from an unknown source because of the fear of being duped.

Market Segments

Indian Moments catered to three markets-Foreign tourists, Indians based in foreign countries travelling to India and Domestic tourists travelling within India. Apparently the perceived risks of the segments were different; the travel company identified a common value proposition-making the travel a rewarding experience for the customer. The international tourists were attracted towards *Indian Moments* because of their requirement to have a decent amount of planning and arrangement done well in advance prior to their departure, while on the other hand, the domestic tourists planned very close to their travelling dates. Thus, the value sought by the first two segments was assurance while the third segment sought availability. *Indian Moments* customized plans and offers based on the needs of each target group.

Product Offerings

Indian Moments provided a comprehensive basket of products and services including air tickets, hotel reservations, car/taxi bookings, vacation packages, road-trips and weekend breaks. It attracted customers by offering quality service and bundling products like flight ticket bookings with hotel booking, car rental, heritage accommodation, tent living, hot air ballooning, and entertainment at the destination. It covered major tourism circuits of the country. It attempted to cover both on and off-beat destinations, exhibiting India's exotic flavours and amazing lifestyles.

Table-1 highlights selected tour packages offered by the company covering four corners of the country. Through its website it attempted to highlight the spiritualism and rich diverse culture of the country by striking a chord with the travelers by showcasing mighty Himalayas, purity of river Ganga, divine celebrations, unique festivities, India's forests and lifestyle, Indian dressing styles, varied cuisine and diverse culinary habits and performing arts. One of its tour packages "Glimpses of India" had been designed in a way that it enticed the foreign tourists by taking them through the colourful journey of old Rajasthan, providing them opportunities to mingle with local people, showcase the traditions and rhythms of the region and explore local customs, legends and celebrations. To discover some of the real highlights of Rajasthan *Indian Moments* took the travelers to some off-beaten trails covering least-visited World Heritage sites of the state, experiencing regional fairs to familiarize guests with traditions and contrasts of the fairs; to ascertain hidden art treasures in Hadoti and join pilgrim devotions on the full moon night.

To keep the customers hooked over the years, the company added a few innovative ventures like mobile luxury-tents known as 'Camp Bliss', 'Haveli of experimental living', 'Hot Air Ballooning' etc. Camp Bliss was unique combination of luxury camping with real desert adventure. Like the nomads of the Thar, it moved between mesmerizing and culturally authentic desert locations while Haveli in the small Shekhawati village of Mukundgarh was a beautiful 1850s old painted mansion, off the well-travelled touristic circuits thoughtfully restored to its past glories to serve their customers better and provide a differential experience of discovering old Rajasthan of camel carts and ancient wells, rural roads and small town bazaars.

Every year during the Camel Fair at Pushkar the population of the town increased from 21,500 to around 400,000, so managing comfortable accommodation for customers became challenging for the company. To entice their guests with a stylish and luxurious experience of the fair they came up with the idea of 'Camp Bliss' which were luxury tents set up in a peaceful gooseberry orchard, strategically located at a short walking distance from the fair ('mela' in local language) ground. These camps were exclusive and offered a high standard of accommodation with authentic hospitality. To provide a welcoming and friendly atmosphere clubbed with excellent service 'Camp Bliss' were run and managed by company's staff. One of the features of Camp Bliss had been special events – light installations by visiting artists, yoga sessions, excursions to places in the locality, informal talks by historians, authors and photographers.

The Camp Bliss tents offered everything for luxury living under canvas. Their spacious Swiss tents were of traditional hand block-printed heavy canvas in typical Rajasthani style. The interiors had space for sleeping and dressing and a separate bathroom. The tents were well-furnished with teak-wood beds, chairs and a writing desk. Tents were fully carpeted and environment-friendly materials were used throughout. Bedlinen and towels were changed daily and each tent had its own outdoor relaxation area with relaxed teak loungers. Delicious vegetarian meals were prepared and served by their talented young chefs. Freshly and safely prepared food included varied menus and regional specialities.

After successful launch of the tents at Pushkar they further experimented with them at Thar desert camp at Shiv in the remote district of Barmer district held in the months of January and February and at regional mela Nagaur Fair held in January. They chose Nagaur, another desert town of the state to lure travelers to the cattle fair where they saw people from rural communities in colourful attires and even more camels than one can see at Pushkar. Chandrabhaga Fair at Jhalarapatan, in the less visited Hadoti region, another of Rajasthan's great trading fairs and the regional equivalent of Pushkar Fair was also catered to by the 'Camp Bliss' concept. At Chandrabhaga held in the month of November Camp Bliss Nomad tents featured in a breathtaking location, in the grounds of the impressive old summer palace of the erstwhile Maharajas.

Each evening around the campfire guests were entertained by evening performances featuring musicians and dancers from the region. Authentic performers and the private setting were the highlight of the camps. The nightly programme also included traditional puppet shows as well as performances from magicians, desert musicians and gypsy dancers. Some of the performers came from semi-nomadic communities who wandered the Thar desert and camped outside towns and villages with their musical traditions being handed down from generation to generation. Their resident group of Manganiyar musicians from Barmer district provided authentic traditional music in the mornings. Around the campfire in the evening, they served an assortment of local snacks, with an option to try some traditional street food dishes from the mela.

Indian Moments hosted *'Wild Books'* – their Camp Bliss (mini) Pushkar Literature Festival where they organized evening events with special guests who shared their knowledge and extraordinary experiences of Indian culture and wildlife. Each year their guests and non-resident dinner guests had the opportunity to meet amazing authors whose lives in the wild places of India had featured in books and TV documentaries and they shared some of their experiences with tigers, snakes, crocodiles and camels. In the past they had organized interfaces with Ilse Köhler-Rollefson, author of *Camel Karma,* Gobind Sagar Bhardwaj, author of *Tracking Tigers in Ranthambhore,* Janaki Lenin, author of *My Husband and Other Animals.*

To provide an exhilarating experience for their guests, *Indian Moments* arranged horse safaris starting from the stunning countryside around Ranakpur and riding to Pushkar Camel Fair on superior Marwari horses. The ride captured the spirit of a traditional journey to the great mela covering between 25–35 km each day visiting villages and temples and travelling through picturesque areas noted for wildlife and colourful villages of the local farming communities. The safari was escorted by a friendly, skilled team who took exceptional care of both horses and riders. Besides horse safaris they also arranged cycle tours to Pushkar for their guests, and arranged a visit to the Camel Café at the Camel Conservation Centre near Ranakpur, Rajasthan where visitors could savor dishes like, camelatté, camelcino, delicious cheesecakes and cakes, all made from camels milk.

They also arranged for viewing ancient, sacred landscape Pushkar from the air in Hot Air Balloons. The thrill of floating over Pushkar's holy lake, high temples and holy places provided once-in-a-lifetime experience to the travelers. The balloon flights were managed by an experienced team with equipment and training of European and US international safety standards. The pilots trained in UK and US- had thousands of hours of balloon flight experience, internationally and in India.

The staff headed by Pankaj Sharma worked seamlessly as a team, and the IM drivers were competent and trustworthy, to ensure successful experience. IM's approach was customer-focused. They would give advice, but design the itinerary to a traveler's pocket and tastes in a collaborative manner. Another aspect of their planning that has been greatly appreciated is their flexibility during tour operations. In certain situations entire tour circuits were redrawn on request of their guests at incredibly short notice.

With an eye for detail they relentlessly strive to refine the quality of their services such as maintaining most up to date cars with designer's touch from cushions to the specifically ordered flower box. To make long road journeys a pleasurable ride for the travelers the cars are well-equipped with face tissues, towels, magazines and even maps. They have also trained their chauffeurs in interpretation of wayside attractions and it has generated terrific feedback from their guests.

Their product offerings and services have been highly appreciated by their customers. A few complimented them for the once-in-a-lifetime adventure among the camels and horses, exotic experience –forts, Maharajas, singing birds and cattle fair, luxury stay at a palace, tents with the local flavour of the Mela, etc. Some appreciated the amazing staff, mind-blowing musicians, dancers and magician, fantastic food, Camp Bliss is a wonderful ‹home from home›. Excellent service, colour, light, music. A ‹must-return› destination.' RK C – 3/11/14

Business Model

The Internet revolution led to significant changes in the way travel agencies interacted with customers. Travel websites were utilized to different degrees, and for a variety of combinations of pre-transaction, transaction and post-transaction services. A better understanding of how customers interacted with online services helped *Indian Moments* advance service quality to delight customers, and thus generate loyalty. Pankaj Sharma termed Indian Moments business model as a simple Business to consumer (B2C) model. The customers would use company's website to book air tickets, hotel rooms, and travel packages. There were three enabling components: supplier relations, people and process and technology. Strong relationships with suppliers including domestic and international airlines, and hotels would help the company in running the business model effectively. Technology was identified as a cornerstone. *Indian Moments* adopted user-friendly interfaces to simplify the consumer experience: effortless navigation, superior interactivity and time saver quick book options were amongst the most important ones. To simplify the journey of a travel seeker features like painless cancellation, personalized deals, ticket tracking and on-call customer service were added.

Other factors in favour of Business model were: (a) households disposable income has increased resulting in increase spending on vacations; (b) escalating number of credit card transactions likely to impact e-ticketing as well; (c) optimistic growth in all travel segments, i.e., leisure, business, visiting relatives and friends and others; and (d) affirmative spend on business travel by IT companies.

The other key components of the business model were employees possessing do-main-specific skills in order to help the company develop and offer customized suit-able products and services for the travel consumer.

Table III covers the value proposition offered by Indian Moments while Table-IV Summarizes the key facts about Indian Moments.

Table III: Value Proposition and Service Offerings by *Indian Moments*

Value Propositions	Anticipated Outcomes
Empowering the global travellers with rich information and varied options	Rebuilding travel and tour products distribution network
Ascertaining transparency and reliability	Developing efficiency in sales and marketing logistics to pass on benefits to the customer
Providing convenience of buying anytime and anywhere	Stress-free travel related product buying
Differentiated Travel experience	Providing an opportunity to tap the unexplored heritage
Offering customized tour packages	Boosting the reach of the tourism and travel market to remote locations
Providing 24x7 customer service	Stress free service experience

Table IV: Key Facts about Indian Moments

Product Drivers	Products/Services Business Model (Online)	Target Market Characteristics	Branding & Positioning	Competitors & Challenges
• Market growth rates • Bright prospects in e-ticketing business as per evolving customer trends • Rising penetration of internet • Enhanced number of online hotels and ticket booking • Long-term experience in the same business model • Expertise and understanding about India as a destination • Positive customer feedback • Satisfied repeat customers	• Quality of services • Real time booking of rooms in luxury hotels • Holiday packages in India • Road-trips covering major cities of India with interactive maps • Professional and friendly drivers and guides • Car/Taxi, tour bus bookings at special prices for airport transfers and other trips • Options for both long and short stay holidays. • Covering off-beat destinations • Providing camp-living and heritage Haveli living experience • Arranging aerial view of religious fairs through hot air balloons • Travelling through Indian villages on cycles, horses, etc.	• Foreign travelers mainly from Europe and USA • Indians residing abroad • Domestic tourists • Group tours and single female/male tours • Internet-savvy • Adventure seeker • Deal hunters **Segments** • Personal travel & tourism • Business travel	• Motto-"Customization is the key for us to grow, to satisfy and feel satisfied" • Flexibility during tour operations • Comprehensive & complete travel solution and online, one-stop shop • Upto date cars with designer's touch from cushions to the specially ordered flower box. Face tissues, towels, magazines, maps; etc. • Periodically modifying hotels list based on quality of services, deleting many hotels from recommended ones and adding new ones. • Effectively utilizing travel blogs, trip advisors and social networking sites to establish a brand name by encouraging visitors to share their personal travel experiences. These sites help spread positive word of mouth and • enhance the credibility of the portal, resulting in increased lifetime value for their customers.	• Travel agents and tour operators • New players keep entering the market • Supplier's website **Challenges** • E-booking by suppliers • In future hybrid On-line Travel Services (OTS) provider models may pose a threat

Source: Compiled by Authors

Competitive Environment

With the rise in the number of international travelers and recognizing India's potential, many online travel companies invested in the tourism and hospitality sector. Indian Moments faced competition from other OTS providers and suppliers themselves. Pankaj mentioned that when they began way back in 1990's there was not much competition. However, he anticipated competition to be stiff now as multiple well-funded online ventures have cropped up. One plus side of competition was that there would be a positive development for the overall market growth as other companies share the burden of creating awareness among customers regarding the advantage of buying travel products online. Pankaj was secure enough to lead from the front with his experience, more notably his customer base from the west. Prominent players in the sector include:

MakeMyTrip: An online travel company that offered domestic and international travel services including flight, train and bus tickets, hotel reservations, holiday packages and other related products and services.

Cleartrip: It provided online travel services encompassing domestic and international holiday packages, reservations, rail tickets, flight tickets and bus tickets.

Goibibo: It is a one-stop online travel company that featured various travel services and products which allowed the user to explore the largest range of destinations and hotels.

Yatra.com: It provided all the information, availability, pricing details and bookings of domestic and international hotels, packages, train, flights and car rentals across 336 cities.

Ixigo: A travel Guide & trip planner for Indian & International Destinations which provided customers with information & finest booking deals for resorts, hotels, flights, buses, trains.

Expedia: It claimed to offer more than 75000 hotels and over 3000 holiday packages with additional features like maps and weather forecasts of the destination.

Travelguru: Offered the facility to book and explore flight tickets, hotel rooms, cruises and vacation packages suitably.

Thomas Cook: An integrated travel and travel-related financial services company that provided a broad spectrum of services including foreign exchange, corporate travel, leisure travel, insurance, visa & passport services and e-business.

Akbar Travels of India Pvt Ltd.: It has an online portal which assists its users to book flights, rail tickets and hotels at low costs.

Cox & Kings: Provided a gamut of services like outbound tourism, destination management, International and Domestic holiday packages, business travel etc.

Challenges Ahead of Indian Moments

The challenges ahead include:

- Online travel market in India was expanding thus, intensifying competition the number of players was expected to increase.
- Suppliers are now selling their products and services online; posing a threat to *Indian Moments*.
- Hybrid Online Travel Service (OTS) provider models are anticipated to evolve and augment in future.

With these lines covered by Sunday Times Travel Magazine, UK '*Indian Moments can tailor-make just about any Indian adventure you can dream up… make travelling in the most bonkers country on Earth feel effortless – at very competitive prices*' the success saga of the company continues.

References

"*Annual Report (2015–16), Ministry of Tourism, Government of India*" *(PDF). Ministry of Tourism, India, pp. 6, 7. Retrieved 14 October 2016.*

"*Travel & Tourism Economic Impact 2015 India*" *World Travel and Tourism Council. Retrieved 15 April 2016.*

"*Performance of Tourism Sector during December, 2016*" *(PDF). Ministry of Tourism, India, Retrieved 28 February 2017.*

http://www.ibef.org/industry/tourism-hospitality-india.aspx [accessed on 8th July 2016] https://www.statista.com/topics/2076/travel-and-tourism-industry-in-india/ [accessed on 11th February 2017]

Exhibit-I: Selected Tour Packages

Central India	Kerala	Raja-sthan	Western India	Eastern India	North India	South India
A Rich Legacy (12 days)	**A Spicy Affair** (14 days)	**A Rich Legacy** (12 days)	**A Rich Legacy** (12 days)	**Buddha Calling (10 days)**	**A Rich Legacy (12 days)**	**A Spicy Affair (14 days)**
New Delhi, Jaipur, Jaisalmer, Jodhpur, Udaipur, Mumbai.	Trivandrum, Alleppey, Kumarakom, Periyar, Munnar, Kochi.	New Delhi, Jaipur, Jaisalmer, Jodhpur, Udaipur, Mumbai.	New Delhi, Jaipur, Jaisalmer, Jodhpur, Udaipur, Mumbai.	New Delhi, Varanasi, Kushinagar, Patna, Rajgir, Bodhgaya, Kolkata.	New Delhi, Jaipur, Jaisalmer, Jodhpur, Udaipur, Mumbai.	Trivandrum, Alleppey, Kumarakom, Periyar, Munnar, Kochi.
An Affair to Remember (16 days)	**Buddha Calling** (10 days)	**An Affair to Remember (16 days)**	**Close Cousins India & Nepal (22 days)**	**Temple Towns (24 – 29 days)**	**An Affair to Remember (16 days)**	**Buddha Calling** (10 days)
New Delhi, Jaipur, Agra, Gwalior, Orchha, Bhopal, Mandu, Mumbai.	New Delhi, Varanasi, Kushinagar, Patna, Rajgir, Bodhgaya, Kolkata.	New Delhi, Jaipur, Agra, Gwalior, Orchha, Bhopal, Mandu, Mumbai.	Mumbai, Aurangabad, Udaipur, Jaipur, Agra, Khajuraho, Varanasi, Kathmandu, Chitwan, Pokhara, New Delhi.	Kolkata, Bhubaneshwar, Chennai, Thanjavur, Madurai, Mysore, Hassan, Hampi, Badami, Aurangabad, Mumbai.	New Delhi, Jaipur, Agra, Gwalior, Orchha, Bhopal, Mandu, Mumbai.	New Delhi, Varanasi, Kushinagar, Patna, Rajgir, Bodhgaya, Kolkata.

Source: www.indianmoments.com

Impact of Deregulation and Issues of Rajasthan State Road Transport Corporation (RSRTC) with the beginning of Paradigm Shift: Good or Bad

Mahendra Parihar*

Abstract

Increasing competition in a market is always beneficial but the basis must be similar for said competition. Moreover, changes in an existing set-up of any system (to some extent if not completely) is always required to get some effective correction. However, one might observe that bringing changes for correction is not always beneficial for a particular set-up. In recent times, some changes were introduced by concerned authorities/government body, a kind of paradigm shift, for Rajasthan State Road Transport Corporation (RSRTC) by set-up of Bus Port Authority for the betterment of RSRTC. These changes are in the form of deregulation of routes of operation which were previously reserved for RSRTC and opened for private operators by issuing route permits to private operators along with other activities/functions/things related to RSRTC. This particular step relating to the deregulation of routes and its functioning has given rise to several issues directly affecting RSRTC in many ways (might be positively or negatively). Therefore, given the existing set-up along with nature of operation of RSRTC and the basis for set up of RSRTC almost more than 50 years ago especially with the aim of social welfare, we are undertaking in this study, a critical assessment of paradigm shift via set-up of Bus Port Authority and its impact through deregulation of routes and other functions/activities on RSRTC by looking at various issues need to be considered for the betterment of RSRTC.

Keywords: Deregulation, Social Welfare, Competition.

Introduction

In any economic system, the decision of regulation and deregulation of anything (may be goods or services) i.e. whether concerned government need to keep it under its control or to keep it open for private sector also fully or may be in some limited manner depends on the nature of demand of those particular things. This is because the basic aim of the government in any economy is to maximize public/ social welfare and given this concern government undertake various activities and functions accordingly to provide better life to its people. Transport in general and public transport i.e. passenger movement in particular is one of those activities the government undertake to provide basic facilities to meet the travel demand of the

---

*Manipal University Jaipur

people. With this aim, very recently, Government of Rajasthan set up an institutional body for the smooth functioning and betterment of RSRTC along with takeout RSRTC from loss making situation and get rid out of various challenges currently face by RSRTC in maximum possible manner, if not fully.

Further, with reference to the status of SRTU's in our country, Currently more than 18 lakhs buses are on the Indian roads as compare to 15 lakhs in 2009, out of which 80% of the fleet are privately operated and remaining 20% of the fleet operated by the STU's as compare to the earlier situation where around 45% of the fleet operated by government entities and 55% of the fleet by the private players (World Bank, 2005). Thus, it is also said that the movement of passengers in most optimal way is always beneficial for any economy and therefore, in order to provide economical and efficient transportation facilities and services for the movement of people it is required to strengthen SRTU's (Parihar et.al. 2016).

Rajasthan State Road Transport Corporation (RSRTC) in Rajasthan

RSRTC has been established on 1st October, 1964 under the Road Transport Act 1950 with the objective of providing economic, adequate, punctual and efficient services to the travelling public in the State with 8 Depots and 421 Buses plying 45000 kilometres, carrying 29000 passengers per day. Currently more than 4500 buses across 52 depots are plying more than 16 lakhs kilometres and carrying more than 9 lac passengers per day. Moreover, RSRTC serves the role of lifeline across the state of Rajasthan. It has become a household term for transportation. Over past 52 years and so of its existence, it has proved to be a dependable mode of transportation in every nook and corner of the state, especially for poor or lower income group, needy people, etc. It is providing services in most of the rural areas of the state even on non-viable routes also as a community service. It has brought transport service to the doorstep of villagers in most remote parts. However, it has also been observed that today many of the SRTU's and especially RSRTC, are not performing well on many fronts. RSRTC, despite playing an important role in passenger movement in Rajasthan also faces various challenges in this competitive regime i.e. in recent years, RSRTC experienced a difficult situation due to various challenges relating to some factors includes financial and physical performance, operational inefficiency, organizational inefficiency, etc.[1]

Further, the characteristics of the RSRTC in Rajasthan are not very different from the nature and characteristics of many of the SRTU's in India as a whole. For the purpose of the study, stakeholder surveys, discussions, interviews were conducted in Rajasthan and during enroute RSRTC's bus operation also. The objective of the study undertaken in Rajasthan and especially in Jaipur was to examine relevant issues relating to RSRTC especially with reference to the paradigm shift in terms of set-up of Bus port Authority and its impact on RSRTC and its operation in all possible respects in a state like Rajasthan given its largest size in terms of geographical area and socio-economic concerns of movement of people by public transport to achieve maximum social welfare with optimum cost. Also, this study has examined the impact of deregulation of routes which were earlier reserved for RSRTC now open for private operators along with the nature of activities which will be undertaken by said Bus Port Authority for efficient functioning of RSRTC with reference to the development of required infrastructure and facilities to attract more and more passengers towards RSRTC buses. The study also carefully looked at issues which need to be considered for better functioning of RSRTC along with the set-up of Bus port Authority.

RSRTC: Issues need to be considered

The basic requirement/needs of any passenger to travel through any SRTU's or may be RSRTC are good infrastructural facilities especially at bus stands/depots when they arrive to take the bus for their journey, good condition of buses in which they travel, other facilities like food, hygiene, etc. However, it has been observed that almost all the mentioned needs or requirements are not met given the current context of operation of RSRTC. This is one of the major reasons responsible for shifting of passengers from SRTU's to the private bus operators. Thus, in order to revamp the situation of RSRTC and bring it back to the good condition, government has set-up Bus Port Authority in recent time.

Further, given the organizational approach and management with no government support or required necessary support from government officials, RSRTC also faces some of the issues discussed so far. During conduct of the study we found that private bus/taxi operators picking up passengers right from the front of bus depot. We also learnt that there exist some political interference to make RSRTC private to provide benefits to private people because most of the private buses belongs to most influencial people or their relatives. So because of loss incurred by RSRTC since they are supportive of the privatization of RSRTC and are of the opinion that given the operational inefficiency of RSRTC it is making loss year after year and therefore it need to be privatized. However, our study observed that it is not only a problem of operational inefficiency. More than operational inefficiency, it is a problem of managerial inefficiency. Thus, with good or average efficiency but with proper managerial decisions, the debt of RSRTC with some support from government, can be overcome and be converted into profit making from loss in the future.

Moreover, our study also learned that as per the rules, private buses are not allowed within specific area of RSRTC bus depot, but if we take an example of Sindhi Camp bus stand at Jaipur, the scenario is completely different. One can find very easily the buses of private operators/travel companies even inside the specific area of bus depot to take passengers even by calling the passengers who are about to go inside the bus depot to take the bus of RSRTC. This is because very next to Sindhi camp (nearby), around 150 private buses parked near homeopathic college, where residential property is running commercial activities (since the offices of most of the private travel companies in same area/building) and this is adding to congestion and more pollution near Sindhi camp bus stand. RTO is aware of this but is not doing anything because these private buses belongs to highly influencial people. Moreover, especially after 7 pm in the evening there is no place to walk also due to congestion between places like Chandpole to railway station and Vanasthali marg.

RSRTC: Bus Port Authority – A Way Towards Paradigm Shift for RSRTC

Rajasthan State Bus Terminal Development Authority Bill, 2015 was passed by the Assembly allowing the operations of 225 bus terminals under public-private partnership.[1] The bill has the provision of constituting an authority whose mandate would be to create, develop and operate facilities at the notified bus terminals. It would also streamline and facilitate the running of buses by STU's and private bus operators from terminal. Further, it has been presumed that once enacted, the notified terminals that are worth Rs. 15,000 crores to Rs. 20,000 crores, would be transferred to the authority. Apart from operating the buses, authority would develop parking areas, hotels, toilets, banks and other facilities needed by the passengers.[2] Hence, the move will give better facilities to passengers.[3]

Moreover, it has been found that with the setup of Rajasthan State Bus Authority, very soon private buses will run/operate on the routes reserved for RSRTC buses.[4]

---

[1] Now, public-private partnership for 225 State bus terminals: (10/04/2015---Times of India).

[2] "Creation of the authority is a step towards improving the functioning and operation of buses from terminals. It will enhance the convenience and provide modern facilities to the passengers", said the Transport Minister Yunus Khan. He added that no single bus stand had the basic amenities that are needed by the passengers. (Rajasthan Patrika, 10/04/2015)

[3] Further, most members (MLA's) raised their concern over the power that authority will get to sell off the properties transferred. On this, the minister (Mr Yunus Khan) assured that the authority will be accountable to the Government and Assembly. "Even when the bill would be notified, the properties would not go into the hands of private players. It will stay with the government just the way the Airport Authority of India developed facilities at the airports, but property remained with the Government of India". However, the important question is why authority is needed? Because 45496 villages have no bus stand and no agency to develop them. 4500 public buses play 16 lakhs kilometres and carry 10 lakhs passengers every day, (Rajasthan Patrika, 10/04/2015).

[4] Set up of Bus Port Authority-Ask for route wise bus numbers and time table: on the state highways/roads the RSRTC and Private buses will operate on the basis of 60:40 ratio: (RAJASTHAN PATRIKA 19-03-2015)

For this, for any route, the ratio of private buses would be 40% of the maximum RSRTC buses on that particular route. Given this, government has initiated the competition between private buses and government buses on roads. According to Transport Department, to decide ratio and time on routes/roads, they have asked RSRTC management for number of buses route wise and time table. It has been presumed that the information related to time table of RSRTC buses would be provided to RTO's of State. Further, RTO, before the issue of the permit to private operators, they will check RSRTC bus route as well as time table and then they will issue the permit. With this, on same route competition will increase between RSRTC buses and private buses.

However, it has been presumed by the study that the Transport Department will fix-up time for RSRTC buses and private operators on a particular route. But, if private operator operates a bus on same route even at the same time of RSRTC bus, no one is there to stop it or control it. Thus, this will result in an increase in the possibility of conflicts. Because, even earlier also, private bus operators has damaged the buses in rural services. In case if a private bus operator keeps more than one bus on same single route then his people (employee) would be there on entire route and in order to take passengers in their buses they will get into fighting/conflict with RSRTC bus drivers and conductors. It has already happened in past even at Sindhi camp bus stand, Jaipur i.e. conflict between employees of RSRTC and private bus operators.[5]

Further, on the basis of Notification issued regarding public – private partnership i.e. operation of private buses from RSRTC bus depot and RSRTC's route, State Transport Authority has given permission for 40% more buses to be operated on State's road. For this, Transport Division has deregulated the route which was regulated earlier for RSRTC only and 100% banned for private bus operators, but now issued a notification regarding permission to private operators to operate 40% private buses against the ratio of RSRTC buses. However, the terms and conditions for private operators to operate on these routes are not yet finalized. In this regard, the transport department will issue guidelines very shortly. After this, the application will be invited from private operators. The important thing would be under this exercise that no private bus would be operated at the same time of RSRTC bus on same route. However, currently on most of the routes, private operators are operating the buses under party permit and in this way there are almost 4000 to 5000 buses operating. Further, given no mechanism to supervise time schedule of RSRTC and Private operator on entire route, there would be much more possibility of clashes. Although, currently many cases have been registered relating to the conflict between

---

[5] Times of India dated 10th April, 2015.

RSRTC employees and peoples of private operators (similar possibility has been discussed in previous paragraph).[6]

Thus, on the basis of Transport Department's hearing of private bus operators in order to allow them to operate their buses on the routes which were earlier reserved for RSRTC buses only, to connect direct headquarter to capital of State, Rajasthan Public Transport Service have identified some routes in first round work relating to this have been completed in some of the Regional Transport Offices of Dausa, Udaipur, Sikar, Ajmer, etc. The private operators, who have got the permission, have to take permit from concerned Transport Office in 30 days of permission received.[7] The bus colour would be white and red.

The routes identified in first round are given in Table 1 below:

Table 1: Permitted Routes for Private Operators by RTO

Sr.No.	R.T.O.	Routes
1	Dausa	Jaipur – Bharatpur via Dausa, Mahua.
2	Ajmer	Ajmer – Tonk, Devli – Kota, Jodhpur – Bilara – Beawar – Ajmer, Jaipur – Ajmer via Dudu, Kishangarh, Jaipur – Nagaur via Mahala, Jobner, Phulera, Sambhar, Navha, Kuchamancity (Route No. 1).
3	Udaipur	Udaipur – Beawar via Kailashpuri, Delwara, Nathdwara, Kankroli, Gomti, Diver, Kamlighat Circle, Devgarh, Bheem (Route No. 31) and link Ajmer – Jaipur via Dudu and Kishangarh.
4	Sikar	Jaipur – Bikaner via Chomu, Sikar, Salasar, Sujangarh, Nokha, etc.

Source: Rajasthan Patrika News Paper dated 2nd and 11th December, 2015.

Further, the private operators will be operating their buses on terms and conditions, given below[8]:

Colour of the buses would be off-white, red colour strip on left, right and front with logo and name of Rajasthan Public Transport Service should be written.

There would be one permit for one route. However, separate charges would be applicable for different-different routes.

[6] Now in state 40% more buses will run/operate: "private buses are given permission to operate on Roadways (RSRTC)'s route- Notification issued :- (Rajasthan Patrika-5/6/15)
[7] "Private Buses on RSRTC's Route": (Rajasthan Patrika dated 02/12/15 and 11/12/15)
[8] *Rajasthan Patrika News Paper dated 11thDecember, 2015.*

GPS (Global Positioning System) would be installed in the buses to supervise the route and schedule. However, fitness certificate for the buses would be given by RTO only.

Sleeper coach buses would be operated only for night services/travelling. No license would be issued to non-sleeper/normal buses to operate between 10:00 pm to 4:00 am.

Private operators have to issue printed, online and e-tickets only.

The tenure of permit is 5 years i.e. after 5 years the permit would be terminated/cancelled automatically.

Thus, it has been observed that this move of the State Government will create tough competition for RSRTC, who are already facing financial losses. It has been estimated that there would be an operation of 3000 or more private buses over and above the existing RSRTC buses from Sindhi Camp bus stand and nearby areas.

Further, it has been also understood through the relevant sources that despite this move of the government to allow private operators to operate on the routes earlier reserved for RSRTC through deregulation, the response of private operators is not so good i.e. fewer application have been received from private operators against the notification. However, government is planning to issue more than 5000 permits to private operators but given the reduced demand government is able to issue only 77 permits i.e. government has issued so far around 77 permits for Lok Parivahan (under private operators). This is because the private operators only apply for the permit for the route which is viable and not for the non-viable route. The only reason is that they are here to make profit not for the social services as being done by RSRTC. Very recently, it is learnt that government has issued some more permits to private operators (i.e. Lok Parivahan Seva) for the operation of around 467 buses on 140 routes out of total 467 routes which were earlier only for the operation of RSRTC. Given this, now around 1434 (earlier 967 buses and now 467 buses under Lok Parivahan Seva) private buses will also operate along with the buses of RSRTC in the State.

On the contrary, it has been observed that the RSRTC employees are not happy with this move i.e. public – private partnership. Further, to save RSRTC, they conducted a march to protest against privatization at Sindhi Camp Bus Stand, Jaipur in the month of April, 2015.[9] Thus, to protest against the privatization of roadways,

---

[9] "Save Roadways", a march-rally to show protest against privatization by RSRTC employees at Sindhi Camp Bus Stand, Jaipur: (28/04/2015)-Rajasthan Patrika.

the employees of Rajasthan Roadways registered their protest via march-rally. This protest was jointly called by Bhartiya Parivahan Majdoor Mahasangh (BPMS) and Rajasthan Parivahan Nigam Sayukt Karamchari Federation (RPNSKF). National head of BPMS revealed that on one side government says that they will not shut-down/close RSRTC and on other hand banned the purchase of new buses as well as new recruitment. This simply reflects their self-interest at the cost of convenience of general public.[10] Moreover, the RSRTC employees went on strike against the move of government to privatize RSRTC and many other issues relating to certain provisions of Road Safety Bill. This strike of RSRTC employees affected almost 11 lakhs passengers in the State. Only in Jaipur, more than 58000 passengers with inward and outward movement got affected along with the loss of revenue by around Rs. 5 crores.[11] It has also been observed that during the strike of RSRTC, the private bus operators and jeep operators took undue advantages of this by charging and increased fare by 2–3 times more than the regular fare. For example, fare for Kota is about Rs. 200 to Rs. 300 but these private operators charged upto Rs. 600 due to strike of RSRTC. Even, roadways officers asserted that the policy of privatization of roadways by government caused the strike and ultimately it affects general public.

Again, given the decision of government to allow private operators opposed by many labour unions relating or concerned with RSRTC employees, many labour organizations of RSRTC registered their protest against this move/decision of government at Sindhi Camp bus stand Jaipur and other bus stands in entire State. It was a state wide protest. The leaders of this joint protest asserted that this move/decision of the government is against the public interest and there will be protests against this move/decision of the government at all levels. Moreover, given this, one of the largest and busiest bus stand of Jaipur i.e. Sindhi Camp was shut down for 3 hours to register the protest against the decision of government by RSRTC's joint labour organization committee.[12] However, our survey revealed that the concerned government despite taking some positive steps to help RSRTC in terms of improving on quality of services by putting more money on infrastructural development and other facilities via proper and efficient management, are only creating more problems for RSRTC.

Further, our study is also of the opinion that the private player always look/operate for the profit rather than more social welfare as compared to RSRTC whose basic aim is to maximize social welfare and then for profit, if possible. Thus, even on specific routes, if private operators are applying for permits and once they get them and agree to operate on that particular route, it simply means that there exists demand for

[10] Rajasthan Patrika (28/04/2015).
[11] Rajasthan Patrika dated 30th April, 2015 and 1st May, 2015.
[12] Rajasthan Patrika (14/12/15 & 15/12/15).

travel on that route which may make them a good profit. If this is the case, then why is there no government support for RSRTC to operate more and better quality services on that particular route so that they can earn more revenue and minimize their losses and further earn some more profit for its better future. It's all about proper planning and efficient execution of planning with effective decisions. Therefore, the study is of the opinion that government should revisit/rethink permitting private bus operator to operate on routes reserved for RSRTC.

Conclusion

The study concludes that in order to enhance or bringing the correction i.e. with reference to the various issues faced by RSRTC especially related to operational management covering facilities, infrastructure, managerial and performance efficiency (financial, physical, etc.), constitute the Bus Port Authority with the mandate to create, develop and operate facilities at the notified bus terminals. It would also streamline and facilitate the running/operation of buses from terminals along with developing the parking areas, hotels, toilets, banks and other facilities needed by passengers. The study also concludes that the government has deregulated the routes of operation which were earlier solely for RSRTC i.e. government has opened the routes for private operators through the deregulation of routes. However, it has been assumed that in order to provide better facilities for the passengers (as mentioned above in the paper), the move of the government i.e. set up of Bus Port Authority would prove a right decision in future but there are still some issues or contradiction on the decision of deregulation of routes. Although, government has assured that there would be proper supervision and execution of tasks related to the deregulation of routes but some of the recent incidences (also mentioned in the paper earlier/above) raise many questions on this.

Therefore, in this regard, firstly, the Bus Port Authority would revamp all the bus stands and depots with reference to provide more and more facilities to the passengers. Secondly, the concerned authority would insist on more improvement of managerial efficiency for the effective decision to bring out RSRTC from losses. Thirdly, more precisely, Bus Port Authority would look at all the consequences of deregulation of routes to avoid and solve the problems (clashes among employees, time schedule and management of bus operation of STU's, basically RSRTC, and private operators) arising out of it and provide necessary support to RSRTC in all possible manners, which ultimately could enhance the competition with reference to the passenger movement i.e. operation of buses (public and private). Moreover, despite deregulation of routes, the response of private operators is not as expected by the authority. This is because the private operators are applying for permits on only those routes which are viable in operation i.e. routes on which enough travel demand is there so they can make profit. On the other hand RSRTC is running its services on viable as well as non-viable routes as a social obligation with the aim of maximizing the social welfare rather than maximizing profit. This results in the negative impact on the financial position of RSRTC in the absence of necessary and required support. Hence, in this regard a detailed study is called for.

References

Buses Not Operating, Passengers Upset. (2015, December 15). *Rajasthan Patrika*, pp. 02.

CIRT. (2012). *Service Quality Management for RSRTC Operations.*Pune: Central Institute of Road Transport.

GOI. (2012).*Working Group Report on Road Transport Twelfth Five Year Plan.* New Delhi:Planning Commission Government of India.

Hire More, Deficit Still Growing. (2015, April 10). *Rajasthan Patrika*, pp. 03.

NCAER. (2007).*State Policies Affecting Competition: Passenger Road Transportation Sector.* New Delhi: National Council for Applied Economic Research.

New Public Private Partnership for 225 State Bus Terminal. (2015, April 10). *Times of India*, pp. 01–02.

Now Let's Enjoy Travelling in Red and White Buses. (2015, December 02). *Rajasthan Patrika*, pp. 11.

Parihar, M. (2015). Employment Potential Road Transport Industry in India. *Supply Chain Pulse, ITM (Institute of Technology & Management), Navi Mumbai, Maharashtra, Vol.6 Issue 3.*

Parihar, M., Gupta, S. & Sharma, R. (2016). *An Economic Analysis of State Transport Undertaking: A Case of Rajasthan State Road Transport Corporation (RSRTC).* Jaipur: Manipal University Jaipur.

Private Buses Will Run on Roadways Buses Reserved Routes Soon. (2015, March 19). *Rajasthan Patrika*, pp. 19.

Roadways Employees Opposed Bus Stand Authority. (2015, April 28). *Rajasthan Patrika*, pp. 07.

Roadways Employees Perform on Privatization. (2015, June 05). *Rajasthan Patrika*, pp. 04.

Ramesh & Ramanaya. (2007). Economic Contribution of Public Passenger Transport Organizations – An Application of EVAR Methodology. *Vision – The Journal of Business Perspective, Volume II, No. 3.*

Sriraman, S., Anand, V., Manisha, K. (2007).*Competition Issues in the Road Goods Transport Industry in India with Special Reference to the Mumbai Metropolitan Region*, New Delhi: Competition Commission of India.

Stuck Wheel, Passenger Stray. (2015, April 30). *Rajasthan Patrika*, pp. 01.

The Knock on the Path of the Private Corporation. (2015, December 11). *Rajasthan Patrika*, pp. 05.

Three Hours Getting Off Roadways Bus. (2015, December 14). *Rajasthan Patrika*, pp. 01.

Vehicle Passengers Suffering from Strike. (2015, May 01). *Rajasthan Patrika*, pp. 12.

Trivedi, S. (2012). Performance review of Gujarat State Road Transport Corporation. *International Journal of Social Science and Interdisciplinary Research, Volume 1, Issue 9.*

World Bank. (2005).*Road Transport Service Efficiency Study*. Washington D.C., World Bank,

"Is Green The New Black?"

Rahul Agarwal* & Divya Kakkar*

Abstract

In today's life, the social media has its own importance, especially amongst the youth. This is a common trend across nations, ethnicity, culture, language, education and financial sectors. Social presence is as vital for today's youth to their very existence. This is noticed, researched and leveraged by the marketers to position their product correctly and consistent with the social image of the consumer.

Another important trend is so called sensitivity towards going green and projecting an environment-friendly image where one strives to look sensitive for the environment.

This research involves discovering how important social image is for youth. The goal is to understand to what extent our young generation is becoming more concerned about the environment. The paper also tries to find out whether this concern is for real or merely to improve their social image and to check whether going green is a felt social responsibility or a 'trend' that young people want to follow.

This exploratory study uses implications of concepts of self-image used for business and marketing, which attracts many young customers.

The anticipated outcome of this study is the identification of areas that may influence the idea of 'Going Green' amongst youth in this true sense. The findings may be useful in understanding the reality of the green wave and thereby contributing to creating a socially responsible society.

Keywords: Pollution, Increasing Concern For Environment, Green Marketing And Green Washing.

Introduction

Environment friendly/Eco Friendly/Green are terms that refer to objects, services, laws and rules that either do not harm the environment or do very little harm to it. (Longman, 2010)

---

* AMITY University, Jaipur

Youth nowadays is becoming very concerned about the environment and it has been seen that there is a tremendous rise in sales of the products which are friendly to the environment in the past few years because of the customers being environment friendly.

Before investigating the role that youth can play in addressing environmental issues, it is important to provide some background and establish a clear context by identifying the current state of the environment.

- Pollution kills more than 1 million seabirds and 100 million mammals every year.
- The garbage dumped in the ocean every year is roughly around 14 billion pounds. Plastic is the major constituent.
- 5000 people die every day as a result of drinking unclean water.
- United States produces 30% of the world's waste and uses 25 % of the worlds natural resources
- The Mississippi River dumps 1.5 million metric tonnes of nitrogen pollution in the Gulf of Mexico every year.
- More than 3 million kids under the age of 5 years die every year due to environmental factors like pollution.
- Almost 80% of urban waste in India is dumped in the river Ganges.
- There are around 73 various kinds of pesticides in the groundwater, which is used as drinking water.
- There are more than 500 million cars in the world and by 2030 the number will rise to 1 billion. This means pollution level will be more than double.
- House owners use chemicals that are 10 times more toxic per acre, than the amount used by the farmers.
- In India, the Ganges water is gradually becoming septic, especially due to dumping of half burnt dead bodies and enshrouded babies. (Rinkesh, 2009)

Human beings have a tremendous negative impact on the planet, including that of pollution. **Pollution** is the introduction of contaminants into the environment, either chemicals, foreign substances, or even light and noise. Environmental pollution produces a number of negative effects, including ocean acidification, global warming, acid rain, and habitat loss for plant and animal species. Additionally, environmental pollution has a number of adverse health effects on human beings.

It has been estimated that about *400 million metric tons* of pollution is produced annually, of which the United States alone produces 250 million metric tons. Motor vehicle emissions are one of the leading causes of environmental pollution in the atmosphere. There are, of course, other sources of carbon dioxide that constitute pollution to the environment. The United States, despite having less than five percent of the world's population, produces one-quarter of the world's carbon dioxide. (Paper Masters, 2015)

Review of Literature

During the latter half of the 1980's, environmental concern became translated into a specific activity of green consumerism. Surveys show that there has been a permanent change in consumer's attitudes. The eco-labelling of products seems to be an effective means of communicating the green message to the increasingly responsive customers. (Sharpley, 2001)

But there is a contradiction as it is also seen that it is the customers' need to maintain their cultural capital,their social image more than a genuine concern for the environment.

Witherspoon's research from 1994 also supports this idea. Witherspoon observed that upto one half of those who claim to embrace green values never transfer these beliefs into their behaviour, and there is a difference between the declarative and actual environment sensitivity. (Tuohino, 2003)

FOMO

Youth care deeply about what others do and think and they feel left out and which results in FOMO (Fear of missing out). Past research indicates FOMO includes irritability, anxiety and feelings of inadequacy, which had worsened with the increasing use of social media sites (Wortham, 2011)

Thus, this research paper tries to find answers to a few questions. Has green become the new black for youth and this is why they want to go green or is it a felt social responsibility? (WORTHAM, 2011)

Increasing Concern For Environment

It has been seen that there is a rising awareness among customers about sustainability and environment protection.Two thirds of consumers consciously choose to avoid specific brands or items due to environment concerns, a figure that has increased by 26% in the last six years, according to Tetra pack's latest environmental research, which involved surveying 6000 consumers across 12 countries including the US.

The transition from consumer concern to consumer action is also driving a positive change in the green industry.Companies around the world are making environmental stewardship a top priority and using it to transform every aspect of their business. (Kennell, 2015)

Green Marketing And Green Washing

Businesses are in unique position to capitalize on the environmental anxieties of the millennial. It often happens that people buy eco-friendly products not because they are concerned about the environment but because they want to keep pace with the trend of 'GOING GREEN'. A lot of customers are not aware of the positives and negatives that a particular product poses on the environment.

Just by looking at the eco labels they buy a particular product and then showcase it on their social media to match it with their self concept of 'green'.

Companies around the world are making environmental stewardship a top priority and using it to transform every aspect of their businesses and this is supported by the following data:

- Starbucks has green advocates smiling about its "bean-to-cup" approach, which stresses top efficiency at each link of its global supply chain. By all measures the program appears to be a great success, with the company's decision to use coffee cup sleeves made of recycled paper saving roughly 78,000 trees per year since 2006. Starbucks has also partnered up with many environmental organizations, from Conservation International to the Earthwatch Institute, in efforts to do right by the communities it operates in. (Business Pandit, 2008)
- Coca-Cola has narrowed down 3 environmental goals on which to focus their efforts: water stewardship, sustainable packaging, and climate & energy protection. In just a few years, Coca-Cola has already gotten itself involved in community recycling programs and a complete, sustainability-focused overhaul of its packaging designs.
- In 2009, the largest CSD manufacturer in the world, Coca-Cola, introduced PlantBottle for its water brand Dasani. PlantBottle uses about 30% PET resin from sugarcane and is thus more eco-friendly than traditional plastic bottles.
- Sales of Dasani have increased by 20% since the launch of PlantBottle. The company also plans to introduce bottles made completely out of plant-based resinin the coming few years. This move could further boost sales of Dasani, which currently has a market share of ~10% in the still water category with retail sales of over $900 million in FY2013. (Team, 2014)

- TESCO-This British grocery chain has enlisted its customer base in the fight to go green by offering savings to shoppers who bring reusable shopping bags to their stores. The company has also turned each of its stores into wind-powered, high-recycling, biodiesel truck delivered epicentres of environmental sustainability,
- Possibly the most hated name in the entire green movement, Wal-Mart is now positioned to make all but the most dogmatic of its detractors eat their words. According to Sustainablog, Wal-Mart has launched an ambitious long-term plan to eventually power each and every one its stores using 100% renewable energy sources. As per the company's executives, Wal-Mart is committed to using its waste-eliminating corporate philosophy to make its own operations eco-friendlier than ever.US retailer Wal-Mart addressed the issues of excess packaging of products and greenhouse gas emissions by introducing a 'packaging scorecard' concept,through which it expects to reduce packing across its global supply chain.
- Companies such as Tesco and Wal-Mart are not committing to environmental goals out of the goodness of their hearts. The reason for their actions is a simple yet powerful realization that the environmental and economic footprints are most often aligned.
- When M&S launched its "Plan A" sustainability programme in 2007, it was believed that it would cost more than £200m in the first five years. However, the initiative had generated £105m by 2011/12 according the company's report. (Das, 2012)

As a 2015 study by the Nielson company suggests, despite high unemployment rates and low wages, people are willing to spend more for products that are environment friendly. Just over the span of one year, people are willing to spend more for products that are environment friendly and the number of people willing to pay more for products and services from companies committed to positive environmental and social change has increased from 55% in 2014 to 72% in 2015.

Such a rapid expansion in green conscious customers has spurred the surge of companies making green claims, sparking gridlock at the US patent and trademark office. Between 2006 and 2007, filing for eco friendly labels has doubled and stores offered 73% more green products in 2010 compared to 2009.

People often look at these symbols and buy the products thinking that these are eco friendly and thus companies manufacturing such products leverage this notion of customers to earn profits. A lot of big organisations have switched to an environment friendly production and **'GREEN MARKETING'**-Marketing of products that are presumed to be environmentally safe. Thus, green marketing incorporates a broad range of activities, including product modification, changes to production process and most importantly 'GREEN ADVERTISING'

Companies may not be committed to environmental goals. The reason for their action is simple yet powerful realization that the environmental and economic footprints are most often aligned.

When M&S launched its plan A sustainability programme in 2007,it was believed that it would cost a lot but however the initiative generated 105M pounds by 2011 according to the company's report.

Business also use terms like sustainable, carbon neutral and compostable which leaves consumers guessing about the real environmental impact of the products they see. This also creates an incentive for companies to greenwash their products with false, deceptive or unsubstantiated eco-friendly claims. (walker, 2013)

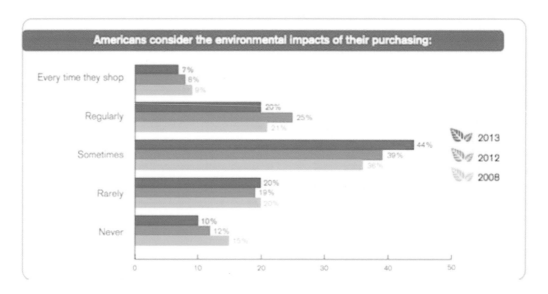

Source: https://www.environmentalleader.com/2013/04/71-of-consumers-think-green-when-purchasing/

Changing Buyer Behaviour

- As a 2015 study by The Nielsen Company suggests, despite high unemployment rates and low wages, people are willing to spend more for products that are environmentally friendly. Just over the span of one year, people are willing to pay more for products and services from companies committed to positive environmental and social change increased from 55% in 2014 to 72% in 2015.

- Although seen by some as a niche minority, eco-minded consumers are now a major concern and opportunity for marketing departments across the country. Such a rapid expansion in green-conscious customers has spurred a surge of companies making green claims, sparking gridlock at the United States Patent and Trademark Office. Between 2006 and 2007, filings for eco-friendly labels doubled and stores offered 73% more green products in 2010 compared to 2009. Thus, even if a business owner does not believe the threat of climate change is real, businesses nevertheless invest in eco-friendly practices so they may advertise and sell to green-minded customers.

- The assumption that customers only use environment friendly products to uplift their social image is also supported by the record that 71 percent of Americans consider the environment when they shop, according to research from Cone Communications but only 7 percent consider the environment every time they shop, according to the 2013 Cone Communications Green Gap Trend Tracker.

- Even as thinking "green" is increasingly at the forefront of consumers' minds, Americans still struggle with their role in the lifecycle of products with an environmental benefit. Nine in 10 respondents say they believe it's their responsibility to properly use and dispose of these products, but action isn't aligning with intent

- Only 30 percent say they often *use* products in a way that achieves the intended environmental benefit. Some 42 percent say they *dispose* of products in a way that fulfills the intended environmental benefit.

Their social media usage patterns also direct towards the same trends – (Delzio, 2016)

- 24% of teens go online "almost constantly," aided by the convenience and constant access provided by mobile devices, especially smartphones,

- Youth generally post pictures of whatever they do on their social media accounts and thus Going green has also become a fashion for them which they can wear and showcase on their snapchat and face book accounts.

- Every day, between 300 and 350 million photos are uploaded to Facebook. With an audience of 1.59 billion and 1.04 billion monthly active users, the portion of the audience participating by uploading photos is less than 35%.

- In comparison, 65% of Snapchat users upload their own photos daily. They're engaged with the platform, viewing it as an extension of their own personal brand rather than just a place to passively receive information

- People share 1.3 million pieces of content on Facebook every minute of every day.

- Total 500 million tweets are sent per day.
- 88% of B2B marketers are using Twitter for sharing content.
- 37% Twitter users are aged between 18 to 29.
- 92% of all Pinterest posts are photos.
- There are 75 million daily active users on Instagram.
- Almost 85 million videos and photos people are uploaded everyday.
- More than 500,000 advertisers growing their businesses on Instagram.

The assumption that customers only use environment friendly products to uplift their social image is also supported by the record that 71% of Americans consider the environment when they shop but only 7% consider the environment when actually they shop, according to research from cone communication.

Social media usage patterns also direct towards same trend.

Discussion and Suggestions

As we saw in the past, there are many more rules, laws, conventions are made for protecting the environment but there is no effective implementation.

Young people constitute a large part of the world's population and young people will have to live longer with the consequences of current environmental decisions than will their elders. Future generations will also be affected by these decisions and the extent to which they have addressed concerns such as the depletion of resources, biodiversity loss, and long-lived radioactive wastes.

Young people can play an active role in protecting and improving the environment. They can change their lifestyle and how it affects the environment. They can make their homes, schools and youth organizations more environmentally friendly by adopting environmentally friendly practices, recycling of different materials as well as preserving resources such as water and electricity. Engaging youth in environmental protection not only creates direct impact on changing youth behaviours and attitudes, but possibly influence their parents, relatives and families.

Youth are back bone of the nation. They can change the future of the society with their well-being and courageous behaviour. Unfortunately today we find the youth those who are more interested in other places which are not useful to them as well as nationally. They choose to spend their days doing drugs and playing video games. They spend their nights partying and living it up, so to speak. More and more young men of this age group are sitting at home in front of their televisions playing games all day instead of bettering themselves or going to work. They have no vision and if they do have dreams they do not have the drive to make any attempt at achieving them.

The environment is simply defined as our surrounding, including both living and non-living things and youth are the young people. Environmental protection is a broad subject Environmental problems are rising day by day and everyone is concerned about global warming and climate change as globally but local and national environmental problems are less concerned. Protecting the environment starts with pollution control therefore, youth can help reduce waste by paying attention to minor details in their daily lives, for example, not to take extra plastic bags when we go shopping. Actually there are many other tips for greener environment.

By applying the greening knowledge at home and schools, we can help to make city, a greener city. Discarding computers, electrical appliances and rechargeable batteries can seriously harm the environment. Youth role is to implement recycling programs for used computers and electrical appliances. You can arrange for collection services with them. There are also many collection points for recycling of rechargeable batteries, so do not simply throw them away. Youth have a role to play in environmental and conservation efforts that will improve livelihoods.

Green Tips:

➢ **Going Green in House**

- Close the running tap water, when not needed.
- Use the dishwasher, when the dishes are full. Try to avoid using it more often i.e. for each single plate.
- Try to be cautious in using water. Turn off taps when not used. By this way, it is estimated every home can save more than a gallon of water, which is very high when combined in a local.
- Turning off Lights and saving electricity as much as possible is also a way to go green. During the daytime, it is good to open windows and screens to let sunlight in and fill house with warmth. After all, sunlight is essential for body in the form of vitamin A.
- The local power company would be able to provide a free presentation on how to make the home a better energy efficient home.

➢ **Going Green with Recycling and Reusing**

- Giving away unwanted or unusable materials to free service organizations is a better way to start going green.

- Reusing the furniture would save some extra money spent on newer furniture. For example, one can remodel a table by adding sheets of wood to it and create his own wardrobe.
- Recycling paper, plastics, glass and metals could also be done by making use of the local trash pickup service.
- Instead of simply throwing older items, one can use his creativity in creating the essence out of them. For example, the older screen cloth could be stitched with flat sheets and made as curtains or cloth piece covering the shades of the lamp. They are easy and cheap in terms of interior decorating materials.
- Choosing reusable water bottles in comparison with plastic bottles every month is a nice way to avoid using plastics and reusing the water bottles. They may be expensive at the beginning, but once getting used to it, they would prove worthy providing health and hygiene besides going green.

➤ Going Green with Transport

- Carpooling or vehicle pooling is the best way to save environment from three or four times the pollution. Carpooling can be done with friends, neighbours, or relatives working in the same direction as yours, not necessarily the same company.
- Maintaining the vehicle regularly and providing it for service near a service station would help minimize its pollution output.
- Many companies have started offering the plan 'Work while you are at home'. Enjoying this benefit not only saves green, but also enables one to spend quality time together in a family and allowing to save costs of travelling and fuel. (Acharya, 2013)

The earth provides all the necessary resources for human beings to survive and prosper. But as the global population grows and develops, the demand for energy and consumer goods increases. This has led to increased pollution and misuse of natural resources, causing great damage to the environment. In turn, people's health, food supplies and livelihoods are increasingly threatened. The release of greenhouse gases into the atmosphere that contribute to climate change, the overuse of agricultural soil that deteriorates the ground and often leads to deforestation, the contamination of water through bacteria and chemicals or the loss of biodiversity – environmental challenges are plentiful.

Today, many people speak about "sustainability" when highlighting an alternative model of how human beings can develop economically and socially without putting too much strain on the environment. Sustainable development is defined as "development that meets the needs of the present generation without compromising the ability of future generations to meet their own needs." This clearly shows that youth are at the heart of the sustainability debate. As politicians sometimes lack the necessary long-term thinking that is needed to effectively address pressing environmental issues, it's key that global youth have a say in environmental policies, which have a direct impact on the current and future environment they live in.

Present day youth know that this is not the time to sit back and expect things to change themselves. Therefore almost every day we hear about a new movement or story of youth participation ranging from deforestation, disaster management or discouraging animal ill treatment. Engaging youth in organised effort to promote environmental sustainability has implications for youngsters themselves as well as for their communities. It is high time for youth to analyse their needs and decide what are their true priorities are. We have plenty of resources. But the demand is increasing day by day. It is the responsibility of the youth to manage it efficiently.

Youth participation should be increased for the environment protection. The participation of youth can be sought at all levels ranging from grass root activism to policy bodies to non-Governmental organizations (NGOs).

Their role can be institutionalised in policy making through advisory bodies such as Youth councils. The deterioration of the natural environment is one of the principal concerns of young people world-wide as it has direct implications for their well-being both now and in the future.

The natural environment must be maintained and preserved for both present and future generations. The causes of environmental degradation must be addressed. The environmentally friendly use of natural resources and environmentally sustainable economic growth will improve human life. Sustainable development has become a key element in the programmes of youth organizations throughout the world. While every segment of society is responsible for maintaining the environmental integrity of the community, young people have a special interest in maintaining a healthy environment because they will be the ones to inherit it.

In order to turn your backs to such corporate, consumer boycotts and protests can be the most effective, eventually causing polluting companies to rethink their corporate strategy. Apart from having a greater stake in the more distant future, young people are properly poised to promote environmental awareness simply due to the fact that they often have better access to information about the environment than their elders. The youth have lived all their lives in an era in which environmental issues have loomed large. They can introduce fresh ideas and outlook to environment-related issues because anti-ecological ways of thinking and behaving are not ingrained in them. A major reason why the youth ought to take the lead in protecting the environment is stronger awareness of the issues and a greater stake in long-term sustainability. They will obviously face challenges as pressures are brought to bear in the opposite direction. Commercialization in every aspect of life is severely affecting the youth of today. In addition to these effects, on the whole, technologies that increasingly distance people from the environmental effects of their consumption decisions are growing with globalization, acting as an impediment to environmental awareness.

Governments and youth organizations should initiate programmes to promote participation in tree planting, forestry, combating desert creep, waste reduction, recycling and other sound environmental practices. The participation of young people and their organizations in such programmes can provide good training and encourage awareness and action. Waste management programmes may represent potential income-generating activities which provide opportunities for employment.

Young people should be involved in designing and implementing appropriate environmental policies. Women and children are the worst sufferers of climate change and pollution in many countries of the world. Women should be encouraged to fight climate change and pollution and their active participation is necessary to make the world a better place to live in. With the use of digital technology such as internet, mobile and social media youth can bring revolution in the world and protect environment with youth power. (verma, 2016)

References

Acharya, R. (2013, JUNE 25). *Role of Youth for A Cleaner and Greener Environment.* **Retrieved from www.ypard.net: http://www.ypard.net/2013-june-25/role-youth-cleaner-and-greener-environment**

Business Pandit. (2008, July 29). *25 Big Companies That Are Going Green.* Retrieved from www.businesspundit.com: http://www.businesspundit.com/25-big-companies-that-are-going-green/

Das, S. (2012, may 28). *Is going green just a fad?* Retrieved from business-standard. com: http://www.business-standard.com/article/management/is-going-green-just-a-fad-112052800059_1.html

Delzio, S. (2016, FEBRUARY 17). *Snapchat Gains Momentum: New Research.* Retrieved from socialmediaexaminer.com: http://www.socialmediaexaminer.com/snapchat-gains-momentum-new-research/

Kennell, B. (2015, 09 10). *Environmental Concern Empowers the People.* Retrieved from www.huffingtonpost.com: http://www.huffingtonpost.com/brian-kennell/environmental-concern-emp_b_8105580.html

Longman. (2010). *Longman Dictionary of Contemporary English.* Retrieved from ldoceonline.com: http://www.ldoceonline.com/dictionary/environmentally-friendly

Paper Masters. (2015). *Environmental Pollution.* Retrieved from www.papermasters.com: https://www.papermasters.com/environmental-pollution.html

Rinkesh. (2009). *Conserve energy future.* Retrieved from www.conserve-energy-future.com: http://www.conserve-energy-future.com/various-pollution-facts.php

Team, T. (2014, jan 30). *Beverage Companies Go Green In Hope To Sell More Water.* Retrieved from www.forbes.com: https://www.forbes.com/sites/greatspeculations/2014/01/30/beverage-companies-go-green-in-hope-to-sell-more-water/#1292e92be516

Tuohino, A. (2003). *Environmental awareness and environmentally friendly behaviour.* Retrieved from www2.uef.fi: https://www2.uef.fi/documents/1145891/.../anja.../bee22e7c-afa0-49ee-85af-10baca9e6f41

verma, P. (2016, MARCH 09). *Youth participation in environment protection.* Retrieved from www.worldpulse.com: https://www.worldpulse.com/en/community/users/priya-verma/posts/65057

walker, l. (2013, APRIL 03). *71% of Consumers Think Green When Purchasing.* Retrieved from www.environmentalleader.com: https://www.environmentalleader.com/2013/04/71-of-consumers-think-green-when-purchasing/

WORTHAM, J. (2011, APRIL 09). *Business day.* Retrieved from www.nytimes.com: http://www.nytimes.com/2011/04/10/business/10ping.html

Cyanobacterial Mycosporine-Like Amino Acids and Their Derivatives as Natural Sunscreen

Shikha Jain*, Ganshyam Prajapat**, Akhil Agrawal** & Lalita Ledwani*

Abstract

Ultraviolet radiation is harmful to living systems; causing damage to biological macromolecules. An important strategy for dealing with ultraviolet exposure is the biosynthesis of mycosporine-like amino acids by several organisms. Mycosporine-like amino acids are the most common group of ultraviolet radiation absorbing intracellular secondary metabolites with a maximum absorbance between 310 and 362 nm. These molecules have wide phylogenetic distribution. However, it is presumed that the enzymatic machinery to synthesize these molecules was inherited from cyanobacterial ancestors via endosymbiosis, as cyanobacteria are primitive photosynthetic oxygen-evolving prokaryotes that appeared on the earth when there was no ozone layer to protect them from harmful ultraviolet radiation. Cyanobacteria might have faced the most deleterious ultraviolet radiation, which leads to an evolution of ultraviolet protecting molecules for efficient selection in the environment. Due to the putative role of mycosporine-like amino acids in ultraviolet photo protection, they are the promising candidates for use in pharmaceutical and cosmetic applications. In the last three decades, scientists have investigated various cyanobacteria for novel mycosporine-like amino acids, applying different induction techniques. This review organizes all the cyanobacterial groups that produce various mycosporine-like amino acids including their sunscreen activity.

Keywords: Mycosporine-like amino acids, cyanobacteria, ultraviolet radiation, shinorine, mycosporine glycine.

Introduction

Solar radiation reaching the Earth consists of infrared (>800 nm), visible or photosynthetically available (PAR, 400–750 nm), ultraviolet-A (UV-A, 320–400 nm),and the more energetic ultraviolet-B (UV-B, 280–320 nm) wavelengths. Highly energetic ultraviolet-C radiation (UV-C, 200–280 nm) does not reach the Earth because it is absorbed by atmospheric ozone and O_2.UV radiation can induce acute skin reactions like erythema but produces also long term effects such as premature skin aging (photoaging)and carcinogenesis. The more energetic UV-B is absorbed

---

* Manipal University Jaipur, Jaipur, Rajasthan, India ** Central University of Rajasthan

in the epidermis where it can cause acute sunburn,DNA mutation or even cancer. Although less energetic, the longer wavelengths in the UV-A region can penetrate much deeper into the skin. UV-A reaches the dermis where it is responsible for the premature skin aging effects of sunlight. Various synthetic sunscreens are available but they might be problematic for the everyday application(Schlumpf et al., 2001) in particular with respect to reproduction and ontogeny. We examined six frequently used UVA and UVB screens for estrogenicity in vitro and in vivo. In MCF-7 breast cancer cells, five out of six chemicals, that is, benzophenone-3 (Bp-3. There is a need of potential natural UV-screening substances to protect the skin against photoaging. The strongest UV-absorbing compounds in nature are the mycosporine-like amino acids (MAAs).MAAs are widely distributed in nature, thought to have great importance to ancient forms of life on Earth, functioning as a primary sunscreen. They are found in various organisms from tropical to polar regions (Shick & Dunlap, 2002). These are present typically in organisms that are exposed to high-intensity light, such as cyanobacteria and other prokaryotes, eukaryotic micro-organisms (e.g., microalgae and fungi), marine macroalgae (both green and red algae), corals, terrestrial lichens, and other marine organisms that accumulate MAAs from their feed (Sinha, Singh, & Häder, 2007). These MAAs are thought to be efficient natural sunscreens that can prevent damages induced by UV radiation.

Synthetic Sunscreens: Their Demerits

Because of growing public concern about skin damage by UV light, the use of synthetic sunscreens is increasing, even though the benefit with respect to prevention of melanoma remains controversial (Autier, Mezzetti, & Doré, 1998; Bigby, 1999). The chemicals used in sunscreens are highly lipophilic and therefore can be expected to bioaccumulate in the environment. In 1991 and 1993,six different sunscreens were identified in fish of the Meerfelder Maar lake (Eifel, Germany) at total concentrations of 2 mg/kg lipid in perch and 0.5 mg/kg lipid in roach (Nagtegaal, Ternes, Baumann, & Nagel, 1997). Both fish species were contaminated with sunscreens,polychlorinated biphenyls and DDT at comparable levels.

Humans can be exposed to sunscreens by dermal absorption (Aghazarian, Tchiakpe, Reynier, & Gayte-Sorbier, 1999; Hagedorn-Leweke & Lippold, 1995; Hayden, Roberts, & Benson, 1997; Jiang, Roberts, Collins, & Benson, 2001) or through the food chain. The sunscreen benzophenone-3(Bp-3) and its metabolite 2,4-dihydroxybenzophenone have been detected in human urine from 4 hours after application of commercially available sunscreen products to the skin (Felix, Hall, & Brodbelt, 1998; Hayden et al., 1997). Bp-3 has also been found to be readily absorbed from the gastrointestinaltract(Kadry, Okereke, Abdel-Rahman, Friedman, & Davis, 1995). There are evidences for bioaccumulation of sunscreen in human stem cells(Hany & Nagel, 1995). In five out of six samples of human milk, Bp-3 and/ or octyl methoxycinnamate were present in detectable amounts.From these results it appeared that sunscreens are relevant environmental contaminants and concern for human health.

Mycosporine-Like Amino Acids

Mycosporine-like amino acids (MAAs) are ultraviolet (UV) absorbing small molecules. They are colorless and water-soluble substances, which exhibit molecular weight ranging from 188 to 1050 Daltons (Wada, Sakamoto, & Matsugo, 2015). They are characterized by a cyclohexenone or cyclohexenimine chromophore (Favre-bonvin & Arpin, 1976) conjugated with the nitrogen substituent of an amino acid or its imino alcohol, having absorption maxima ranging from 268 to 362 nm (Wada et al., 2015). These were first discovered and named mycosporine because of light mediated fungal sporulation (Dehorter, Brocquet, Lacoste, & Alais, 1980; Favre-bonvin & Arpin, 1976; Trione, Leach, & Mutch, 1966). However, the real interest in MAAs has tremendously grown in recent years because of their potential in absorbing UV radiations. In addition to acting as sunscreen agents, recently MAAs have also been found to play multiple roles in many other biological processes, including UV photo-protection of organisms (Bandaranayake & Des Rocher, 1999; Mason, Schafer, Shick, & Dunlap, 1998; Neale, Banaszak, & Jarriel, 1998; Aharon Oren & Gunde-Cimerman, 2007; Shick & Dunlap, 2002) and their embryos (Adams & Shick, 2001), antioxidant and ROS scavenging property (Rastogi, Sonani, Madamwar, & Incharoensakdi, 2016), osmotic regulation (Kogej, Gostinčar, Volkmann, Gorbushina, & Gunde-Cimerman, 2006; A Oren, 1997; Anne Portwich &Garcia-Pichel, 1999; Singh, Kumari, Rastogi, Singh, & Sinha, 2008; Sinha& Häder, 2003; Waditee-Sirisattha, Kageyama, Sopun, Tanaka, & Takabe, 2014)Israel. This is the first report of the occurrence of MAAs in a halophilic cyanobacterial community. Two MAAs were detected, one with an absorption maximum at 332 nm, and one at 362 nm. Intracellular MAA concentrations in the cyanobacterial community were estimated to be at least 98 mM, and this already high value is probably an underestimation. With an average molecular weight of around 300, MAAs should contribute at least 3% of the cell wet weight. While MAAs have been shown to absorb ultraviolet (UV, desiccation (Feng, Zhang, Feng, & Qiu, 2012; Olsson-Francis, Watson, & Cockell, 2013)for decades researchers have tried to cultivate N. flagelliforme but have failed to get macroscopic filamentous thalli. In this study, single trichomes with 50 to 200 vegetative cells were induced from free-living cells by low light and used to investigate the morphogenesis of N. flagelliforme under low UV-B radiation and periodic desiccation. Low-fluence-rate UV-B (0.1 W m(-2, defense against oxidative and thermal stresses (Michalek-Wagner, 2001; Shick & Dunlap, 2002).

MAAs in Cyanobacteria

Cyanobacteria, also referred as blue-green algae, are phylogenetically a primitive group of Gram-negative prokaryotes with a long evolutionary history and the only prokaryotes that perform plant-like oxygenic photosynthesis (Stewart, 1980). They are the oldest photosynthetic organisms on earth that originated approximately 2.6–3.5 billion years ago (Hedges, Chen, & Kumar, 2001). The existence of cyanobacteria precedes the existence of the present ozone shield. Therefore, to withstand the detrimental effects of solar UV radiation, these prokaryotes have evolved several lines of defense and various tolerance mechanisms, including avoidance, antioxidant production, DNA repair, protein re-synthesis, programmed cell death and the synthesis of UV-absorbing/screening compounds, such as MAAs and scytonemin (Sinha, Klisch, Gröniger, & Häder, 1998).

A number of cyanobacteria isolated from freshwater, marine or terrestrial habitats contain MAAs (Garcia-Pichel & Castenholz, 1993; Karsten & Garcia-Pichel, 1996). However, the first report of the accumulation of large amounts of MAAs in cyanobacteria *Microcoleus* was reported in 1969 (Shibata, 1969). Shibata found out that the extract of cyanobacteria in the UV region showed strong absorption band at 322 nm with a shoulder at 362 nm, and the peak at 322 nm was 23 times higher than the highest phycobilin band at 545 nm. Later, a number of cyanobacterial isolates from various extreme environments like Antarctica and halophilic lakes found to contain MAAs (A Oren, 1997; Quesada & Vincent, 1997)Israel. This is the first report of the occurrence of MAAs in a halophilic cyanobacterial community. Two MAAs were detected, one with an absorption maximum at 332 nm, and one at 362 nm. Intracellular MAA concentrations in the cyanobacterial community were estimated to be at least 98 mM, and this already high value is probably an underestimation. With an average molecular weight of around 300, MAAs should contribute at least 3% of the cell wet weight. While MAAs have been shown to absorb ultraviolet (UV. Here, we will discuss all the cyanobacteria reported till date having/producing MAAs.

Section- Nostocales

Large numbers of studies have been done regarding presence of MAAs and their biosynthesis on the members of Nostocales; especially on *Anabaena* sp. and *Nostoc* sp. The first report of the existence of MAA in a rice-field cyanobacterium, *Anabaena* sp. was obtained in 1999 (Sinha, Klisch, & Häder, 1999). An ultraviolet-absorbing MAA had been detected in this filamentous and heterocyst cyanobacterium, isolated from a rice paddy field near Varanasi, India. Only one MAA, shinorine was detected with an absorption maxima at 334 nm. Sinha et al. also studied the MAA profile of other *Anabaena* sp. and revealed the presence of only shinorine having same retention time and absorption maxima. The results indicated that *Anabaena* sp. may protect itself from deleterious short wavelength solar radiation by its ability to synthesize a MAA in response to UV-B radiation and thereby screen the negative effects of UV-B (R. P. Sinha, Sinha, Gröniger, & Häder, 2002; Sinha, Klisch, Walter Helbling, & Häder, 2001). Similar results were also obtained by Roshan et al. when using filtered natural solar radiation on *Anabaena* sp. (Khanipour Roshan, Farhangi, Emtyazjoo, & Rabbani, 2015).

Later in 2008, Singh and his coworkers studied the MAA profile of *Anabaena doliolum*. They revealed the biosynthesis of three MAAs, mycosporine-glycine (λ_{max} 310 nm), porphyra- 334 (λ_{max} 334 nm) and shinorine (λ_{max} 334 nm) (Singh, Sinha, Klisch, & Häder, 2008). This was the first report for the occurrence of mycosporine-glycine and porphyra-334 in addition to shinorine in *Anabaena* strains studied so far. *Anabaena* strains of rice-fields investigated before this study, produce a single MAA, shinorine, in response to UV radiations under experimental conditions (Singh, Klisch, Sinha, & Häder, 2008). A possible explanation for the presence of mycosporine-glycine in one strain of *Anabaena* and its absence in the other strain could be due to differences exists in the expression of enzymes responsible for the conversion of mycosporine-glycine to shinorine.

Another study on *Anabaena variabilis* PCC 7937 was done to check the effects of several factors like UV radiation, heat, salinity and ammonium ions on MAA induction (Singh, Klisch, Häder, & Sinha, 2008). The study indicated that heat as a stress factor had no effect on shinorine production, whereas; salt and ammonium treatment had synergistic effects with UV stress. These results suggested that MAAs may have others functions in addition to photoprotection in this organism. Similarily, Singh et al. also reported the role of nutrient deficiency in bioconversion of MAAs (Singh, Klisch, Sinha, & Häder, 2010b)\u03bbmax = 334 nm. They showed for the first time that bioconversion of a primary MAA into a secondary MAA is regulated by the sulfur deficiency in the cyanobacterium *Anabaena variabilis* PCC 7937. This cyanobacterium synthesizes the primary MAA shinorine (λ_{max} 334 nm) under normal conditions (PAR + UVA + UV-B); however, under sulfur deficiency, a secondary MAA palythine-serine (λ_{max} 320 nm) appears. This was also the first report for the synthesis of palythine-serine by cyanobacteria, which has generally been reported; only found in corals.

A bioinformatics study was conducted by Singh et al. to identify the possible genes involved in MAA biosynthesis by analyzing the genome of MAA-synthesizing and non-synthesizing cyanobacteria (Singh, Klisch, Sinha, & Häder, 2010a). They studied four cyanobacteria, *Anabaena variabilis* PCC 7937, *Anabaena* sp. PCC 7120, *Synechocystis* sp. PCC 6803 and *Synechococcus* sp. PCC 6301. The MAA induction experiment and HPLC analysis revealed that out of the four cyanobacteria only *A. variabilis* PCC 7937 has the capability to synthesize MAA. Genome mining identified a combination of genes, *YP_324358* (predicted *DHQS* gene) and *YP_324357* (*O-MT* gene)*,* which were present only in *A. variabilis* PCC 7937 and missing in the other studied cyanobacteria. This study provided the first insight into the genes of cyanobacteria involved in MAA biosynthesis and thus widens the field of research for molecular, bioinformatics and phylogenetic analysis of the MAAs. Based on the results, they proposed that *YP_324358* and *YP_324357* gene products are involved in the biosynthesis of the common core (deoxygadusol) of all MAAs. However, the whole gene cluster involved in the synthesis of MAA shinorine in the cyanobacterium *Anabaena variabilis* American Type Culture Collection (ATCC) 29413 was revealed by Balskus and Walsh in 2010 (Balskus & Walsh, 2010). A cluster of four genes (*Ava_3858* to *Ava_3855*) was shown to be responsible for MAA biosynthesis from sedoheptulose-7-phosphate in the Calvin-Benson cycle. Genes *Ava_3858* and *Ava_3857* encode demethyl 4-deoxygadusol synthase and O-MT enzyme, respectively, to synthesize 4-deoxygadusol. The product of *Ava_3856* catalyzes the addition of glycine to 4-deoxygadusol to produce mycosporine-glycine. Further condensation of serine onto mycosporine-glycine yields shinorine, which is catalyzed by the product of *Ava_3855* encoding a nonribosomal peptide synthetase (Rahman et al., 2014).

After 2010, it is well known that 4-deoxygadusol is the parent core structure of MAAs, which, in cyanobacteria, is derived from the conversion of the pentose phosphate pathway intermediate sedoheptulose-7-phosphate by the enzymes 2-epi-5-epivaliolone synthase, and O-MT. However, it was found out that deletion of the 2-epi-5-epivaliolone synthase gene from *Anabaena variabilis* ATCC 29413 have little effect on MAA production, thus suggesting that MAA biosynthesis is not exclusive to the pentose phosphate pathway (Spence, Dunlap, Shick, & Long, 2012). By using pathway-specific inhibitors, Pope et al. in 2015 demonstrated that MAA biosynthesis occurs also via the shikimate pathway. Complete in-frame gene deletion of the O-MT gene from *A. variabilis* ATCC 29413 revealed that the pentose phosphate and shikimate pathways are inextricably linked to MAA biosynthesis in this cyanobacterium. Furthermore their proteomic data showed that the shikimate pathway is the predominate route for UV-induced MAA biosynthesis (Pope et al., 2015).

Cosmopolitan distributed *Nostoc* sp. is another most studied cyanobacteria for the presence of MAAs in this section. Scherer et al. were first to conduct the study for the presence of MAAs in *Nostoc commune* collected from semiarid and human areas of the People's Republic of China (Scherer, Chen, & Böger, 1988). They found out the presence of UV-absorbing compounds in *N. commune*when colony was grown under solar radiation. Analysis of these UV-absorbing compounds showed that these are higher content of polysaccharide and nitrogen content having molecular weight of 1500 and 3000 Da. These compound also have two different chromophores with absorption maxima at 312 and 330 nm.

Böhm et al. found UV-absorbing pigments in *N. commune* var. Vaucher (Böhm, Pfleiderer, Boger, & Scherer, 1995). The pigments constitute a complex mixture of monomers with a molecular mass of up to 1801 Da and have two different chromophores linked to amino acids threonine and serine. Authors found oligosaccharides attached to the UV-absorbing pigments are galactose, glucose, xylose, glucuronic acid and glucosamine. This was the first report on covalently linked oligosaccharide MAAs production. During experiment, outdoor grown colony was collected and methanolic extraction was done for the extraction of UV-absorbing pigments. From the extract protein content and other impurities were removed and further separation was done by reverse phase HPLC. For the analysis of attached oligosaccharides, glycoside analysis was done. The 335 and 312 nm chromophores were found out to be 1,3-diaminocyclohexene and 3-aminocyclohexen-1-one derivatives, respectively.

Glycosylated MAAs in *Nostoc commune* sp. were further reported after a decade (Matsui et al., 2011). MAAs were directly isolated from dried *N. commune* colony and the extract was subjected to UV-visible spectrophotometry. MAAs were purified and subjected to HPLC, MALDI-TOF MS and LC-MS analysis. Result showed that these colonies have two novel glycosylated MAAs having absorption maximum at 335 nm and another molecule have absorption maxima at 312 and 340 nm. One molecule was pentose bound porphyra-334 of 478 Da and another is unique 1050 Da MAA. 1050 Da MAA was found to have two chromophores, 3-aminocyclohexene-1-one and 1,3-diaminocyclohexene. Two chromophores feature extended the UV-absorbing window covering both UV-A and UV-B radiations. These MAAs also have *in vitro* radical scavenging activity. UV protection and antioxidant properties of these MAAs favor the anhydrobiosis in *N. commune*. Further, Nazifi et al. studied the glycosylated porphyra-334 and palytine-threonine in another strain of *N. commune* (Nazifi et al., 2013). HPLC chromatogram showed that this colony has three different MAAs with molecular weights of 508, 450 and 612 Da. These MAAs were found to have absorption maxima at 334, 322 and 322 nm, respectively. Sugar moiety in all the three MAAs was investigated as hexose. All studied MAAs were observed to have radical scavenging activity. Nazifi et al. also studied two more strains of *N. commune* collected from Kakuma Campus of Kanzawa University (Nazifi et al., 2015). They examined the two genotype of *N. commune* for the presence of glycosylated MAAs. Genotype A cyanobacteria contained four different types of MAAs; 478 Da pentose bound (β-arabinose) porphyra (λ_{max} 335 nm, 62%), 464 Da pentose bound shinorine (λ_{max} 332 nm, 15%), 508 Da hexose bound porphyra-334 (λ_{max} 334 nm, 3%), and 347 Da porphyra-334 (λ_{max} 333 nm, 1%). Genotype B consisted of 1050 Da MAA (λ_{max} 312 and 340 nm, 43%), 880 Da MAA (λ_{max} 331 nm and 312 nm, 16%), and 273 Da MAA (λ_{max} 310 nm, 8%). Double absorption maxima showing MAAs were found to have two distinct chromophores, 3-aminocyclohexen-1-one and 1,3-diaminocyclohexene linked to 2-O-(b-xylopyranosyl)-b-galactopyranoside and two pentose and hexose sugars. This study showed that different genotypes of same cyanobacteria have their own characteristic glycosylated MAAs profile that could be a chemotaxonomic marker for classification of organisms.

Sinha et al. studied N_2-fixing cyanobacteria, *Anabaena* sp., *N. commune* and *Scytonema* sp. for the presence of MAAs induction by solar UV radiation (Sinha et al., 2001). They found a single bisubstituted MAA, shinorine in all the studied cyanobacteria. Interestingly, another UV-absorbing brownish compound secreted in the medium by *Scytonema* sp. having absorption maxima at 315 nm. Wavelength and salt stress dependent induction of MAAs and role of inhibitors in MAAs synthesis in *N. commune* species was also studied by Sinha et al. They found that shinorine production was induced by UV-B but not by salt stress. Inhibitors of the shikimate pathway, photosynthesis, protein synthesis, pterin synthesis and a quencher of the excited state of flavin and pterin reduced the MAAs synthesis in *N. commune* (Sinha, Ambasht, Sinha, & Häder, 2003).

Gao and Garcia-Pichel showed the involvement of ATP grasp ligase in the formation of MAA in *Nostoc punctiforme* ATCC 29133 (Gao & Garcia-Pichel, 2011). The study showed that shinorine in this cyanobacteria was synthesized by *Npr5597* gene encoded ATP grasp ligase. They expressed the whole gene cluster responsible for shinorine synthesis of *N. punctiforme* ATCC 29133 in heterologous host *E. coli*.

Richa et al. studied the presence of MAAs in two *Nostoc* sp.; HKAR-2 and HKAR-6 isolated from the hot springs of Rajgir, India and rice paddy field of Varanasi, India, respectively (Richa & Sinha, 2014). These strains showed the presence of shinorine and porphyra-334. From the both the strains, HKAR-2 was found to be the better source for the production of MAAs. HKAR-2 also had another unknown MAA having absorption maxima at 334 nm.

Roshan et al. studied *Anabaena* and *Nostoc* species isolated from rice paddy fields of Northern Iran. Both the isolates showed the production of shinorine (Khanipour Roshan et al., 2015), when induction was done by solar radiation for 3 days. MAA was quantified using the peak area and the molar extinction coefficient. In *Anabaena* sp. 0.11±0.002 mg/ml shinorine and in *Nostoc* sp. 0.22 ± 0.003 mg/ml shinorine of dry weight was observed.

Rastogi et al. studied the presence of different MAAs in cyanobacterial mat collected from the old temple located in the Phra Nakhon district, Bangkok, Thailand (Rastogi, Madamwar, & Incharoensakdi, 2015). They found that this mat contains shinorine, porphyra-334, mycosporine-glycine and palythiol along with two unknown MAAs having absorption maxima at 320 and 329 nm. The organism constitutes of mats showed the presence of *Synechocystis* sp., *Scytonema* sp., *Nostoc* sp., *Gloeocapsa* sp. and *Gloeocapsopsis* sp. UV photoprotection function of extracted MAAs were checked by applying crude extract on grown *E. coli* cell culture. The result showed that survival of *E. coli* cells was significantly increased in presence of MAAs extract.

Biological crusts collected from various sites of Varanasi, India such as roof top, bark of *Mangifera indica*, window ledge and agricultural field were studied for the presence of MAAs by Pathak et al. (Pathak, Sonker, Kannaujiya, & Sinha, 2015). These biological crusts primarily contained *Scytonema* sp., *Lyngbya* sp. and *Nostoc* sp. and showed the presence of mycosporine-taurine (λ_{max} 309 nm), mycosporine-glycine (λ_{max} 310 nm), asterina (λ_{max} 330 nm) and palythinol (λ_{max} 332 nm). Very recently, Shukla et al. studied lichens collected from high altitude region of Himalaya, India. *Nostoc* species present in these lichens were found to be rich in oxo and imino MAAs (Shukla, Kumari, Patel, & Upreti, 2016).

Apart from *Anabaena* sp., *Nostoc* sp. and *Scytonema* sp. another members of this section were also studied regarding presence of MAAs. *Calothrix* sp., *Spirulina* sp., *Tolypothrix* sp. were found to have UV-absorbing MAAs (Garcia-Pichel & Castenholz, 1993). MAAs shinorine and porphyra-334 were observed in three filamentous and heterocystous cyanobacterial strains of *Nodularia; N. baltica, N. harveyana* and *N. spumigena* (Sinha, Ambasht, Sinha, Klisch, & Häder, 2003). Porphyra-334 was also isolated from the aquatic cyanobacterium *Aphanizomenon flos-aquae* (Torres, Enk, & Hochberg, 2006).

Section – Chroococcales

Some members of this section were found to protect themselves from high UV radiations by synthesizing MAAs as important defense mechanisms.Terrestrial cyanobacterium *Gloeocapsa* sp. strain C-90-Cal-G isolated from limestone quarry wall in Calafell, Spain was found to accumulate intracellular MAAs when exposed under UV-320 radiation (Garcia-Pichel & Castenholz, 1993). Accumulated MAA was having the maximum absorbance at 326 nm. No extracellular accumulation of sunscreen compound was revealed. The level of intracellular MAA increased with the incident of UV-320. This suggested the role of MAAs in the process of photoadaptation to UV radiation in *Gloeocapsa* sp.

Kedar et al. studied unicellular cyanobacterium *Euhalothece* sp. strain LK-1 isolated from the upper layer of a gypsum crust developing on the bottom of a hypersaline saltern pond in Eilat, Israel (Kedar, Kashman, & Oren, 2002). Isolated cyanobacterium when exposed to high light intensity, two MAAs were expressed, having maximum absorption at 331 nm and 362 nm. Compounds were purified by high performance liquid chromatography (HPLC) and structure elucidation was done by nuclear magnetic resonance (NMR) and mass spectrometry (MS). MAA absorbing at 331 nm was identified as mycosporine-2-glycine. Mycosporine-2-glycine was first described from the sea anemone *Anthopleura elegantissima* (Stochaj, Dunlap, & Shick, 1994)320 to 400 nM. However, this was the first report of the presence of mycosporine-2-glycine in cyanobacteria. The second MAA compound present in strain LK-1, absorbing at 362 nm, was found to have the molecular mass of 330 Da and was identified as a novel compound, Euhalothece-362 (Volkmann & Gorbushina, 2006).

Another member of this section, *Synechocystis* sp. PCC 6803 was studied to characterize and investigate the MAAs (Zhang, Li, & Wu, 2007). Induction by UV-A and UV-B irradiation revealed the production of three major MAAs. HPLC and MS analysis identified compounds as mycosporine-tau and two novel compounds, dehydroxylusujirene and mycosporine-343. Mycosporine-tau was induced by both UV-A and UV-B while the other two compounds were induced only by UV-A. However, a comparative study of genome mining of MAAs synthesizing and non-synthesizing cyanobacteria, revealed that *Synechocystis* sp. PCC 6803 and *Synechococcus* sp. PCC 6301 were not found to have genes required for the synthesis of MAAs (Singh et al., 2010a). The probable reason for not finding the genes of MAA synthesis in the *Synechocystis* sp. PCC 6803 is the presence of another set of homologous genes that were not searched.

Study for the distribution of MAAs along the surface water meridional transect of the Atlantic revealed that MAAs were ubiquitous along the transect, although the composition of the MAAs was variable (Llewellyn, White, Martinez-Vincente, Tarran, & Smyth, 2012)000-km meridional transect (52\u00b0 N to 45\u00b0 S. The phytoplankton in this region consisted of mainly cyanobacteria *Synechococcus* sp., *Prochlorococcus* sp. and the nitrogen fixing filamentous cyanobacteria *Trichodesmium*.

Waditee-Sirisattha et al. identified the MAAs and their biosynthetic genes in halotolerant cyanobacteria *Aphanothece halophytica*. Using HPLC and time of flight-mass spectrometry (TOF-MS) analysis; mycosporine-2-glycine was identified in *A. halophytica*. Under salt stress condition accumulation of mycosporine-2-glycine was more stimulated than UV-B radiation. They also identified the genes involved in the biosynthesis of MAAs in *A. halophytica*. It was found that *A. halophytica* contains a unique organization of MAA biosynthetic genes. The *Aphanothece-demethyl-4-deoxyguadusol synthase* (*Ap-DDG*) gene was separated from the other three genes *Aphanothece-O-methyl transferase* (*Ap-OMT*), *Aphanothece-CNligase* (*Ap-CNligase*) and *Aphanothece-D-alanine-D-alanine Ligase* (*Ap-AAligase*). In general, MAAs synthesizing four genes are arranged consecutively. Therefore, this study was the first example to show that a far-separated gene, the *Ap-DDG* gene, was involved in the biosynthesis of a MAA. Heterologous expression of *A. halophytica* MAAs biosynthetic gene in *E. coli* and *Synechococcus* cells produced large amount mycosporine-2-glycine under salt stress condition (Waditee-Sirisattha et al., 2014).

Rahman et al. analyzed the proteins that are involved in the production of MAAs in *Synechocystis* PCC 6803. According to them, protein 3-phosphoshikimate-1-carboxyvinyl transferase involved in producing mycosporine–glycine in this cyanobacterium (Rahman et al., 2014). Recently, Rastogi and coworkers studied MAAs production in cyanobacteria *Gloeocapsa* sp. CU-2556 isolated from the autotrophic biofilm covering stone monuments located in the Phra Nakhon district, Bangkok. After induction with 395 {Photosynthetic Active Radiation (PAR)}, 320 (PAR + UV-A) and 295 (PAR + UV-A + UV-B) nm cut-off filters two MAAs were identified. HPLC revealed that two MAAs were, shinorine (λ_{max} 333 nm) and an unknown MAA designated as mycosporine-307 (λ_{max} 307 nm). Production of MAAs was significantly increased with exposure of UV-B. The biosynthesis of mycosporine-307 was more dominant in this unicellular cyanobacterium compared to shinorine (Rastogi & Incharoensakdi, 2014b).

Section – Oscillatoriales

The first reported cyanobacteria containing MAA was *Microcoleus* sp. belongs to this section (Shibata, 1969). Other studies have been performed on members of Oscillatoriales regarding MAAs are discussed below.

Karsten et al. applied the chemotaxonomy with carotenoids and MAAs profile to solve the problems of low-rank cyanobacterial systematics. They found presence of MAAs in 21 isolates of genus *Microcoleus*(Karsten & Garcia-Pichel, 1996). All studied *Microcoleus* sp. were found to contain shinorine while *M. chthonoplastes* and *M. paludosus* were observed to have four different types of MAAs apart from shinorine. Later *M. chthonoplastes* isolated from Baltic Sea, North Sea and Brittany was also found to have UV-absorbing MAAs (Pattanaik, Roleda, Schumann, & Karsten, 2008).

UV radiation effect on the two Antarctic cyanobacterial communities composed of *Leptolyngbya* sp. and *Phormidium* sp. was studied by enhanced UV radiations levels by UV-B lamp at 30 cm distance (George, Murray, & Montiel, 2001). Only one type of MAA was present having absorbance maxima at 332 nm. The concentration of chlorophyll a, carotenoids and MAA revealed higher UV absorbing compounds to chlorophyll a ratio in *Phormidium* mat than *Leptolyngbya* mat.

Mckenzie and Deole studied the genome of *Oscillatoria limnetica* strain Solar Lake for the presence of MAAs biosynthesis related genes. They identified a predicted 3-dehydroquinate synthase (DHQS) and O-methyltranferase (O-MT) in *O. limnetica* draft genome. DHQS and O-MT were present in one open reading frame (Mckenzie & Deole, 2013). N_2-fixing *Trichodesmium* isolated from Atlantic ocean was found to have shinorine, asterina-332, mycosporine glycine, porphyr-334 and two unidentified MAAs (Subramaniam, Carpenter, & Falkowski, 1999).

Wu et al. studied the presence of UV-absorbing compound in *Arthrospira platensis* due to the impact of solar UV radiation (Wu, Gao, Villafañe, & Watanabe, 2005). Rastogi and Incharoensakdi investigated the biosynthesis of MAAs in *Arthrospira* sp. CU2556 (Rajesh P Rastogi & Incharoensakdi, 2014). HPLC revealed the presence of UV-absorbing compound mycosporine-glycine with absorption maxima at 310 nm. This was the first report on the occurrence of mycosporine-glycine in *Arthrospira* strains. The induction of mycosporine-glycine was found more significant under UV-B radiation. The mycosporine-glycine was found to be highly stable under UV radiations, heat, strong acidic and alkaline conditions. It also exhibited good antioxidant activity and photoprotective ability by detoxifying the *in vivo* reactive oxygen species (ROS) generated by UV radiation. Results indicated that the studied cyanobacterium may protect itself by synthesizing the UV-absorbing/screening compounds as important defense mechanisms, in their natural brightly-lit habitat with high solar UV-B fluxes.

Rastogi and Incharoensakdi also explored the UV-absorbing/UV-screening compounds of *Lyngbya* sp. CU2555 isolated from the bark of a rain tree *Albizia saman* (Jacq) Merr, Bangkok, Thailand (Rastogi & Incharoensakdi, 2014a). Based on the HPLC and mass spectrophotometry, the compounds were identified as palythine (λ_{max} 319 nm; m/z 245), asterina (λ_{max} 330 nm; m/z 289), scytonemin (λ_{max} 384 nm; m/z 544), and reduced scytonemin (λ_{max} 384 nm; m/z 547). This was the first report for the occurrence of palythine, asterina, and an unknown MAA, mycosporine-312 (λ_{max} 312 ± 1 nm), in addition to scytonemin and reduced scytonemin in *Lyngbya* strains studied so far. Induction of MAAs and scytonemin was significantly more prominent upon exposure to UV-A + UV-B radiation. Both MAAs and scytonemin were highly resistant to UV-B, heat, and a strong oxidizing agent and exhibited strong antioxidant activity.

Section – Stigonematales

Few members of this section (e.g. *Stigonema, Chlorogloeopsis*) are capable of producing a UV-absorbing protective pigment (scytonemin) in the extracellular sheaths (Garcia-Pichel & Castenholz, 1991). *Chlorogloeopsis* sp. was also found to synthesize MAAs (Anne Portwich & Garcia-Pichel, 1999).In thermophilic cyanobacteria *Chlorogloeopsis* PCC 6912, synthesis of mycosporine-glycine and shinorine was observed in the presence of osmotic and UV-B stress. In normal/ uninduced condition these MAAs were not synthesized in the cells. When both salt and UV stress conditions were applied in combination, a significant enhancement of MAAs synthesis was observed. It was found out that shinorine concentration was enhanced by UV-B while synthesis of mycosporine-glycine was activated by osmotic shock. This was the first report of the presence of MAAs in *Chlorogloeopsis* PCC 6912. In *Chlorogloeopsis* differential synthesis was studied and revealed that each stress factor induced the particular biosynthetic pathway and regulate particular metabolites differentially. As in this organism MAA synthesis is not only induced by UV-B stress but also by osmotic stress. So they distinguished between the photo-sensory and the purely biochemical requirements of MAA synthesis (A Portwich & Garcia-Pichel, 2000). They prove neither visible light nor UV radiation required for the biosynthesis process of MAAs by incubating the cells in the dark on sucrose containing media providing all the conditions required for the MAAs synthesis. An action spectrum of the MAA synthesis showed a distinct peak of shinorine at 310 nm. They proposed pterin to be the UV-B photoreceptor for MAA induction. To investigate the pterin role in UV-B sensing which is responsible for the shinorine synthesis, cells were grown in the presence of pterin inhibitors N-acetylserotenin (NAS) and 2,4-diamino-6-hydroxypyrimidine (DAHP) and after 3 days they were exposed under UV and salt stress for 72 h for MAAs induction. There occurred significant reduction in MAAs synthesis in medium containing DAHP in both stress conditions, while in medium containing NAS significant reduction in MAAs concentration occurred only in UV stress cells. They also used phenylacetic acid, which is known to quench excited states of pterin. No effect was observed on the salt-induced MAA production but there was reduction of shinorine concentration in UV-B exposed cell. These experiments revealed that both inhibitors and quencher of pterins, only depressed the photosensory efficiency of induction but not chemosensory efficiency.

Conclusions

MAAs discovered in cyanobacteria also have many other important biological functions as secondary metabolites. In addition to be UV protectant molecules, they also have role in osmotic regulation (Kogej et al., 2006; A Oren, 1997; Anne

Portwich & Garcia-Pichel, 1999; Singh, Klisch, Sinha, et al., 2008; Sinha et al., 2003; Waditee-Sirisattha et al., 2014), desiccation (Feng et al., 2012; Olsson-Francis et al., 2013), against oxidative (Yakovleva & Hidaka, 2004) and thermal stress (Michalek-Wagner, 2001; Shick, Dunlap, Pearse, & Pearse, 2002). Also, their induction under different abiotic stresses (Rastogi, Richa, Sinha, Singh, & Häder, 2010) other than UV radiation indicates that they might have some other roles including the key role in solar UV-photoprotection. It was demonstrated that MAAs can dissipate absorbed radiation as heat without producing ROS and can also block the production of both 6–4 photoproducts and pyrimidine dimer formation (Rastogi & Incharoensakdi, 2014b), therefore; are potential candidates for commercial application in the cosmetic industry. In similar manner, MAAs multifunction can be biotechnologically exploited for various commercial applications e.g. dietary supplements, medicine, functional organic devices and others. Hence, commercialization of multipurpose MAAs is a promising future endeavor.

Acknowledgements

This work was supported by a WOS-A grant (SR/WOS-A/LS-1360/2014 G) provided by Department of Science and Technology, India.

References

Adams, N. L., & Shick, J. M. (2001). Mycosporine-like amino acids prevent UVB-induced abnormalities during early development of the green sea urchin *Strongylocentrotus droebachiensis.Marine Biology, 138*, 267–280.

Aghazarian, V., Tchiakpe, L., Reynier, J. P., & Gayte-Sorbier, A. (1999). Release of Benzimidazole and Benzylidene Camphor from Topical Sunscreen Formulations. *Drug Development and Industrial Pharmacy, 25*, 1277–1282.

Autier, P., Mezzetti, M., Doré, J. F., Zantedeschi, E. (1998). Sunscreen use, wearing clothes, and number of nevi in 6-to 7-year-old European children. *Journal of the National Cancer Institute, 90*(24), 1870–1872.

Balskus, E. P., & Walsh, C. T. (2010). The genetic and molecular basis for sunscreen biosynthesis in cyanobacteria. *Science, 329*, 1653–1656.

Bandaranayake, W. M., & Des Rocher, A. (1999). Role of secondary metabolites and pigments in the epidermal tissues, ripe ovaries, viscera, gut contents and diet of the sea cucumber *Holothuria atra. Marine Biology, 133*, 163–169.

Bigby, M. (1999). The sunscreen and melanoma controversy. *Archives of dermatology*, *135*(12), 1526–1527.

Böhm, G. A., Pfleiderer, W., Boger, P., & Scherer, S. (1995). Structure of a novel oligosaccharide-mycosporine-amino acid ultraviolet A/B sunscreen pigment from the terrestrial cyanobacterium *Nostoc commune. Journal of Biological Chemistry*, *270*, 8536–8539.

Dehorter, B., Brocquet, M. F., Lacoste, L., Alais, J.1980). Influence de la lumière et de la mycosporine sur la composition stérolique du *Nectria galligena* au cours de la morphogenèse sexuée. *Phytochemistry*, *19*(11), 2311–2315.

Favre-Bonvin, J., Arpin, N., & Brevard, C. (1976). Structure de la mycosporine (P 310). *Canadian Journal of Chemistry*, *54*(7), 1105–1113.

Felix, T., Hall, B. J., & Brodbelt, J. S. (1998). Determination of benzophenone-3 and metabolites in water and human urine by solid-phase microextraction and quadrupole ion trap GC–MS. *Analytica Chimica Acta*, *371*(2), 195–203.

Feng, Y. N., Zhang, Z. C., Feng, J. L., & Qiu, B. S. (2012). Effects of UV-B radiation and periodic desiccation on the morphogenesis of the edible terrestrial cyanobacterium *Nostoc flagelliforme. Applied and Environmental Microbiology*, *78*, 7075–7081.

Gao, Q., & Garcia-Pichel, F. (2011). An ATP-grasp ligase involved in the last biosynthetic step of the iminomycosporine shinorine in *Nostoc punctiforme* ATCC 29133. *Journal of Bacteriology*, *193*(21), 5923–5928.

Garcia-Pichel, F., & Castenholz, R. W. (1993). Occurrence of UV-absorbing, mycosporine-like compounds among cyanobacterial isolates and an estimate of their screening capacity. *Applied and Environmental Microbiology*, *59*, 163–169.

Garcia-Pichel, F., & Castenholz, R. W. (1991). Characterization and biological implications of scytonemin, a cyanobacterial sheath pigment. *Journal of Phycology*, *27*(3), 395–409.

George, A. L., Murray, A. W., & Montiel, P. O. (2001). Tolerance of Antarctic cyanobacterial mats to enhanced UV radiation. *FEMS Microbiology Ecology*, *37*, 91–101.

Hagedorn-Leweke, U., & Lippold, B. C. (1995). Absorption of Sunscreens and

Other Compounds Through Human Skin inVivo: Derivation of a Method to Predict Maximum Fluxes. *Pharmaceutical Research, 12*, 1354–1360.

Hany, J., & Nagel, R. (1995). Nachweis von UV-filtersubstanzen in muttermilch. *Deutsche Lebensmittel-Rundschau, 91*(11), 341–345.

Hayden, C. G., Roberts, M. S., & Benson, H. A. (1997). Systemic absorption of sunscreen after topical application. *The Lancet, 350*(9081), 863–864.

Hedges, S. B., Chen, H., Kumar, S., Wang, D. Y., Thompson, A. S., & Watanabe, H. (2001). A genomic timescale for the origin of eukaryotes. *BMC Evolutionary Biology, 1*(1), 4.

Jiang, Roberts, Collins, & Benson. (2001). Absorption of sunscreens across human skin: an evaluation of commercial products for children and adults. *British Journal of Clinical Pharmacology, 48*, 635–637.

Kadry, A. M., Okereke, C. S., Abdel-Rahman, M. S., Friedman, M. A., & Davis, R. A. (1995). Pharmacokinetics of benzophenone-3 after oral exposure in male rats. *Journal of Applied Toxicology, 15*, 97–102.

Karsten, U., & Garcia-Pichel, F. (1996). Carotenoids and Mycosporine-like Amino Acid Compounds in Members of the Genus *Microcoleus* (Cyanobacteria): A Chemosystematic Study. *Systematic and Applied Microbiology, 19*, 285–294.

Kedar, L., Kashman, Y., & Oren, A. (2002). Mycosporine-2-glycine is the major mycosporine-like amino acid in a unicellular cyanobacterium (*Euhalothece* sp.) isolated from a gypsum crust in a hypersaline saltern pond. *FEMS Microbiology Letters, 208*, 233–237.

Khanipour Roshan, S., Farhangi, M., Emtyazjoo, M., & Rabbani, M. (2015). Effects of solar radiation on pigmentation and induction of a mycosporine-like amino acid in two cyanobacteria, *Anabaena* sp. and *Nostoc* sp. ISC26. *European Journal of Phycology, 50*, 173–181.

Kogej, T., Gostinčar, C., Volkmann, M., Gorbushina, A. A., & Gunde-Cimerman, N. (2006). Mycosporines in extremophilic fungi – Novel complementary osmolytes? *Environmental Chemistry, 3*, 105–110.

Llewellyn, C. A., White, D. A., Martinez-Vincente, V., Tarran, G., & Smyth, T. J. (2012). Distribution of Mycosporine-Like Amino Acids Along a Surface Water

Meridional Transect of the Atlantic. *Microbial Ecology*, *64*, 320–333.

Mason, D. S., Schafer, F., Shick, J. M., & Dunlap, W. C. (1998). Ultraviolet radiation-absorbing mycosporine-like amino acids (MAAs) are acquired from their diet by medaka fish (*Oryzias latipes*) but not by SKH-1 hairless mice. *Comparative Biochemistry and Physiology – A Molecular and Integrative Physiology*, *120*, 587–598.

Matsui, K., Nazifi, E., Kunita, S., Wada, N., Matsugo, S., & Sakamoto, T. (2011). Novel glycosylated mycosporine-like amino acids with radical scavenging activity from the cyanobacterium *Nostoc commune*. *Journal of Photochemistry and Photobiology B: Biology*, *105*, 81–89.

Mckenzie, A., & Deole, R. (2013). Genome mining of the draft genome of *Oscillatoria limnetica* reveals mycosporine like amino acids genes, *Recent Development in Biotechnology*, *8*, 2134–2138.

Michalek-Wagner, K. (2001). Seasonal and sex-specific variations in levels of photo-protecting mycosporine-like amino acids (MAAs) in soft corals. *Marine Biology*, *139*, 651–660.

Nagtegaal, M., Ternes, T., Baumann, W., & Nagel, R. (1997). UV-Filtersubstanzen in Wasser und Fischen UWSF-Z Umweltchem Ökotox 9: 79–86. *Find This Article Online*.

Nazifi, E., Wada, N., Asano, T., Nishiuchi, T., Iwamuro, Y., Chinaka, S. (2015). Characterization of the chemical diversity of glycosylated mycosporine-like amino acids in the terrestrial cyanobacterium *Nostoc commune*. *Journal of Photochemistry and Photobiology B: Biology*, *142*, 154–168.

Nazifi, E., Wada, N., Yamaba, M., Asano, T., Nishiuchi, T., Matsugo, S., & Sakamoto, T. (2013). Glycosylated porphyra-334 and palythine-threonine from the terrestrial cyanobacterium *Nostoc commune*. *Marine Drugs*, *11*, 3124–3154.

Neale, P. J., Banaszak, A. T., & Jarriel, C. R. (1998). Ultraviolet sunscreens in *Gymnodinium sanguineum* (Dinophyceae): Mycosporine-like amino acids protect against inhibition of photosynthesis. *Journal of Phycology*, *34*, 928–938.

Olsson-Francis, K., Watson, J. S., & Cockell, C. S. (2013). Cyanobacteria isolated from the high-intertidal zone: A model for studying the physiological prerequisites for survival in low Earth orbit. *International Journal of Astrobiology*, *12*, 292–303.

Oren, A. (1997). Mycosporine-like amino acids as osmotic solutes in a community of halophilic cyanobacteria. *Geomicrobiology Journal, 14,* 231–240.

Oren, A., & Gunde-Cimerman, N. (2007). Mycosporines and mycosporine-like amino acids: UV protectants or multipurpose secondary metabolites? *FEMS Microbiology Letters.*

Pathak, J., Sonker, A. S., Kannaujiya, V. K., & Sinha, R. P. (2015). Isolation and partial purification of scytonemin and mycosporine-like amino acids from biological crusts. *Journal of Chemical and Pharmaceutical Research, 7,* 362–371.

Pattanaik, B., Roleda, M. Y., Schumann, R., & Karsten, U. (2008). Isolate-specific effects of ultraviolet radiation on photosynthesis, growth and mycosporine-like amino acids in the microbial mat-forming cyanobacterium *Microcoleus chthonoplastes. Planta, 227,* 907–916.

Pope, M. A., Spence, E., Seralvo, V., Gacesa, R., Heidelberger, S., Weston, A. J. (2015). O-methyltransferase is shared between the pentose phosphate and shikimate pathways and is essential for mycosporine-like amino acid biosynthesis in *Anabaena variabilis* ATCC 29413. *ChemBioChem, 16,* 320–327.

Portwich, A., & Garcia-Pichel, F. (1999). Ultraviolet and osmotic stresses induce and regulate the synthesis of mycosporines in the cyanobacterium *Chlorogloeopsis* PCC 6912. *Archives of Microbiology, 172,* 187–192.

Portwich, A., & Garcia-Pichel, F. (2000). A novel prokaryotic UVB photoreceptor in the cyanobacterium *Chlorogloeopsis* PCC 6912. *Photochemistry and Photobiology, 71*(4), 493–498.

Quesada, A., & Vincent, W. F. (1997). Strategies of adaptation by Antarctic cyanobacteria to ultraviolet radiation. *European Journal of Phycology, 32*(4), 335–342.

Rahman, M. A., Sinha, S., Sachan, S., Kumar, G., Singh, S. K., & Sundaram, S. (2014). Analysis of proteins involved in the production of MAA's in two Cyanobacteria *Synechocystis* PCC 6803 and *Anabaena cylindrica. Bioinformation, 10,* 449–53.

Rastogi, R. P., & Incharoensakdi, A. (2014). Analysis of UV-absorbing photoprotectant mycosporine-like amino acid (MAA) in the cyanobacterium *Arthrospira* sp. CU2556. *Photochemical & Photobiological Sciences, 13*(7), 1016–1024.

Rastogi, R. P., & Incharoensakdi, A. (2014a). Characterization of UV-screening compounds, mycosporine-like amino acids, and scytonemin in the cyanobacterium *Lyngbya* sp. CU2555. *FEMS Microbiology Ecology, 87*, 244–256.

Rastogi, R. P., & Incharoensakdi, A. (2014b). UV radiation-induced biosynthesis, stability and antioxidant activity of mycosporine-like amino acids (MAAs) in a unicellular cyanobacterium *Gloeocapsa* sp. CU2556. *Journal of Photochemistry and Photobiology B: Biology, 130*, 287–292.

Rastogi, R. P., Madamwar, D., & Incharoensakdi, A. (2015). Sun-screening bioactive compounds mycosporine-like amino acids in naturally occurring cyanobacterial biofilms: Role in photoprotection. *Journal of Applied Microbiology, 119*, 753–762.

Rastogi, R. P., Richa, Sinha, R. P., Singh, S. P., & Häder, D.-P. (2010). Photoprotective compounds from marine organisms. *Journal of Industrial Microbiology & Biotechnology, 37*, 537–558.

Rastogi, R. P., Sonani, R. R., Madamwar, D., & Incharoensakdi, A. (2016). Characterization and antioxidant functions of mycosporine-like amino acids in the cyanobacterium *Nostoc* sp. R76DM. *Algal Research, 16*, 110–118.

Richa, & Sinha, R. P. (2014). Biochemical characterization of sunscreening mycosporine-like amino acids from two *Nostoc* species inhabiting diverse habitats. *Protoplasma, 252*, 199–208.

Scherer, S., Chen, T. W., & Böger, P. (1988). A new UV-A/B protecting pigment in the terrestrial cyanobacterium *Nostoc commune. Plant Physiology, 88*(4), 1055–1057.

Schlumpf, M., Cotton, B., Conscience, M., Haller, V., Steinmann, B., & Lichtensteiger, W. (2001). In vitro and in vivo estrogenicity of UV screens. *Environmental Health Perspectives, 109*, 239–244.

Shibata, K. (1969). Pigments and a UV-absorbing substance in corals and a blue-green alga living in the Great Barrier Reef. *Plant and Cell Physiology, 10*(2), 325–335.

Shick, J. M., Dunlap, W. C., Pearse, J. S., & Pearse, V. B. (2002). Mycosporine-like amino acid content in four species of sea anemones in the genus *Anthopleura* reflects phylogenetic but not environmental or symbiotic relationships. *Biological Bulletin, 203*, 315–330.

Shick, & Dunlap. (2002). Mycosporine-like amino acids and related gadusols: Biosynthesis, acumulation, and UV-protective functions in aquatic organisms. *Annual Review of Physiology, 64*, 223–262.

Shukla, V., Kumari, R., Patel, D. K., & Upreti, D. K. (2016). Characterization of the diversity of mycosporine-like amino acids in lichens from high altitude region of Himalaya. *Amino Acids, 48*, 129–136.

Singh, S. P., Klisch, M., Häder, D. P., & Sinha, R. P. (2008). Role of various growth media on shinorine (mycosporine-like amino acid) concentration and photosynthetic yield in *Anabaena variabilis* PCC 7937. *World Journal of Microbiology and Biotechnology, 24*, 3111–3115.

Singh, S. P., Klisch, M., Sinha, R. P., & Häder, D. P. (2008). Effects of abiotic stressors on synthesis of the mycosporine-like amino acid shinorine in the cyanobacterium *Anabaena variabilis* PCC 7937. *Photochemistry and Photobiology, 84*, 1500–1505.

Singh, S. P., Klisch, M., Sinha, R. P., & Häder, D. P. (2010a). Genome mining of mycosporine-like amino acid (MAA) synthesizing and non-synthesizing cyanobacteria: A bioinformatics study. *Genomics, 95*, 120–128.

Singh, S. P., Klisch, M., Sinha, R. P., & Häder, D. P. (2010b). Sulfur deficiency changes mycosporine-like amino acid (MAA) composition of *Anabaena variabilis* PCC 7937: A possible role of sulfur in MAA bioconversion. *Photochemistry and Photobiology, 86*, 862–870.

Singh, S. P., Kumari, S., Rastogi, R. P., Singh, K. L., & Sinha, R. P. (2008). Mycosporine-like amino acids (MAAs): Chemical structure, biosynthesis and significance as UV-absorbing/screening compounds. *Indian Journal of Experimental Biology, 46*, 7–17.

Singh, S. P., Sinha, R. P., Klisch, M., & Häder, D. P. (2008). Mycosporine-like amino acids (MAAs) profile of a rice-field cyanobacterium *Anabaena doliolum* as influenced by PAR and UVR. *Planta, 229*, 225–233.

Sinha, R. P., Ambasht, N. K., Sinha, J. P., & Häder, D. P. (2003). Wavelength-dependent induction of a mycosporine-like amino acid in a rice-field cyanobacterium, *Nostoc commune*: role of inhibitors and salt stress. *Photochemical & Photobiological Sciences, 2*(2), 171–176.

Sinha, R. P., Ambasht, N. K., Sinha, J. P., Klisch, M., & Häder, D. P. (2003). UV-

B-induced synthesis of mycosporine-like amino acids in three strains of *Nodularia* (cyanobacteria). *Journal of Photochemistry and Photobiology B: Biology, 71,* 51–58.

Sinha, R. P., & Häder, D. P. (2003). Biochemistry of mycosporine-like amino acids (MAAs) synthesis: Role in photoprotection. *Recent Research Development in Biochemistry, 4,* 971–983.

Sinha, R. P., Klisch, M., Gröniger, A., & Häder, D. P. (1998). Ultraviolet-absorbing/ screening substances in cyanobacteria, phytoplankton and macroalgae. *Journal of Photochemistry and Photobiology B: Biology, 47,* 83–94.

Sinha, R. P., Klisch, M., & Häder, D. P. (1999). Induction of a mycosporine-like amino acid (MAA) in the rice-field cyanobacterium *Anabaena* sp. by UV irradiation. *Journal of Photochemistry and Photobiology B: Biology, 52,* 59–64.

Sinha, R. P., Klisch, M., Walter Helbling, E., & Häder, D. P. (2001). Induction of mycosporine-like amino acids (MAAs) in cyanobacteria by solar ultraviolet-B radiation. *Journal of Photochemistry and Photobiology B: Biology, 60,* 129–135.

Sinha, R. P., Singh, S. P., & Häder, D. P. (2007). Database on mycosporines and mycosporine-like amino acids (MAAs) in fungi, cyanobacteria, macroalgae, phytoplankton and animals. *Journal of Photochemistry and Photobiology B: Biology, 89,* 29–35.

Sinha, R. P., Sinha, J. P., Gröniger, A., & Häder, D. P. (2002). Polychromatic action spectrum for the induction of a mycosporine-like amino acid in a rice-field cyanobacterium, *Anabaena* sp. *Journal of Photochemistry and Photobiology B: Biology, 66,* 47–53.

Spence, E., Dunlap, W. C., Shick, J. M., & Long, P. F. (2012). Corrigendum: Redundant Pathways of Sunscreen Biosynthesis in a Cyanobacterium. *ChemBioChem, 13*(4), 497–497.

Stewart, W. D. P. (1980). Some aspects of structure and function in N fixing cyanobacteria. *Annual Reviews in Microbiology, 34*(1), 497–536.

Stochaj, W. R., Dunlap, W. C., & Shick, J. M. (1994). Two new UV-absorbing mycosporine-like amino acids from the sea anemone *Anthopleura elegantissima* and the effects of zooxanthellae and spectral irradiance on chemical composition and content. *Marine Biology, 118,* 149–156.

Subramaniam, A., Carpenter, E. J., & Falkowski, P. G. (1999). Bio-optical properties of the marine diazotrophic cyanobacteria *Trichodesmium* spp. II. A reflectance model for remote-sensing. *Limnology and Oceanography*, *44*, 618–627.

Torres, A., Enk, C. D., Hochberg, M., & Srebnik, M. (2006). Porphyra-334, a potential natural source for UVA protective sunscreens. *Photochemical & Photobiological Sciences*, *5*(4), 432–435.

Trione, E., Leach, C., & Mutch, J. (1966). Sporogenic substances isolated from fungi. *Nature 212*, 163–164.

Volkmann, M., & Gorbushina, A. A. (2006). A broadly applicable method for extraction and characterization of mycosporines and mycosporine-like amino acids of terrestrial, marine and freshwater origin. *FEMS microbiology letters*, *255*(2), 286–295.

Wada, N., Sakamoto, T., & Matsugo, S. (2015). Mycosporine-Like Amino Acids and Their Derivatives as Natural Antioxidants. *Antioxidants*, *4*, 603–646.

Waditee-Sirisattha, R., Kageyama, H., Sopun, W., Tanaka, Y., & Takabe, T. (2014). Identification and upregulation of biosynthetic genes required for accumulation of mycosporine-2-glycine under salt stress conditions in the halotolerant cyanobacterium *Aphanothece halophytica*. *Applied and Environmental Microbiology*, *80*, 1763–1769.

Wu, H., Gao, K., Villafañe, V., & Watanabe, T. (2005). Effects of solar UV radiation on morphology and photosynthesis of filamentous cyanobacterium *Arthrospira platensis*. *Applied and Environmental microbiology 71*, 5004–5013.

Yakovleva, I., & Hidaka, M. (2004). Diel fluctuations of mycosporine-like amino acids in shallow-water scleractinian corals. *Marine Biology*, *145*, 863–873.

Zhang, L., Li, L., & Wu, Q. (2007). Protective effects of mycosporine-like amino acids of *Synechocystis* sp. PCC 6803 and their partial characterization. *Journal of Photochemistry and Photobiology B: Biology*, *86*, 240–245.

Corporate Social Responsibility* –
Dilemma for Environmental Conservation

Sugandha Shanker & *Richa Mishra**

Abstract

CSR is the buzzword in today's corporate sector. The corporates are feeling that investing in activities like school education for slum kids, woman empowerment, health camps and tree plantation etc. will fulfill their responsibility and give them the competitive edge of being socially responsible as well as fulfil the legal norms of investing 2 percent of the profit for social causes. This is evident through the secondary data collected from the websites of approximately 50 multinational and national organisations.

However, deeper analysis points towards the fact that CSR is acting as an umbrella and is overshadowing the actual environmental issues like pollution of air, water, soil and detoriation of bio diversity, forests and most importantly human health which should be addressed by the companies with more rigor and be a part of the CSR mandates. The present research proposes that there is a strong need for development of separate policies within the CSR framework which should address the need for environmental problems and concerns related to specific industries and sectors.

Keywords: CSR, Environment, Policy, India.

Introduction

In our desire to grow and develop, we have somewhere forgotten our responsibility towards the environment. We take the environment for granted and believe that the environment is maintenance free. This notion is the root cause of many environmental problems existing today. Our greed has made us reach unsustainable levels since we do not have clean air, water, soil and food which form the basis for the existence of life on the planet.

Therefore, environmental concerns should be our utmost priority in today's time. We need to preserve, protect and make this environment livable for generations to come, the answer lies in formulating strategic policies and developing mechanisms for effective implementation of these policies.

---

* JK Lakshmipat University, Jaipur

In addition to getting profits, the policies and actions of the corporate organizations and governments should be proactive. They should provide enough space for development of environmental conservation. One important step towards achieving the goal of clean and sustainable world is through the formulation of separate environmental regulations within the Corporate Social Responsibility act commonly known as CSR.

Currently, many organizations across the globe are focusing on the aspects of CSR because it is felt that life on earth can only be sustainable if everyone including corporates realize their responsibility of maintaining a balance between people, planet and profit (3 P's). This could be easily monitored and implemented through a CSR mandate.

In 2013 the government of India implemented a policy which says that organizations have to spend 2% of their net profit in 3 years for the purpose of CSR. This policy is formulated for generating a harmonious balance between the 3 P's. However, this policy has been used by the corporates in a way that doesn't benefit the environment. Most of the corporates perform activities like slum education, funding to NGO's or tree plantation under the CSR mandate and get rid of their legal responsibility. Nonetheless, these activities do not actually benefit the environmental conditions which are detoriating day by day.

In order to assess the proportion of actual CSR benefits for the environment the present work analyzed research papers, magazines reviews and two annual reports published by IIM-Udaipur. The results of which are presented below.

Literature Review

The term CSR itself came into common use in the early 1970s. The last decade of the twentieth century witnessed a shift in focus from charity and traditional philanthropy towards more direct engagement of business in mainstream development and concern for disadvantaged groups in the society. In India, there is a growing realization that business cannot succeed in isolation and social progress is necessary for sustainable growth.

Over the past few years CSR, as a concept, has been the focus of many deliberations and research. It has grown in importance both academically as well as in the business sense. The Organization for Economic Co-operation and Development (OECD) established a set of guidelines for multinational enterprises in 1976, and was thus a pioneer in developing the concept of CSR. The purpose of these guidelines was to improve the investment climate and encourage the positive contribution of multinational enterprises who can contribute in economic and social progress.

Initially, this can just be CSR since the author has already explained the term was a concept where companies integrate social, environmental and health concerns in their business strategy (policy) and operations in their interactions with stakeholders on a voluntary basis. The social responsibility of business encompasses the economic, legal, ethical, and discretionary expectations that society has for organizations at a given point in time (Carroll, 1979).

Ideal CSR practice should have both ethical and philosophical dimensions, particularly in India where there exists a wide gap between sections of society in terms of income and standards as well socio-economic status (Bajpai, 2001).

It was quite evident from the literature review that researches in the area of CSR are focusing on the reporting of economic aspects of CSR. Limited research has been conducted on environmental aspects under the CSR banner. However IIM Udaipur annually compiles a report of 200 top companies in India regarding their CSR status. It focuses on four major aspects i.e. governance, disclosure, stakeholders and sustainability. These reports as well as some magazines & research papers published in the year 2015 and 2016 serve as the basis for this work.

CSR mandates have changed the way corporates looked at philanthropy. Now it has become more of a responsibility which is being imposed on them through a legal mechanism in the form of 2% compulsory spend of their profit. Legal mechanisms are forcefully imposed because in the past the corporate world specially the manufacturing sector did not focus on maintaining the balance between the three P's. They only cared for profit generation through all means which lead to destruction and over exploitation of natural resources, human resources and depleting human health. The legal impositions are looked at by international organisations as a much needed requirement for environmental conservation, protection of biodiversity and natural resources as well as generating of positive impact on the society. However, in reality the situation is slightly different. Despite, legal enforcements and mandates the results of such initiatives do not show a positive picture.

Discussion

The two reports by IIM-Udaipur and most company websites, informal discussion with some of the representatives as well as presentations by companies point towards the trend that most companies consider CSR as a philanthropic tool and focus on using the money under this banner for activities like cleanliness drive, slum education and health awareness camps.

The only concern about environmental issues under the CSR banner is limited to tree plantations and waste management for most of the organisations. This, fact is supported by the two reports which states that sustainability does not use the major proportion of CSR funds and aspects like green supply chain, green buildings, biodiversity conservation, energy conservation, water treatment etc. are at the least priority. However, today there is a need for more focused environmental actions in terms of adapting these new technologies for a sustainable future.

The analysis of the reports and articles stated a clear difference between the term CSR and sustainability which are generally understood interchangeably. The report clearly makes a point that CSR and sustainability are two different terms The focus of CSR is on giving back to the society over and above the ordinary course of business. CSR is looked at as a philanthropic, community-centered approach, whereas sustainability includes activities like reduction in emissions to diminish the impact of climate change, waste and water management and a move towards renewable sources of energy.

Only the top 10 companies out of the 200 studied during the report have developed and adopted technologies specifically for environmental management and are working toward environmental conservation under the CSR. The work analysed that companies apart from the top 10 focus on environmental issues of waste management and tree plantation.

Secondly, the work finds that organisations do not link the CSR's environmental side with the overall business strategy due to which the focus on various aspects of environmental management like green supply chain, green logistics are not fully integrated.

Thirdly, the companies do not actually understand the meaning of sustainability and cannot relate to the long term negative impacts of not following a sustainable approach now and the long term financial benefits of developing a sustainable policy now.

Discussion

This work analysed that CSR initiatives in India have grown after being made mandatory, organisations have atleast started to think about initiating CSR related policies and are also working towards it. However, CSR still remains an act of philanthropy rather than an act of responsible behavior towards society and environment.

On the whole, environmental conditions within the CSR framework have a very small presence and organisations except the top ones do not have the protection of the environment as its priority despite the CSR mandate. The authors recommend that environmental or sustainability related considerations should be dealt separately within the CSR mandate and a separate policy describing the clear cut norms for environment needs to be developed so that a large proportion of the funds should go to developing green technologies and rebuilding the losses to environment.

Conclusion

India is the first country in the world to make CSR expenditure mandatory which was done via section 135 of company's act, 2013. According to CII, 1,270 companies spend mainly on health, sanitation, education, rural development and skill development (Venkateswaran, S. & Chaudhuri, A., 2017). This shows an ignorance towards environmental protection and resource conservation in fulfilling the CSR mandate.

Majority of the companies contribute mostly towards other activities unmindful of the fact that sustainability of their own operations depends on externalities such as non depletion and conservation of natural resources like water, forest, food security which are the basis of most industries.

Top corporate leaders across the globe and specially India point out that CSR has to be liberated from the traditional approach of charity and philanthropy and focus on generating more sustainable business models which not only protect the environment, improve livelihood but also generates profit.

References

Bajpai, G. N. (2001). Corporate Social Responsibility in India and Europe: Cross Cultural Perspective. *Retrieved on April, 17,* 2011.

Carroll, A. B. (1979). A three-dimensional conceptual model of corporate performance. Academy of management review, 4(4), 497–505.

Desai, M., &Dharmapala, D. (2006). Corporate social responsibility and taxation: The missing link. Leading Perspectives,(Winter), 4–5. http://indiacsr.in/green-initiatives-of-corporations-and-environmental-csr/

Dhaliwal, D. S., Li, O. Z., Tsang, A., & Yang, Y. G. (2011). Voluntary nonfinancial disclosure and the cost of equity capital: The initiation of corporate social responsibility reporting. *The accounting review, 86*(1), 59–100.

Karnani, A.(2017, May). A Catalyst for change?. *Indian Management*, 56 (5) 14–18

Majmudar,U., Rana,N., Sanan, N. (2015). India's Top Companies for CSR & Sustainability 2015. Retrieved from https://iimu.ac.in/upload_data/main_containts/about/Social-Responsibility/IIMU_CSR_REPORT.pdf

Majmudar,U., Rana,N., Sanan, N. (2016). Gearing Up for Responsible Growth. Retrieved from https://iimu.ac.in/upload_data/Publications/IIMU_CSR_REPORT_2016_FINIAL.pdf

Servaes, H., & Tamayo, A. (2013). The impact of corporate social responsibility on firm value: The role of customer awareness. *Management Science*, *59*(5), 1045–1061.

Singh,S.(2017, May).Break away from the Traditional. *Indian Management*, 56 (5) 28–29

Sundar, P.(2017, May).Unequal balance. *Indian Management*, 56 (5) 24–27

Venkateswaran, S., Chaudhuri, A., & Sons, T.(2017, May). Beyond Compliance. *Indian Management*, 56 (5) 20–23

Wilson, R. J. (2009). An examination of corporate tax shelter participants. *The Accounting Review*, *84*(3), 969–999.

An Overview of Drivers Responsible for Implementation of Green Practices in Manufacturing Companies

*Shruti Vadukiya**

Abstract

The past few decades have witnessed an increase in practices of green supply chain management (GSCM). GSCM is a method of reducing the harmful impacts of supply chains on environment. This is done through process improvements, adaptation of new technologies, developing recycling and adaptation of strategies for mitigating environmental risks.

GSCM does not happen just by the notion of responsibility towards environment, it has many other drivers which force the organizations to change their existing processes and adapt new ones. These changes are meant to reduce the harmful impacts, and generate more profits and provide competitive advantage.

The adaptation of GSCM processes is becoming a key component for organisations making it essential for us to study the drivers behind the fast change towards GSCM. Therefore, this paper aims to identify key drivers for adapting the green practices in the supply chain especially in the manufacturing sector.

The work is based on literature review of selected research papers, articles and books from various databases like 'Google scholar', 'EBSCOhost', 'Proquest' etc. These works suggest that most organizations today want to adapt green supply chain practices in order to be compliant with the changing environmental & health regulations. Organizations also adapt GSCM because such practices help them in long term profit generation, provide competitive & marketing advantage and help them in their CSR initiatives.

Keywords: Green Supply Chain Management (GSCM), Performance, Green supplier, Drivers, Implementation of Green Supply Chain Management.

Introduction

Green supply chain management is becoming popular day by day and is taking an important place in the formulation of corporate strategy (Mutingi, Mapfaira, & Monageng, 2014). It is on the agenda list of most organizations big or small

---

* JK Lakshmipat University, Jaipur

because it is no more a matter of pride or just a philanthropical concern. Today, it has become an essential tool for the organizations that want to survive in the changing scenarios.

The manufacturing organisations specifically could be on the verge of extinction if they do not comply with the changing needs of environmental requirements for example: Deforestation and unavailability of water can drastically affect the raw material availability (Kurien & Qureshi, 2011) and reduce the profits of businesses by upto US$906 billion (Simpsom, 2016) and $14 billion respectively (Makower, 2017).

If we believe these estimates, it is very alarming for many supply chains because the raw material availability and green house gas emissions can lead to not only loss of business and negatively impact human health but can lead to permanent closure of many businesses. Thereby, generating a strong need for organisations to shift from regular practices to greener ones.

Companies should incorporate the principles of close loop supply chain which is a part of green supply chain process and helps the organisations in improving their environmental footprint as well as generate sustainable profit. Companies have to act at a very fast pace because the time lapse between planning and execution could lead to severe damages in terms of resource depletion and competitive advantage.

Motivated by the importance of the green supply chain in the domain of supply chain management, this research was conducted with an objective to analyse the major drivers behind implementation of green practices in supply chain management. The study was maily conducted through a literature review of research papers, articles and books. The drivers identified through literature review are discussed in the paper.

Review of literature

In order to understand the drivers related to GSCM practices, the author has reviewed papers, articles and books published in various jornals of repute like International Journal of Industrial Organization, International Journal of Logistics Management, International Journal of Physical Distribution & Logistics Management, Journal of Business Logistics, Journal of Operation Management, International Journal of Operations & Production Management, Supply Chain Management: An International Journal, synopsis of which are presented below in Table – 1.

Table – 1: Research in Green Supply Chain Management

Author(s) & Year	Title/Research Objective	Research Findings
(Ali & Om, 1984)	Exploring Green supply chain performance measures framework for Indian Manufacturing Practices	Authors bring forward the research direction for implementation of GSCM practices required in Indian Manufacturing companies and medium scale Enterprises
(K. Green, Morton, & New, 1998)	Green purchasing and supply policies: do they improve companies' environmental performance?	Green Purchasing can result in financial benefits to firms
(Hoek, 1999)	Research note From reversed logistics to green supply chains	There is need of framework or theory to find out factors responsible for sustainable practices.
(Hervani, Helms, & Sarkis, 2005)	Performance measurement for green supply chain management	GSCM system guidelines for ISO 14000 were followed as per company requirement
(K. W. Green, McGaughey, & Casey, 2006)	Does supply chain management strategy mediate the association between market orientation and organizational performance?	Found that Structure Equation Modeling can help to find out the relationship between market orientation and financial performance of an organization
(Vachon & Klassen, 2006)	Extending green practices across the supply chain: The impact of upstream and downstream integration	For green supply chain practices technological collaboration is required at primary supplier
(Simpson, Power, & Samson, 2007)	Greening the automotive supply chain: a relationship perspective	Found from study of Australian Automotive industries that non-strategic supplier should get certified by EMS system or ISO 14000 certification to follow the norms
(Cheng, Yeh, & Tu, 2008)	Trust and knowledge sharing in green supply chains	Inter Organizational knowledge is helpful to follow GSCM with the associated supplier and customer

(Cheng et al., 2008)	Competitiveness Review: An International Business Journal Article information:	Green purchasing play a great role to organizations for economic benefits while reverse logistics is beneficial at social level
(S. S.-Y. Lee, 2008)	The effects of green supply chain management on the supplier's performance through social capital accumulation	Findings provide that environmental issues help to improve social capital by implementation of green concept in firms
(Holt & Ghobadian, 2009)	An empirical study of green supply chain management practices amongst UK manufacturers	The legislative internal factors and drivers for GSCM implementation in manufacturing company of UK has been listed and guidelines developed for the framework and model
(Kiridena, Hasan, & Kerr, 2009)	Exploring deeper structures in manufacturing strategy formation processes : a qualitative inquiry	Researcher has outlined the conceptual model to be tested with large sample of data using statistical technique
(Olugu & Wong, 2009)	Supply chain performance evaluation: trends and challenges	After the review of supply chain strategies and fuzzy logic concept, gap was observed in knowledge of supply chain management measurement
(Beamon, 2010)	Designing the green supply chain	Found out that in order to achieve GSCM implementation, organization must follow basic principles established by ISO 14000
(Jung, Chan, Chen, & Chow, 2010)	Greening of the supply chain : An Empirical study for SMES in Philippine context	It was found that theoretical framework can be developed to study Green concept by applying factors like Cleaner, Inbound logistics, Outbound logistics and reverse logistics
(Mollenkopf, Stolze, Tate, & Ueltschy, 2010)	Green, Lean and Global Supply Chain	Four major factor motivates organization to implement the concept of green, lean and global are: cost reduction, customer demands, ISO Standard 9001 and ISO 14000 standards

(Shaw, Grant, & Mangan, 2010)	Developing environmental supply chain performance measures	PDCA cycle concept is observed to develop a framework to analyze GSCM/PMS of an organization
(Toke, Gupta, & Dandekar, 2010)	Green Supply Chain Management : Critical Research and Practices	GSCM drivers observed within the green supply chain are found in: Green purchasing, in bound logistics, out bound logistics and distribution
(Beer & Lemmer, 2011)	A critical review of "green" procurement	Organization has to follow the guidelines for green supply chain procurement which will give ultimate benefit to manufacturer and consumer both
(Duarte, Cabrita, & Machado, 2011)	Exploring Lean and Green Supply Chain Performance Using Balanced Score card Perspective	Balance Score Card aligns lean and green business objectives. It helps the firm to generate the Performance Management Systems for their lean & green practices
(K. W. Green, Zelbst, Bhadauria, & Meacham, 2011)	Do environmental collaboration and monitoring enhance organizational performance?	Outlined that by doing environmental collaboration with supplier and customer, financial and environmental performance can be measured and enhanced
(Kurien & Qureshi, 2011)	Study of performance measurement practices in supply chain management	Outlined the desirable characteristic & Model for Performance Management Systems for manufacturing firm
(Kirchoff, 2011)	A Resource-Based Perspective on Green Supply Chain Management and Firm Performance	Qualitative methods are beneficial to measure the Performance Management Systems of GSCM and collect the data from firms. Likert scale based survey need to get validated by secondary survey such as annual reports, press reports, public information
(Saadany, Jaber, & Bonney, 2011)	Environmental performance measures for supply chains	Gap has been identified to develop a model which can measure financial benefit similar to environmental

(Björklund, Martinsen, & Abrahamsson, 2012)	Performance measurements in the greening of supply chains	Environmental logistics have effect on performance measurement of organizations
(Giovani & Giuliano,2012)	Identifying effective PMS's for the deployment of "green"	Researchers have reviewed the example of Green Practices implication in FIAT Automotive company Group for PMS framework and found out that PMS includes environmental dimension as well as other competitive factors for system to develop a model for "green" measurement
(G.P., 2012)	Performance measurement systems for green supply chains using modified balanced score card and analytical hierarchical process	ISO 14031 and modified BSC model incorporate an additional guideline for GSPMS Results suggest that BSC model solely not applicable to make comparisons within and across the firm to measure GS factors
(Kenneth W. Green Jr., Zelbst, Meacham, & Bhadauria, 2012)	Green supply chain management practices: impact on performance	Necessary prerequisites for GSCM are : green purchasing, cooperation, customers, and eco design
(Kumar & Chandrakar, 2012)	Overview of green supply chain management: Operation and environmental impact at different stages of the supply chain	GSCM practices recommended to manufacturing firm to protect earth from detrimental effect on environment
(Hitchcock, 2012)	Low carbon and green supply chains: the legal drivers and commercial pressures	There is need of education for green product to supplier and also an agreement between customer and supplier to follow regulatory guidelines in order to implement green supply chain
(Perotti, Zorzini, Cagno, & Micheli, 2012)	Green supply chain practices and company performance: the case of 3PLs in Italy	Economical, operational and environmental performance is associated with Green supply chain performance

(Sarkis, 2012)	A boundaries and flows perspective of green supply chain management	Outlines that multidimensional framework can be developed based on social and economic factors.
(Shi, Koh, Baldwin, & Cucchiella, 2012)	Natural resource based green supply chain management	Scrutinized from empirical study that theoretical framework can be applied to achieve low carbon, sustainable and green business objectives in GSCM
(Youn, Yang, & Roh, 2012)	Extending the efficient and responsive supply chains framework to the green context	To measure green supply chain performance two type of framework can be developed. 1.Eco Efficient or 2.Eco Responsive
(Chen et al., 2013)	Green organizational identity and green innovation	Green practices and implementation observed lower in SME's and medium sized organization compared to large enterprises in Taiwan.
(Chen, Chang, & Chen, 2013)	Green organizational identity and green innovation	The result suggested that companies have to enhance their green Organizational identity and green innovation performance
(Jensen, 2013)	Chasing value offerings through green supply chain innovation	Waste generated in organization can be managed by green supply chain concept and innovative concept of reverse logistics.
(Pazirandeh, Jafari, Pazirandeh, & Jafari, 2013)	Making sense of green logistics	Economic Performance can be measured in terms of product price increase, Market profit, Sales and share values in concern to green practices.
(Wang & Sarkis, 2013)	Investigating the relationship of sustainable supply chain management with corporate financial performance	ESCM practices lead to involvement of upstream, downstream and reverse logistics to complete close looping activities.
(Yaghoubipoor, 2013)	World Journal of Entrepreneurship, Management and Sustainable Development Article information	Besides improving organisations financial & operational aspects, implementation of GSCM will also fulfill sustainable objectives of the organisation.

(Wu, 2013)	The influence of green supply chain integration and environmental uncertainty on green innovation in Taiwan's IT industry	It has been identified that in IT companies green innovation can be upgraded by implication of GSCI for environmental uncertainty.
(Beske & Seuring, 2014)	Putting sustainability into supply chain management	Five factors have been identified for successive sustainable growth: Orientation, Continuity, Collaboration, Risk Management and Pro activity
(Kumar Sahu, Datta, & Sankar Mahapatra, 2014)	Green supplier appraisement in fuzzy environment	Green performance to be considered in the supplier selection criterion
(Mutingi et al., 2014)	Developing performance management systems for the green supply chain	Researchers has identified indicators for measurement of performance of GSCM at Social and economic level and outlined a framework also for the same
(Ortas, Moneva, & Álvarez, 2014)	Sustainable supply chain and company performance: A global examination	Identified a gap that need of examination of some factors like stake holder evaluation and sustainable performance is required for organizational growth.
(Rostamifard et al., 2014)	Identifying the Drivers of Green Supply Chain Management in Tile	Reviewed the practice of GSCM in tile industries and that implementation of environmental standard such as ISO 14000 reduce energy, material consumption and train employees about environment issues
(Varsei, Soosay, Fahimnia, & Sarkis, 2014)	Framing sustainability performance of supply chains with multidimensional indicators	Business requires an assessment framework to measure performance at multidimensional level for sustainable growth of a firm

(Gurtu, Searcy, & Jaber, 2015)	An analysis of keywords used in the literature on green supply chain management.	Green supply chain and sustainable supply chain are the part of reverse logistics
(Yu, Chavez, Feng, & Wiengarten, 2014)	Integrated green supply chain management and operational performance	Operational performance can be measured in terms of flexibility, quality, cost and delivery of the product.
(S.-Y. Lee, 2015)	Drivers for the participation of small and medium-sized suppliers in green supply chain initiatives	The SME supplier is more associated with the GSCM practices compare to large enterprises

The above table is a summary of research work suggesting the importance and status of green supply chain management across the globe. This forms the basis for finding major drivers of the work discussed subsequently.

Research Methodology

This work is based on literature review of various research papers, books & articles related to GSCM practices. These were analysed in order to assess the major drivers for GSCM practices. The method used for this analysis was literature review and secondary data evaluation.

Green Performance Mesurement Drivers

The work by various authors discussed in table 2, especially Wang & Sarkis, 2013, suggests that GSCM practices lead to involvement of upstream, downstream and reverse logistics and completely close the loop. For this purpose, business require an assessment framework to measure performance at multidimensional level (Varsei et al., 2014). It was found during the literature review that GSCM awareness is high and is perceived as a competitive advantage for companies in the manufacturing sector. Adoption of GSCM practices is highest in areas where there is a correlation to efficiency, cost saving and sustainability but lower in SME's.

Table – 2: Summary of Literature Specifying Important Drivers & Dimensions

S. No.	GSCM Practice Drivers	Author(s) & Year	Important Dimensions
1	Green Process & Product Design	(Dwayne Whitten, Green, & Zelbst, 2012), (K. W. Green et al., 2011), (Deshmukh & Sunnapwar, 2013), (Bhool & Narwal, 2013), (Dandekar, 2012), (Abu Seman, 2012), (Ali & Om, 1984), (Anil S. Dube & R. r.gawande, 2012), (Baroto, 2013),(Duarte et al., 2011), (Hervani et al., 2005)	• Enviornmental Cost • Eco Design • CO_2 Emission • Waste disposal • Supplier Pressure • Consumer Pressure • Energy Use • Operational Cost • Product Modification • Process Modification.
2	Regulatory norms	(Bhool & Narwal, 2013),(Dandekar, 2012)(Hervani et al., 2005), (Baroto, 2013), (Perotti et al., 2012),(S.-Y. Lee, 2015), (K. W. Green et al., 2011), (K. Green et al., 1998)	• Cost of Sales • Non Financial Factors • Ravenue • Investor & Share Holder Pressure. • ROE • Disosal Norms • Recycling • Government Rules & legislation • ISO 14000 Guidelines
3	Green Purchasing	(G.P., 2012), (Bhool & Narwal, 2013), (K. Green et al., 1998), (Perotti et al., 2012), (Varsei et al., 2014), (Wang & Sarkis, 2013), (Anil S. Dube & R. r.gawande, 2012)	• Green Procurement (Eco product) • Supplier Awareness • Supplier Audit • Certified Supplier • ISO 14000 Certified
4	Green Logistics	(Duarte et al., 2011), (Hervani et al., 2005), (Dwayne Whitten et al., 2012), (Kurien & Qureshi, 2011)	• Green Fuels • Eco product lifecycle • Geen Packaging • Lead Time • Green Disposal
5	Firm's Performance	(Perotti et al., 2012), (Wang & Sarkis, 2013), (Anil S. Dube & R. r.gawande, 2012),(Duarte et al., 2011), (Hervani et al., 2005).	• Customer Satisfaction • Market Share • Competetativeness • Major Award Received

Results & Discussions

The above literature review depicted in Table1&2 reveals that the main drivers behind implementation of green supply chain practices across the globe are: adherence to legislative regulations, gaining competitive advantage, as a marketing strategy, compliance with CSR, fear of shrinking raw materials and sustainable profit generation.

Most researchers consulted for this review agree that globally the major drivers for implementing Green supply chain are following:

Changing regulations for environmental, health & safety – This is a very important driver because the governments across the globe are making environmental norms tougher due to pressure for reduction of carbon emissions as well as increasing health related issues & deaths due to growing pollution levels. Secondly, the environmental norms are globally accepted and it becomes difficult to import & export goods if they are not compliant with these norms. Thirdly, non compliance with these laws could lead to severe punishment in terms of cash, kind and closure of units.

Competitive advantage – Competitive advantage has emerged as an important driver for implementation of GSCM as the organizations which follow GSCM practices tend to gain advantage over their competitors because firstly, they can market their products as eco-friendly which is preferred by environmentally conscious customers. Secondly, reduction in cost leads to more profit generation. Thirdly, they are more sustainable in the future.

Cost reduction – Organizations tend to adapt GSCM because they have realized the fact that in the longer run, GSCM can be more profitable since it reduces wastage, helps in recycling of products which saves energy & revenues. Thirdly, it closes the loop reducing uncertainties.

Quality Improvements – GSCM practices help an organisation to maintain quality and gain certifications of environmental health and safety. During the process of implementing GSCM, organisations undergo process change, product design change which not only improve their processes but makes them a market leader for better quality.

The above mentioned drivers are mainly in the context of global scenarios and still there is a strong need to develop these drivers to motivate Indian manufacturing and SME's. However, this is slowly progressing, yet lot is required to be accomplished in this direction.

Conclusions

This literature review conducted by reviewing reputed research papers, articles, books etc. which have been cited several times revealed that GSCM practices across the globe have taken a new form in the past decade and the corporates have started looking at GSCM practices from a different perspective. It is no more considered a philanthrophical act, however, it is being aligned with business strategies and organisations are designing their operations according to the GSCM requirements. The major drivers for this change evident from the literature search were compliance with regulations, competitive advantage, sustainability in the market, profit generation and stability.

These drivers although very powerful have not yet forced all organisations across sectors to fully adapt the GSCM practices because of lack of knowledge and financial constraints.

Limitations and future research directions

The major limitation of the present work is that it is based on literature review and requires validation from primary data. Secondly, most of the papers reviewed talked about the global scenario and only very few papers could be found dealing specifically with India which needs to be further investigated.

In order to validate empirical findings a case study approach could also be considered for future research as there are many manufacturing companies which have successfully implemented GSCM. Benchmarking the practices of such companies could benefit the strategic formulation for GSCM.

References

Abu Seman, N. A. (2012). Green Supply Chain Management: A Review and Research Direction. International Journal of Managing Value and Supply Chains, 3(1), 1–18.

Bai, C., Sarkis, J., Wei, X., &Koh, L. (2012). Evaluating ecological sustainable performance measures for supply chain management. Supply Chain Management: An International Journal, 17(1), 78–92.

Beamon, B. M. (2010). Designing the green supply chain. Logistics Information Management, 12(4), 332–342.

Beer, S., & Lemmer, C. (2011). A critical review of "green" procurement. Worldwide

Hospitality and Tourism Themes, 3(3), 229–244.

Beske, P., &Seuring, S. (2014). Putting sustainability into supply chain management. Supply Chain Management, 19(3), 322 – 331.

Bhool, R., &Narwal, M. S. (2013). An Analysis of Drivers Affecting the Implementation of Green Supply Chain Management for the Indian Manufacturing Industries, 242–254.

Björklund, M., Martinsen, U., & Abrahamsson, M. (2012). Performance measurements in the greening of supply chains. Supply Chain Management: An International Journal, 17(1), 29–39.

Chen, C. C. Y., Chang, C., & Chen, Y. (2013). Green organizational identity and green innovation. Management Decision Vol. 51(5), 1056 -1070.

Chen, H. J., Yan Huang, S., Chiu, A. A., &Pai, F. C. (2012). Industrial Management & Data Systems Article information : Industrial Management & Data Systems, Vol. 112(1), 83–101.

Cheng, J.-H., Yeh, C.-H., &Tu, C.-W. (2008). Trust and knowledge sharing in green supply chains. Supply Chain Management: An International Journal, 13(4), 283–295.

Dandekar, M. (2012). An empirical study of green supply chain management in Indian perspective. International Journal of Applied Science and Engineering Research, 1(2), 372–383.

Deshmukh, S. P., &Sunnapwar, V. K. (2013). Development and Validation of Performance Measures for Green Supplier Selection in Indian Industries, (5), 105–109.

Duarte, S., Cabrita, R., & Machado, V. C. (2011). Exploring Lean and Green Supply Chain Performance Using Balanced Scorecard Perspective. International Conference on Industrial Engineering and Operations Management, 520–525.

Dwayne Whitten, G., Green, K. W., &Zelbst, P. J. (2012). Triple-A supply chain performance. International Journal of Operations & Production Management, 32(1), 28–48.

G.P., K. (2012). Performance measurement systems for green supply chains using modified balanced score card and analytical hierarchical process. Scientific Research and Essays, 7 (36), 3149 – 3161.

Green, K.W., McGaughey, R., & Casey, K. M. (2006). Does supply chain management strategy mediate the association between market orientation and organizational performance? Supply Chain Management: An International Journal, 11(5), 407–414.

Green, K. W., Zelbst, P. J., Bhadauria, V. S., & Meacham, J. (2011). Do environmental collaboration and monitoring enhance organizational performance ? Emerald Group Publishing Limited, 112(2), 186–205.

Green, K.W., Morton, B., & New, S. (1998). Green purchasing and supply policies: do they improve companies' environmental performance? Supply Chain Management: An International Journal, 3(2), 89–95.

Gurtu, A., Searcy, C., &Jaber, M. Y. (2015). An analysis of keywords used in the literature on green supply chain management. Management Research Review, 38(2), 166–194.

Hervani, A., Helms, M., &Sarkis, J. (2005). Performance measurement for green supply chain management. Benchmarking, 12(4), 330–353.

Hitchcock, T. (2012). Low carbon and green supply chains: the legal drivers and commercial pressures. Supply Chain Management: An International Journal, 17(1), 98–101.

Hoek, R. I. Van. (1999). Research note from reversed logistics to green supply chains. Supply Chain Management: An International Journal, 4(3), 129–135.

Hsu, C.-C. (2013). Supply chain drivers that foster the development of green initiatives in an emerging economy. International Journal of Operations & Production Management, 33(6), 656–688.

Jensen, J. K. (2013). Chasing value offerings through green supply chain innovation. European Business Review, 25(2), 124–146.

Jung, D., Chan, F., Chen, G., & Chow, C. (2010). Journal of Asia Business Studies. Journal of Asia Business Studies, 4(2), 73 – 79.

Kenneth W. Green Jr., Zelbst, P. J., Meacham, J., &Bhadauria, V. S. (2012). Green supply chain management practices: impact on performance. Supply Chain Management: An International Journal, 17, 290–305.

Kim, I. supply chain efficiency from a green perspective, & Min, H. (2011).

Measuring supply chain efficiency from a green perspective. Management Research Review, 34(11), 1169–1189.

Kumar, S. N., Datta, S., & Sankar,M,S. (2014). Green supplier appraisement in fuzzy environment. Benchmarking: An International Journal, 21(3), 412–429.

Kumar, R., &Chandrakar, R. (2012). Overview of green supply chain management: Operation and environmental impact at different stages of the supply chain. International Journal of Engineering and Advanced …, (3), 2–7.

Kurien, G. P., & Qureshi, M. N. (2011). Study of performance measurement practices in supply chain management. International Business, Management and Social Sciences, 2(4), 19–34.

Laosirihongthong, T., Adebanjo, D., Tan, K. C., &Choon Tan, K. (2013). Green supply chain management practices and performance. Industrial Management & Data Systems, 113(8), 1088–1109.

Lee, S. M., Rha, J. S., Choi, D., & Noh, Y. (2013). Pressures affecting green supply chain performance. Management Decision, 51(8), 1753–1768.

Lee, S. M., Tae Kim, S., Choi, D., Kim, S. T., & Choi, D. (2012). Green supply chain management and organizational performance. Industrial Management & Data Systems, 112(8), 1148–1180.

Lee, S. S.-Y. (2008). Drivers for the participation of small and medium-sized suppliers in green supply chain initiatives. Supply Chain Management: An International Journal, 13(3), 185–198.

Lee, S.-Y. (2015). The effects of green supply chain management on the supplier's performance through social capital accumulation. Supply Chain Management: An International Journal, 20(1), 42–55.

Lee, T.-R. (Jiun-S., Le, T. P. N., Genovese, A., &Koh, L. S. C. (2012). Using FAHP to determine the criteria for partner's selection within a green supply chain: The case of hand tool industry in Taiwan. Journal of Manufacturing Technology Management, 23(1), 25–55.

Mollenkopf, D., Stolze, H., Tate, W. L., &Ueltschy, M. (2010). Green, lean, and global supply chains. International Journal of Physical Distribution & Logistics Management, 40(1/2), 14–41.

Mutingi, M., Mapfaira, H., &Monageng, R. (2014). Developing performance management systems for the green supply chain, 1–20.

Olugu, E. U., & Wong, K. Y. (2009). Supply chain performance evaluation: trends and challenges. American Journal of Engineering and Applied Sciences, 2(1), 202–211.

Ortas, E., Moneva, J. M., &Álvarez, I. (2014). Sustainable supply chain and company performance: A global examination. Supply Chain Management: An International Journal, 19(3), 332–350.

Perotti, S., Zorzini, M., Cagno, E., &Micheli, G. J. L. (2012). Green supply chain practices and company performance: the case of 3PLs in Italy. International Journal of Physical Distribution & Logistics Management, 42(7), 640–672.

Rao, P. H. (2014). Across a Green Supply Chain :, 39(March), 57–74.

Rostamifard, M., Shekari, H., &Eslami, S. (2014). Identifying the Drivers of Green Supply Chain Management in Tile, 4(4), 851–860.

Saadany, a M. a El, Jaber, M. Y., &Bonney, M. (2011). Environmental performance measures for supply chains. Management Research Review, 34, 1202–1221.

Sarkis, J. (2012). A boundaries and flows perspective of green supply chain management. Supply Chain Management: An International Journal, 17(2), 202–216.

Shaw, S., Grant, D. B., &Mangan, J. (2010). Developing environmental supply chain performance measures. Benchmarking: An International Journal, 17(3), 320–339.

Shi, V. G., Koh, S. C. L., Baldwin, J., &Cucchiella, F. (2012). Natural resource based green supply chain management. Supply Chain Management-an International Journal, 17(1), 54–67.

Simpson, D., Power, D., & Samson, D. (2007). Greening the automotive supply chain: a relationship perspective. International Journal of Operations & Production Management, 27(1), 28–48.

Toke, L. K., Gupta, R. C., &Dandekar, M. (2010). Green Supply Chain Management ; Critical Research and Practices. Green Supply Chain Management; Critical Research and Practices, 1–7

Vachon, S., &Klassen, R. D. (2006). Extending green practices across the supply chain: The impact of upstream and downstream integration. International Journal of Operations & Production Management, 26(7), 795–821.

Varsei, M., Soosay, C., Fahimnia, B., &Sarkis, J. (2014). Framing sustainability performance of supply chains with multidimensional indicators. Supply Chain Management: An International Journal, 19(3), 242–257.

Wang, Z., &Sarkis, J. (2013). Investigating the relationship of sustainable supply chain management with corporate financial performance. International Journal of Productivity and Performance Management, 62(8), 871–888.

Wu, G.-C. (2013). The influence of green supply chain integration and environmental uncertainty on green innovation in Taiwan's IT industry. International Journal of Operations & Production Management, 18(8), 539–552.

Wu, J., Dunn, S., & Forman, H. (2012). A Study on Green Supply Chain Management Practices among Large Global Corporations, 10(1), 182–194.

Yaghoubipoor, A. (2013). World Journal of Entrepreneurship, Management and Sustainable Development Article information : World Journal of Entrepreneurship, Management and Sustainable Development, 9(1), 14–27.

Youn, S., Yang, M. G. (Mark), &Roh, J. J. (2012). Extending the efficient and responsive supply chains framework to the green context. Benchmarking: An International Journal, 19(4/5), 463–480.

Yu, W., Chavez, R., Feng, M., &Wiengarten, F. (2014). Integrated green supply chain management and operational performance. Supply Chain Management: An International Journal, 19(5/6), 683–696.

Zhu, Q., Sarkis, J., &Geng, Y. (2005). Green supply chain management in China: Pressures, practices and performance. International Journal of Operations and Production Management, 25(5), 449–468.

Marketing Mix and Hotel Service Branding Equity: Developing New Forms of Customer Engagement Through Structural Equation Modelling

Ranu Sharma

Abstract

The service sector is rising across the globe including in India. The hotel industry has taken a bigger role in the service sector of late. It is increasingly seen as the strong base to increase the Gross Domestic Product of the Indian economy. It helps the tourism sector for earning revenue from the foreign as well as Indian tourists. In order to study the impact and scope of the hotel industry the author has looked at the region of Jaipur to identify better service provision and customer satisfaction. This study is carried out in the hotel industry with hotel service as the product category. The author has reviewed the service branding literature and has observed that most of the available brand equity models are for goods. Based on this research gap, a service branding model has been proposed and empirically validated. The model represents the relationship between service marketing mix and on certain service brand equity, namely, brand image(s) and perceived service quality and thereby on brand equity. Structural equation modelling is used to test the hierarchical relationship.

The study has established significant relationships among the service marketing mix elements and brand equity dimensions. It contributes significantly to the literature on hotel service branding and provides valuable insights to hotel managers.

Keywords: marketing mix elements, Service branding, brand image and brand equity.

Introduction

The study of customer based brand equity is one of the popular research fields in brand management. Many researchers have interested in brand equity concept and tried to use different approaches to measure it in various industries. This is because of the necessity in today's marketplace to develop, maintain and use service branding to acquire a certain level of competitive advantage. Strong brand offers advantages such as competitiveness position in the markets, more brand loyalty and better reaction toward increase in price by customers. Despite the research which exists on measuring brand equity in physical products, brand equity in the service sector

---

* Poornima School of Management, Jaipur

has not been fully explored. Conceptualization of customer based brand equity and its relation to customer perception of brand are crucial for services, especially for hospitality service sector and its sub sectors such as hotel industry.

This study aims to make a contribution towards the theory of customer based brand equity and its effects on customer perception of brand equity in the hotel service sector of developing countries. To accomplish the stated goals, this paper is organized in the following manner: first, a brief review of the literature in the area of conceptualization and measurement of customer based brand equity and its criteria has been provided. Next, the methodology and the rationale for measuring the customer based brand equity and its effects on customer perception of brand are provided. This is followed by conclusion and operational implications.

Tourist engagement is a psychological theory that involves the satisfaction of the product/service which involves the feeling of well-being and pleasure that results from obtaining what one hopes for and expects from an appealing product and/ services. Customer engagement is the leading criterion to show the quality delivered to customers through the product or services. As suggested by Berkman and Gilson (1986) customer satisfaction is recognized as being of great importance for customer engagement which leads to repeat purchase and word-of-mouth recommendations.

Costumer Based Brand Equity In Service Industry

Though costumer-based brand equity is cited as a multidimensional approach within the marketing literature (Nam et al, 2011), a debate exists as to whether the principles of branding within marketing goods could be directly applied to service dominant brands such as banks, insurance and hotels. Aaker's conceptualization of brand equity is one of the most cited works that identified a variety of dimensions of brand equity (Tang & Hawley, 2009). He viewed brand equity as a multidimensional construct which is made up of perceived quality, brand loyalty, brand awareness, brand association and other propriety assets. Aaker's study didn't tell which quality dimensions should be included in the brand equity model and therefore whether the model is suitable for assessing service dominant brand equity models in the different service industries (Nam et al, 2011). A similar theory was proposed by Keller; according to him, costumer based brand equity consists of two dimensions: brand knowledge and brand awareness.

Many scholars adopted Aaker's framework in their study of costumer based brand equity (Prasad & Dev, 2000; Low & Lamb, 2000). Some of the results state the framework of Aaker in one or two dimensions. Adjustments to the products-based branding models is required to consider the unique characteristics of services

(Namet al, 2011). Yoo and Donthun used four of Aaker's components of brand equity: brand awareness, brand loyalty, perceived quality and brand association excluding the proprietary assets dimension as it is not essential in the measurement of customer based brand equity (Yoo & Donthu, 2001). Some researchers stated that the applications of the products-based brand equity models show poor validity in the tourism industry as one of the service sectors (Boo et al, 2009). In the service sectors distinct dimensions of brand equity emerge when evaluating brands. The dimensions mentioned most frequently for services are employees, facilities, experiences, and word-of-mouth (Namet al, 2011; O'Cass & Grace, 2004). Researchers stated that two service quality dimensions: physical quality and staff behaviour are incorporated to the costumer based brand equity model (Dall'Olmo Riley & Chernatony, 2000). So there is a need to develop an appropriate costumer based brand equity framework in service industries with respect to the specific characteristics of service delivery.

Recently, several hotels have been established in Jaipur, which has turned the hotel industry into a highly competitive sector. However, there is little empirical research actually describing the relationship between brand equity, perceived value and customer revisit intention in the context of budget hotels. Therefore, the aim of this study is to determine the effect of brand equity and perceived value on customer loyalty in the budget hotel industry in Jaipur. Based on the initial premise of this research, my analysis focuses on two research questions: 1) Does brand equity and perceived value have a positive effect on customer loyalty to particular budget hotels in Jaipur? 2) Does the effect of brand equity and perceived value have a positive effect on the intention of the customers in different categories to revisit the same hotel?

Literature Review

The base of the theoretical framework for the current research has been taken from Aaker's model of brand equity. He described five elements in his model; brand awareness, perceived quality, brand loyalty, brand association and other proprietary brand assets such as trademarks, patents, or channel relationships (Atilgan et al, 2005; Kim & Kim, 2004; Yoo et al, 2000). Among these elements, the first four represent customers' evaluations and reactions to the specific brand that can be understood by consumers; these elements have been extensively adopted to measure customer based brand equity in previous researches (Tang & Hawley, 2009). On the other hand, this current research is distinct from earlier published papers as it investigates the relationship between marketing mix elements and brand equity. Therefore first four dimensions of brand equity are meaningful for the extent of the current research. The conceptual framework of the research presented in Figure 1.

The American Marketing Association (AMA) [2015] explained brand as "a name, term, sign, symbol, or design, or a combination of them, which is intended to identify the goods and services of one seller or group of sellers and to differentiate them from those of competitors".

Aaker [2009] explains brand equity as "a set of brand assets and liabilities linked to a brand, its name and symbol that add to or subtract from the value provided by a product or service to a customer". Moreover the nature of differences between product and service, service branding is unlike product branding in terms of the primary brand established in the tourist's mind. Low and Lamb [2000] explained that the company brand is the key brand in the service industry; whereas on the product market, the product is considered the primary brand.

The customer-based brand equity theory is more practical in the sense that the information offers a strategic vision of tourist behaviour and hotel brand managers can develop many plans and strategies accordingly [Kim, Jin-Sun & Kim,2008]; therefore, in the context of this research, I applied a customer-based brand equity perspective as an approach to measure brand equity of Jaipur Hotels.

Brand loyalty measures the core dimension of consumer-based brand equity for management [Keller,1993] since it regards a customer's "deeply held commitment to rebuy prefer a product or service consistently in the future, despite situational influences and marketing efforts having the potential to cause switching behaviour" [Oliver, 1996]. Zeithaml [1988] explains perceived quality as "the consumer's subjective judgment about a product's overall excellence or superiority". Perceived quality can be taken as a customer's personal perception about service experience, specific needs and consumption situations; therefore, their perception will be involved in their consumer decision-making process.

Brand awareness plays an important role in brand equity. It is explained as "the ability of the potential buyer to recognize and recall that a brand is a member of a certain product category" [Aaker, 2009]. The higher level of brand awareness for a service brand, the higher probability of this brand being involved in a customer's buying decision-making process [Hoyer & Brown, 1990; Nedungadi, 1990].

Brand awareness along with strong associations forms a explicit brand image. Brand association is explained by Aaker [2009] as "anything linked in memory to a brand". Brand awareness combined with brand associations are considerably related to service brand equity since they can be a signal of commitment and quality and they provide tourist information about the service brand at the point of purchase.

Zeithaml [1988] suggested that perceived value is a "consumer's overall assessment of the utility of a product or service based on perceptions of what is received and what is given". Perceived value is not measured by the hotel owners, but by the tourist based on their individual perceptions of a product or service compared to the cost they have already paid [Anderson et al., 1994]. Adding to this, Dodds et al. [1991] also explained that perceived value as a "trade-off between benefits and quality they receive in the product or service relative to the sacrifice they perceive in paying the price".

Repurchase intention has been defined as "the individual's judgment about buying again a designated service from the same company, taking into account his or her current situation and likely circumstances" [Hellier et al., 2003]. Butcher [2005] explained that perceived quality, perceived value and brand preference together have a positive significant effect on the tourist's repurchase intention as one of the hotel service outcomes.

Elements Of The Marketing Mix

a) Product

As for services, according to Hirankitti, Mechinda, and Manjing, (2009) the product offer in respect of services can be explained based in two factors: (1) The core service which represents the core benefit; (2) The secondary services which represent both the tangible and augmented product levels. According to Borden, (1984) a product is characterized by quality, design, features, brand name and sizes.

b) Price

According to Kotler, Armstrong, Wong, and Saunders (2008), price is the amount of money charged for a product or service, or the total value that consumers exchange for the benefits of having or using the product or service. Due to the intangible nature of services, price becomes a crucial quality indicator where other information is not lacking or absent (Zeithaml, 1981). Price is considered as the most important measurement of repurchase intentions (Oh, 2000; Parasuraman and Grewal, 2000).

c) Place

This factor is defined by Armstrong and Kotler (2006) as a set of interdependent organizations that caters to the process of making a product available to the consumers. Hirankitti et al., (2009) considers place as the ease of access which potential customer associates to a service such as location and distribution. An organization should pay attention to place decisions, because of the importance of the product and consumption occurring at the same time and at the same place; a place that provides all information of customer, competition, promotion action, and marketing task.

d) Promotion

It is defined as sales promotion, advertising, personal selling, public relations and direct marketing (Borden, 1984) – A decision of how best to relate the product to the target market and how to persuade them to buy it (Lovelock, Patterson and Walker, 1998). A communication program is important in marketing strategies because it plays three vital roles: providing needed information and advice, persuading target customers of the merits of a specific product, and encouraging them to take action at specific times (Lovelock and Wright, 2002). Activities that cater to promotion are advertising, sales promotions, personal selling and publicity; they can all influence consumer's way of thinking, their emotions, their experience as well as their purchasing.

e) Personnel

This factor refers to the service employees who produce and deliver the service. It has long been a fact that many services involve personal interactions between customers and the site's employees, and they strongly influence the customer's perception of service quality (Hartline and Ferrell, 1996: Rust, Zahorik and Keiningham, 1996). Personnel are keys to the delivery of service to customers. In addition, according to Magrath (1986) customers normally link the traits of service to the firm they work for.

f) Process

Process is generally defined as the implementation of action and function that increases value for products with low cost and high advantage to customer and is more important for service than for goods.

g) Physical Evidence

This factor refers to the environment in which the service and any tangible goods that facilitate the performance and communication of the service are delivered. This holds great importance because the customer normally judges the quality of the service provided through it (Rafiq& Ahmed, 1995). The components of the service experience are called the "services-cape"-that is, the ambience, the background music, the comfort of the seating, and the physical layout of the service facility, the appearance of the staff can greatly affect a customer's satisfaction with a service experience (Rust, Zahorik and Keiningham, 1996).

3. Rationale of the Study

As mentioned above, this research will concentrate on measuring customer-based brand equity following Aaker's [2009] model excluding other proprietary asset aspects, which means the first four elements of brand equity will be taken for analysis. Even though a number of research have been involved in brand equity and its components, a very few researchers have developed precise matter measuring the four brand equity components. In the context of this research, the scale for brand association and brand awareness developed by Yoo et al. [2001] was modified because their scale has been most widely established and validated by many researchers [Washburn & Plank, 2002; Kim et al., 2008]. For perceived quality and brand loyalty, the scale of Kim and Kim [2004] was used since it has been established in the quick-service restaurant field in Korea; therefore, it can be suitable to apply the scale to this research. The perceived value and revisit intention scales were modified from Kim et al. [2008] because the research was done in the hospitality industry, which can be easily adopted by the quick-service restaurant field.

Figure 1 shows the proposed four-factor model of brand equity including brandawareness, brand association, perceived quality and brand loyalty;moreover, the effect of brand equity on tourist revisit intention will be mediated byperceived value.

Based on the literature review and the theoretical frame of the research, the following hypotheses were formulated:

The Research Main Hypothesis

Hypothesis Ia: Marketing mix and brand equity are having positive effect on Tourist Engagement.

The Research Subsidiary Hypothesis:

Hypothesis $I_{a1.1}$-The product is having meaningful effect on brand equity

Hypothesis $I_{a1.2}$-The price is having meaningful effect on brand equity

Hypothesis $I_{a1.3}$-The promotion is having meaningful effect on brand equity

Hypothesis $I_{a1.4}$-The distribution is having meaningful effect on brand equity

Hypothesis $I_{a1.5}$People has a positive direct effect on brand equity.

Hypothesis $I_{a1.6}$-Physical Evidencehas a significant positive direct effect on brand equity.

Hypothesis $I_{a1.7}$-Process has a positive direct effect on brand equity.

Hypothesis $I_{a1.8}$-Brand association has a positive direct effect on brand equity.

Hypothesis $I_{a1.9}$-Perceived quality has a positive direct effect on brand equity.

Hypothesis $I_{a1.10}$-Brand loyalty has a significant positive direct effect on brand equity.

Hypothesis $I_{a1.11}$-Brand awareness has a positive direct effect on brand equity.

Objectives of the Study

1. To identify the nature of Jaipur tourists through studying the demographic profiles.

2. To identify the components and characteristics of Jaipur tourism as a product to establish competitive tourism packages that can satisfy tourists, with a focus on the identity of the Jaipur tourist package.

3. To identify the level of the tourism marketing in Jaipur in the current period, also the efficiency of the tourism services and the extent of tourist satisfaction with these services.

4. To study the impact of marketing mix elements on customer based brand equity.

5. To provide recommendations to hoteliers about the role of each element of the tourism marketing mix and the necessity of each element and its Impact on the satisfaction of tourists.

6. To identify the level of satisfaction of the Jaipur tourists about prices of Tourism Products.

7. To study the importance of distribution of the tourism product on their satisfaction level.

Research Methodology

A survey instrument measuring tourists' perceptions for Jaipur city as a tourist destination and tourists' engagement was developed for this research. This research focuses on tourists, who visited Jaipur city between October 2016 and November 2016, as a population of interest. Data were collected through a sample of 300 survey questionnaires from local and foreign tourists. A total of 274 questionnaires were returned from the 300 distributed questionnaires, that is a response rate of 91.3%. Structured questionnaires were categorized as perception, promotional activities, destination image, experiential value, tourist expectation and tourist satisfaction and engagement. There were two main sections in the survey questionnaire. Section A required the respondents to rate a total of 29 items on marketing and brand equity provided by the local players using a 5-point Likert Scale for the destination choice variables, with 5 = absolutely important and 1 = absolutely unimportant. This scale is fairly representative and popular in application for the tourism industry. Finally, Section B is used to collect the personal profile and demographic data of respondents.

To facilitate the research questions, some inferential data analysis techniques were employed: factor analysis, chi square, linear regression and path analysis. Linear regression analysis is a statistical technique utilized to examine the relationship between a set of dependent variable and a single independent variables (Hair et al., 1998); here it is to examine the relationships between revisit intention attributes and brand equity. The dependent variable was the intention to revisit. The independent variables consisted of 5 attributes measuring brand equity of hotels of Jaipur city. Path analysis tests the plausibility of putative causal relationships between one variable and another in non-experimental conditions. In this research, the path analysis was conducted to further validate the tourist's model, which shows that brand equity affects tourist's engagement in terms of revisit intention such as the use of choice preferences. For the global test of model fit, chi-square statistics is often employed in a path analysis.

The Proposed Model

The proposed model of this study presents an integrated framework to build a customer engagement model in Jaipur Tourist Industry. Fig. 1 demonstrates details of the proposed model.

Figure 1: Proposed model

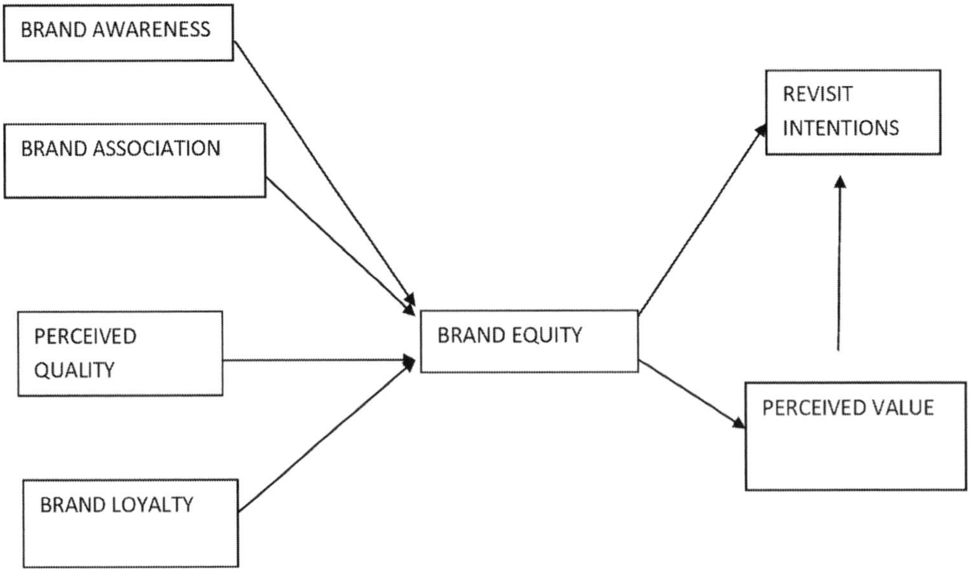

According to Fig. 1, brand awareness, brand association, perceived quality and brand loyalty influence brand equity and revisit intention through perceived value. Intention to revist is analyzed in terms of tourist's satisfaction as well as tourist's commitment and it influenced by perceived value. The proposed research of this paper uses structural equation modelling (SEM) to measure the relationships among different components demonstrated in Fig. 1 in this study. The proposed study designed a questionnaire and distributed it among 300 tourists who came for visit in Jaipur city.

Empirical Results and Discussion

Descriptive Statistics

The data sample for the model test was collected from consumers visiting various hotels in Jaipur city. Data was processed using the SPSS 16.0 and Amos 7.0 software packages. The analyses involved: (1) descriptivestatistics; (2) confirmatory factor analysis (CFA); (3) analysis of structural equation model (SEM).

According to the questionnaire survey, the distribution of population by Ages is: 26–35, 33%36–45, 52%; 46–55, 15%.

Education: mostly university educated (60%). Marital status: mostly married with children (72%).

Employment: housewives make up the largest group (46%).

Table 1 presents the tourist satisfaction variables with their mean and standard deviations.

Table 1: Descriptive Statistics

		Mean	StdDev
1.	FUNCTION	2.0833	.5222
2.	EMOTIONA	4.0694	.7160
3.	NOVELTYV	2.3403	.9473
4.	TOURISTE	3.7639	.8689
5.	SENSE	4.0069	.7432
6.	FEEL	3.6667	.8771
7.	THINK	3.8542	.8525
8.	ACT	3.7014	.9614
9.	RELATE	3.3750	1.1397
10.	SERVICEE	3.6250	1.0301
11.	PHYSICAL	4.0069	.7432
12.	HUMANCON	3.6667	.8771
13.	HOTELSER	3.8542	.8525
14.	FV	3.4514	1.2223
15.	EV	3.3750	1.3216
16.	NV	3.9097	1.1880
17.	PE	2.8750	1.1700
18.	HC	3.2500	1.5667
19.	TOURISTS	2.5000	1.2290
20.	TE	2.6250	1.3216

Reliability

As shown in the Table2A, the reliability coefficient is 0.89 which measures possess sufficient reliability for all dimensions of tourist engagement in Jaipur city.

Table 2A: Reliability Statistics

Cronbach's Alpha	Cronbach's Alpha Based on Standardized Items	N of Items
.8936	.8914	29

Table 2B shows the value of ANOVA Test i.e. 78.24 which is significant and proves the model empirically.

Table 2B: ANOVA

Model		Sum of Squares	df	Mean Square	F	Sig.
	Regression	434.251	16	15.357	78.247	.000(a)
1	Residual	38.236	127	.428		
	Total	472.487	143			

Construct Validity

To validate the quality of the proposed measurement by Luque Martinez et al (2000), factor analysis and reliability analysis were used. A principal components analysis on the set of 29 items and 7 parameters was performed. The result of this analysis is summarized in table 3.

Table 3: Analysis of Variance

Component	Initial Eigenvalues			Extraction Sums of Squared Loadings			Rotation Sums of Squared Loadings		
	Total	% of Variance	Cumulative %	Total	% of Variance	Cumulative %	Total	% of Variance	Cumulative %
1	5.684	28.421	28.421	5.684	28.421	28.421	4.596	22.978	22.978
2	4.659	23.294	51.714	4.659	23.294	51.714	4.197	20.983	43.961
3	1.514	7.572	59.287	1.514	7.572	59.287	2.133	10.667	54.628
4	1.445	7.224	66.511	1.445	7.224	66.511	2.049	10.246	64.873
5	1.313	6.565	73.076	1.313	6.565	73.076	1.586	7.930	72.803
6	1.122	5.612	78.688	1.122	5.612	78.688	1.177	5.884	78.688
7	.856	4.279	82.966	1.011	6.121	83.342	1.023	6.332	83.342
8	.723	3.617	86.583						
9	.536	2.682	89.265						
10	.508	2.541	91.806						

11	.488	2.438	94.244						
12	.320	1.601	95.845						
13	.266	1.330	97.175						
14	.244	1.218	98.393						
15	.181	.905	99.297						
16	.138	.689	99.986						
17	.003	.014	100.000						
18	4.838E-16	2.419E-15	100.000						
19	1.702E-16	8.511E-16	100.000						
20	-1.138E-16	-5.690E-16	100.000						

Above table shows the actual factors that were extracted. If we look at the section labeled "Rotation Sums of Squared Loadings," it shows only those factors that met cut-off criterion (extraction method). In this case, there were six factors with eigenvalues greater than 1. The "% of variance" column tells how much of the total variability (in all of the variables together) can be accounted for by each of these summary scales or factors. Factor 1 accounts for 22% of the variability in all seven variables, and so on.

Kaiser Meyer Olkin (Kmo) And Bartlett's Test (Measures The Strength Of Relationship Among The Variables)

The KMO measures the sampling adequacy (which determines if the responses given with the sample are adequate or not) which should be closer than 0.5 for a satisfactory factor analysis to proceed. Looking at the table below, the KMO measure is 0.537, which is above 0.5 and therefore can be accepted (Table 4). The analysis extracts a 2 factor solution for service quality namely, tourist satisfaction and tourist engagement with eigenvalues above one, and the Bartlett's test for sphericity was given with chi square=2376.302 (p<0.000).

Bartlett's test is another indication of the strength of the relationship among variables. This tests the null hypothesis that the correlation matrix is an identity matrix. An identity matrix is matrix in which all of the diagonal elements are 1 (See Table 4) and all off diagonal elements (term explained above) are close to 0.From the same table, we can see that the Bartlett's Test Of Sphericity is significant (000). That is, significance is less than 0.05 so we can reject the null hypothesis. This means that correlation matrix is not an identity matrix.

Table 4: KMO and Bartlett's Test

Kaiser-Meyer-Olkin Measure of Sampling Adequacy.		.537
Bartlett's Test of Sphericity	Approx. Chi-Square	2376.302
	Df	21
	Sig.	.000

In the below table, the model was found to be significant ($p<.01$). Hence, the direct effects of the predictors significantly explained 79% of the variability in tourist engagement.

Table 5: Model Summary

Model	R	R Square	Adjusted R Square	Std. Error of the Estimate	Change Statistics				
					R Square Change	F Change	df1	df2	Sig. F Change
1	.893(a)	.797	.812	.4032	.813	73.248	16	127	.000

Structure Model Fit and Model Coefficients

A CFA of the constructs of BA, Basso, PQ, BL, BE, PV and RVI were also performed in this study. Employing the covariance matrix among seven measurement items as input and the SEM analysis was conducted to examine the relationships between each pair of constructs as hypothesized. The results of SEM analysis were depicted in the below tables. This structural model confirms that Jaipur tourist's brand equity has stronger significant relationship and positively related to brand awareness, brand association, perceived quality and brand loyalty. Hence, it is concluded that four dimensions of brand equity have greater impact on revisit intention in Jaipur tourism destination. The measurement model was observed for overall fitness by referring to other fit indices as suggested by Byrne (2001), Kline (2005), Schumacker and Lomax (2004), and Tabachnick and Fidell (2007). The fit indices reported in this research were the Root Mean Square Error of Approximation (RMSEA) for model fit, and the Tucker-Lewis Index (TLI) and the Comparative Fit Index (CFI) for model comparison indicate that the model is adequately fit, and the cutoff values are 0.90 or higher for CFI and TLI (Byrne, 2001; Kline, 2005; Schumacker and Lomax 2004), 0.08 or lower for RMSEA, and 0.5 or higher for Parsimony-Adjusted Measures of CFI (PCFI) (Byrne 2001;

Kline, 2005; Schumacker and Lomax, 2005). Kenny, Kaniskan, and McCoach (2011) have noted the RMSEA cut-off value may be closer to .100 or greater in samples compared to populations for which the.08 cut-off was recommended. The model fit was moderately acceptable ($\chi_2(72) = 339.217$, p<.001; CFI = .960, IFI= .861, TLI = .945 RMSEA = .05), providing support for the hypotheses although improvements in fit indices are desirable. The other indices (NFI=.859 and RFI=.908 >0.9,PCFI=0.245 and PNFI=0.702 >0.5) are all within acceptable ranges.The model is areasonable presentation of the data.

Confirmatory Factor Analysis-Customer Experience With Hotel

A second order CFA model is constructed, reflecting the core service, service escape and employee service of the customer experience with the company. The quality of fit indices is shown as in Figure 2, the value of chi-square is 117.047, p=0.000, GFI=1, AGFI=0.851.Hu and Bentler [30] suggest that GFI values over 0.9 and AGFI values over 0.8 indicate good fit. Brown and Cudeck [32] suggest that an RMSEA of 0.05 or less is good, 0.05–0.08 is acceptable, and 0.10 or over is bad. The model's RMSEA is 0.045 which is acceptable. These values are shown in Table 6A. Testing therefore suggests that this two variable model is a good fit for the data.

Figure 2: Customer Experience With Hotel

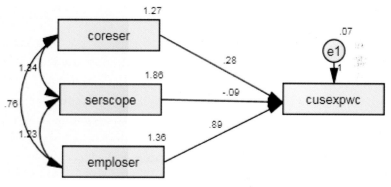

Table 6A: Maximum Likelihood Estimates

			Estimate	S.E.	C.R.	P	Label
coreser	<-->	emploser	.757	.104	7.312	***	
coreser	<-->	Serscope	1.340	.139	9.625	***	
serscope	<-->	emploser	1.225	.137	8.949	***	

Model Fit Summary- RMR, GFI

Model	RMR	GFI	AGFI	PGFI
Default model	.000	1.000		
Saturated model	.000	1.000		
Independence model	.896	.349	.851	.209

Baseline Comparisons

Model	NFI Delta1	RFI rho1	IFI Delta2	TLI rho2	CFI
Default model	.673	.456	.676	.459	.675
Saturated model	1.000		1.000		1.000
Independence model	.000	.000	.000	.000	.000

RMSEA

Model	RMSEA	LO 90	HI 90	PCLOSE
Default model	.615	.578	.653	.000
Independence model	.048	.807	.865	.000

Hotel's Presented Brand Aspects

A second order CFA model is constructed, reflecting the advertising and promotion with company's presented brand aspects of the service encounter. Goodness of fit indices is shown as in Figure 3, the value of chi-square is 415.02, p=0.000, GFI=1, AGFI=.905. Hu and Bentler [30] suggest that GFI values over 0.9 and AGFI values over 0.8 indicate a good fit. Brown and Cudeck [32] suggest that an RMSEA of 0.05 or less is good, 0.05–0.08 is acceptable, and 0.10 or over is bad. The model's RMSEA is .058 which is acceptable. These values are shown in Table 6B. Testing therefore suggests that this five variable model is a good fit for the data.

Figure 3: Hotel's Presented Brand Aspects

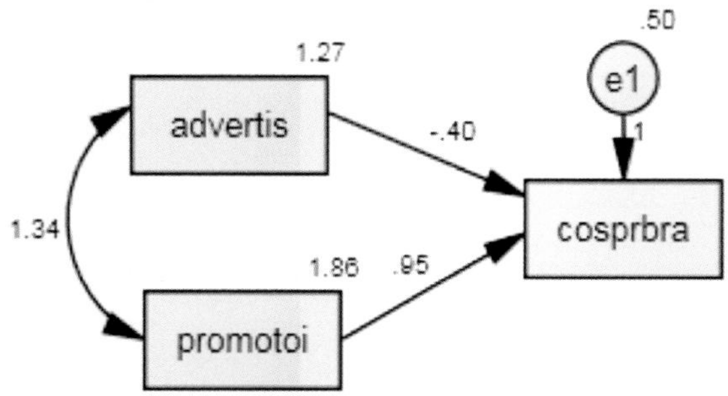

Table 6B: Result (Default model)

			Estimate	S.E.	C.R.	P	Label
cosprbra	<---	Advertis	.405	.087	4.660	***	
cosprbra	<---	promotoi	.950	.072	13.216	***	

Model	RMR	GFI	AGFI	PGFI
Default model	.000	1.000		
Saturated model	.000	1.000		
Independence model	.803	.471	.905	.236

Model	NFI Delta1	RFI rho1	IFI Delta2	TLI rho2	CFI
Default model	1.000		1.000		1.000
Saturated model	1.000		1.000		1.000
Independence model	.000	.000	.000	.000	.000

Model	RMSEA	LO 90	HI 90	PCLOSE
Independence model	.058	.830	.960	.000

External Brand Communications

A second order CFA model is constructed, reflecting the functional, emotional and novelty value of tourist experience value. Goodness of fit indices is shown as in Figure 4, the value of chi-square is 385.23, p=0.000, GFI=1, AGFI=.829. Hu and Bentler [30] suggest that GFI values over 0.9 and AGFI values over 0.8 indicate a good fit. Brown and Cudeck [32] suggest that an RMSEA of 0.05 or less is good,

0.05–0.08 is acceptable, and 0.10 or over is bad. The model's RMSEA is .048 which is acceptable. These values are shown in Table 6C. Testing therefore suggests that this five variable model is a good fit for the data. This model is a good fit for the data.

Figure 4: External Brand Communications

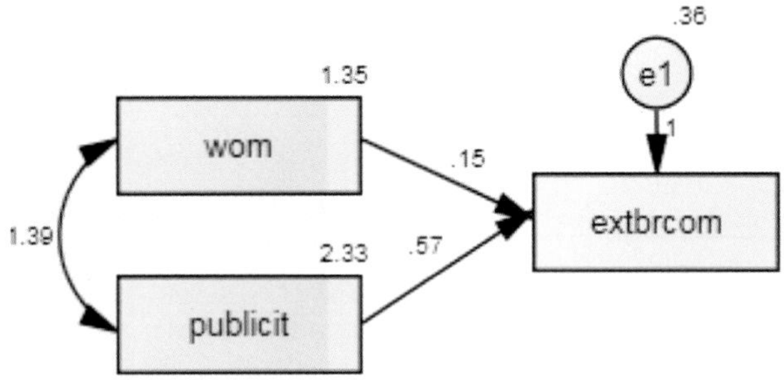

Table 6C: Result (Default model)

			Estimate	S.E.	C.R.	P	Label
extbrcom	<---	wom	.149	.056	2.650	***	
extbrcom	<---	publicit	.570	.043	13.275	***	

Model	RMR	GFI	AGFI	PGFI
Default model	.000	1.000		
Saturated model	.000	1.000		
Independence model	.939	.444	.829	.222

Model	NFI Delta1	RFI rho1	IFI Delta2	TLI rho2	CFI
Default model	1.000		1.000		1.000
Saturated model	1.000		1.000		1.000
Independence model	.000	.000	.000	.000	.000

Model	RMSEA	LO 90	HI 90	PCLOSE
Independence model	.048	.810	.939	.000

Brand Loyalty

A second order CFA model is constructed, reflecting the staff service, brand personality, organization association of brand loyalty. Goodness of fit indices is shown as in

Figure 5, the value of chi-square is 503.21, p=0.000, GFI=1, AGFI=0.851. Hu and Bentler [30] suggest that GFI values over 0.9 and AGFI values over 0.8 indicate a good fit. Brown and Cudeck [32] suggest that an RMSEA of 0.05 or less is good, 0.05–0.08 is acceptable, and 0.10 or over is bad. The model's RMSEA is 0.037 which is acceptable. These values are shown in Table6D. Testing therefore suggests that this five variable model is a good fit for the data. This model is a good fit for the data.

Figure 5: Dimensions Of Brand Loyalty

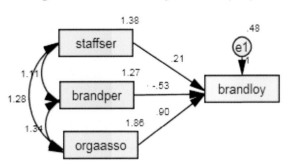

Table 6D: Maximum Likelihood

			Estimate	S.E.	C.R.	P	Label
staffser	<-->	orgaasso	1.280	.140	9.148	***	
staffser	<-->	brandper	1.111	.118	9.414	***	
brandper	<-->	orgaasso	1.340	.139	9.625	***	

Model	RMR	GFI	AGFI	PGFI
Default model	.000	1.000		
Saturated model	.000	1.000		
Independence model	.864	.370	.851	.222

Model	NFI Delta1	RFI rho1	IFI Delta2	TLI rho2	CFI
Default model	1.000		1.000		1.000
Saturated model	1.000		1.000		1.000
Independence model	.000	.000	.000	.000	.000

Model	RMSEA	LO 90	HI 90	PCLOSE
Independence model	.037	.740	.831	.000

6.5.5 Brand Equity

A second order CFA model is constructed, reflecting the product, price, place and promotion of brand equity. Goodness of fit indices is shown as in Figure 6, the value of chi-square is 305.69, p=0.000, GFI=1, AGFI=0.893. Hu and Bentler [30] suggest that GFI values over 0.9 and AGFI values over 0.8 indicate a good fit. Brown and Cudeck [32] suggest that an RMSEA of 0.05 or less is good, 0.05–0.08 is acceptable, and 0.10 or over is bad. The model's RMSEA is 0.049 which is acceptable. These values are shown in Table 6E. Testing therefore suggests that this five variable model is a good fit for the data. This model is a good fit for the data.

Figure 6: Dimensions of Brand LoyaltyAIC

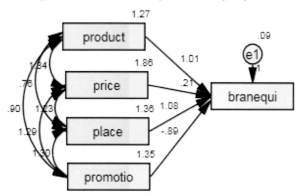

Table 6E: Result (Default model)

			Estimate	S.E.	C.R.	P	Label
price	<-->	place	1.225	.137	8.949	***	
product	<-->	place	.757	.104	7.312	***	
price	<-->	promotio	1.286	.139	9.228	***	
product	<-->	price	1.340	.139	9.625	***	
product	<-->	promotio	.901	.109	8.289	***	
place	<-->	promotio	1.302	.128	10.153	***	

Model	RMR	GFI	AGFI	PGFI
Default model	.000	1.000		
Saturated model	.000	1.000		
Independence model	1.097	.274	.893	.183

Model	NFI Delta1	RFI rho1	IFI Delta2	TLI rho2	CFI
Default model	1.000		1.000		1.000
Saturated model	1.000		1.000		1.000
Independence model	.000	.000	.000	.000	.000

Model	RMSEA	LO 90	HI 90	PCLOSE
Independence model	.049	.892	.963	.000

Customer Engagement

A second order CFA model is constructed, reflecting the product, price, place and promotion of brand equity. Goodness of fit indices is shown as in Figure 7, the value of chi-square is 741.127, p=0.000, GFI=1, AGFI=.967. Hu and Bentler [30] suggest that GFI values over 0.9 and AGFI values over 0.8 indicate a good fit. Brown and Cudeck [32] suggest that an RMSEA of 0.05 or less is good, 0.05–0.08 is acceptable, and 0.10 or over is bad. The model's RMSEA is .048 which is acceptable. These values are shown in Table 6F. Testing therefore suggests that this five variable model is a good fit for the data. This model is a good fit for the data.

Figure7: Customer Engagement

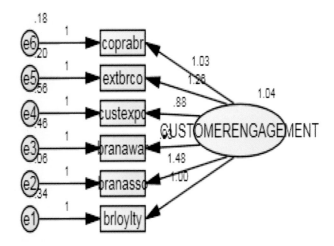

Table 6F: Defult Model

			Estimate	S.E.	C.R.	P	Label
brloylty	<---	CUSTOMERENGAGEMENT	1.000				
branasso	<---	CUSTOMERENGAGEMENT	1.476	.061	24.162	***	
branawar	<---	CUSTOMERENGAGEMENT	.926	.059	15.812	***	
custexpc	<---	CUSTOMERENGAGEMENT	.877	.061	14.363	***	
extbrco	<---	CUSTOMERENGAGEMENT	1.262	.058	21.662	***	
coprabr	<---	CUSTOMERENGAGEMENT	1.026	.049	20.733	***	

Model	RMR	GFI	AGFI	PGFI
Default model	.113	.671	.233	.288
Saturated model	.000	1.000		
Independence model	1.091	.238	.967	.170

Model	NFI Delta1	RFI rho1	IFI Delta2	TLI rho2	CFI
Default model	.673	.456	.676	.459	.675
Saturated model	1.000		1.000		1.000
Independence model	.000	.000	.000	.000	.000

Model	RMSEA	LO 90	HI 90	PCLOSE
Default model	.061	.578	.653	.000
Independence model	.048	.807	.865	.000

Tourist Revisit Intention

A second order CFA model is constructed, reflecting the product, price, place and promotion of brand equity. Goodness of fit indices is shown as in Figure 8, the value of chi-square is 741.127, p=0.000,GFI=1, AGFI=.967. Hu and Bentler [30] suggest that GFI values over 0.9 and AGFI values over 0.8 indicate a good fit. Brown and Cudeck [32] suggest that an RMSEA of 0.05 or less is good, 0.05–0.08 is acceptable and 0.10 or over is bad. The model's RMSEA is .048 which is acceptable. These values are shown in Table 6G. Testing therefore suggests that this five variable model is a good fit for the data. This model is a good fit for the data.

Figure 8: Tourist Revisit Intention

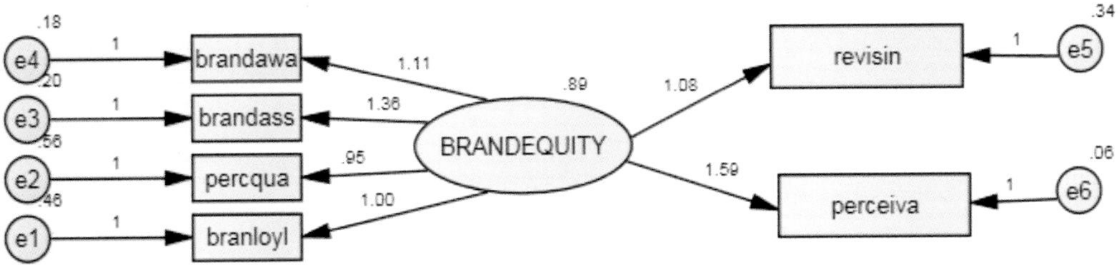

Table 6G: Default Model

			Estimate	S.E.	C.R.	P	Label
branloyl	<---	BRANDEQUITY	1.000				
percqua	<---	BRANDEQUITY	.947	.072	13.198	***	
brandass	<---	BRANDEQUITY	1.363	.075	18.182	***	
brandawa	<---	BRANDEQUITY	1.108	.063	17.622	***	
perceiva	<---	BRANDEQUITY	1.593	.081	19.589	***	
revisin	<---	BRANDEQUITY	1.080	.068	15.812	***	

Model	RMR	GFI	AGFI	PGFI
Default model	.113	.671	.233	.288
Saturated model	.000	1.000		
Independence model	1.091	.923	.067	.170

Model	NFI Delta1	RFI rho1	IFI Delta2	TLI rho2	CFI
Default model	.673	.456	.676	.459	.675
Saturated model	1.000		1.000		1.000
Independence model	.000	.000	.000	.000	.000

Model	RMSEA	LO 90	HI 90	PCLOSE
Default model	.615	.578	.653	.000
Independence model	.038	.807	.865	.000

To sum up, an evident path "Tourist experiential value and Service encounter – satisfaction-tourist engagement" appears in the estimated model (fig3). The results of the hypotheses testing are summarized in Table. Note that tourist attributes influence directly on tourist satisfaction and also influence on tourist engagement. This finding confirms the arguments of previous researches (Alkharabsheh et al, 2011, Chen and Tsai, 2007; Mahadzirah et al, 2011).

Discussion and Conclusion

In this study, I have explained through empirical investigation the effects of various attributes on building tourist engagement through the intention to revisit in the Jaipur tourism industry. The proposed research has determined that all the six variables which were explained earlier influence revisit intention positively. Based on the results of this research, it is suggested that the Jaipur tourism industry enter into market growth by marketing through various agencies. This would help the industry introduce the services to more visitors and help tourists become familiar with different aspects of Jaipur Tourism. This study chose tourists in Jaipur's Railway station, Amber, JLN Marg, Airport area, Bus Stand etc as respondents. This research highlights the importance of marketing mix and brand equity for the intention to revisit Jaipur as a tourist destination. Hence, exploring the phenomenon of perceived and expected quality of hotel services among visitors of Jaipur will broaden the understanding of tourist satisfaction level in Jaipur.

This study contributes to tourist satisfaction and customer engagement research and goes beyond previous researches that were focused on studying the general effect on marketing mix on tourists' satisfaction. This study goes a step further by examining tourist satisfaction and customer engagement in terms of revisit intention through brand equity in Jaipur city. The data come from the hotel industry. The empirical results suggest that the appearance of professionals in the industry has positive significant effect on purchase behavior. The research concludes that tourists in this industry are cautious, and are persuaded by luxurious surroundings or fancy equipment. The key remains human contact with the service providers. This contact makes a significant difference to consumers, making them more likely to purchase. The brand equity, moderated through the perceived value, can significantly increase the likelihood of a revisit intention. Ultimately, the local Jaipur community and the industry players in particular will benefit from this research as it highlights which are the areas in the service delivery that need close scrutiny and improvements.

In this research, it is aimed to reveal which attributes shape the brand equity perception of tourists and the impact of the brand equity perception on the creation of tourist revisit intention. To that end, the consumer based brand equity model has been adapted to the hotel industry. The model of the study has been developed by utilizing Aaker's and Yooatl al, Consumer Based Brand Equity Model. It has measured that brand awareness mentioned in the model is influential on the perceived quality and brand loyalty and therefore brand equity contributes to perceived value and revisit intention. Within this framework, it is possible to emphasize that brand equity is not formed by only one factor, but as a result of total interaction of several attributes. According to this research, brand loyalty is the most influential variable among the parameters determining brand equity. It is also observed that as brand loyalty increases, brand equity and perceived service value also increases. This also demonstrates that there is a positive relationship between brand awareness and intention to revisit and that the brands fixed in the minds of tourists are preferred more intensely on a return visit. When consumers buy a service, they are inclined to buy the brands which they have known in advance or they are familiar with, not the ones they have never heard or seen. Brand association is of capital importance for being a strong brand and raises the possibility of a hotel brand being preferred over other brands. Thus, data relating to the awareness of brands which are easily distinguished contribute to brand equity by creating positive behaviors for the hotel brand. Papu and Quester, (2007) explained that tourists can not have any perception about brand equity and perceived value without brand awareness and therefore it is essential to maintain brand awareness in order to create brand equity. The research findings are well-matched with the findings of other scholars who have carried out earlier works in many countries. In the research model, the relationship between brand equity and brand association is also tested and a positive significant relationship between these two components has been measured. It is a fact that tourists will display loyalty to the hotel brands which they have already known, trusted and perceived as quality brands and that they will continue to prefer this kind of brands. Another result of the study is that brand equity has a direct and positive impact on perceived value. Brand equity contributes to the hotels to understand such functions as preparing and assigning data relating to the hotel brand, differentiating the brand from its competitors and creating positive feelings toward the brand. Hotels aim to increase the number of tourists by creating brand loyalty. The way to achieve this is to generate a brand which has a high awareness level, carries strong and unique brand associations and which is perceived as being high quality. The most important factor measuring the future of Jaipur hotels is not their profitability, but to what extent they satisfy their visitors and how valuable they are for their customers. Thus, the hotels acting with a modern service marketing vision should create a strategy of brand equity by managing well the attributes which determine brand equity in order to protect their present tourists, to find new ones and to regain the lost ones.

Implication

Based on the research findings, this research has the following implications in practice for managers: First, this study can help the hotel managers to understand how brand loyalty together with brand awareness can be used in Jaipur hotels. From that, the hotel industry as well as other service industries can apply experiential marketing and experiencing mechanism in their organization in Jaipur where experiential marketing has not been used popularly. Secondly, this research found that among components of experience, advertising had an indirect effect on tourist satisfaction. So managers should focus on innovating in advertising to increase satisfaction of tourists and to have competitive advantages as well.

This article can provide managers with a new look at marketing, especially in the hotel service industries. Most hoteliers have not considered tourist engagement because they assume their tourists are rational and make decisions based on functional product features, for example, price and quality. This assumption is not completely valid today; hotel managers should, therefore, take account of "excellent and unique experiences" for tourists. The outcome of this research also gives empirical support to implement experiential marketing strategies by managers.

In conclusion, the outcomes of this article should help hotel marketing managers develop suitable strategies to plan and implement brand equity and intention to revisit to satisfy their tourists. On the other hand, tourists also benefit from the memorable experiences they desire. Besides, this research makes contributions to academicians: First, this study presents a good model for understanding tourist engagement and tourist experience in the hotel sector. It is useful for academics to use this model to research other service industries. Second, the model of this research added another dimension to the original model, namely, perceived value and intention to revisit and confirmed the results as expected. These results help academicians understand that any component which can contribute to customer experience is of value for the hotel industry.

Limitation, Recommendation and Future Research

As all research works, this study has some limitations and presents a starting point for future research. The first limitation is that this research is based on collected samples according to convenience method while it should be collected according to random method. Because of limited resources, the author cannot approach the study through a detailed description of each hotel's strategy in Jaipur. As a result, hotels who engage with tourists and those who do not appear together. The second, limitation is that brand loyalty and the perceived value of services have only been considered in this study as a general concept. The study has not specifically explored precise attributes of brand loyalty and perceived value of services by tourists. This study has focused on customer engagement and ignored the service culture and service leadership which are important aspects in service sector (Akesson, et al, 2008). To sum up, this study is limited because of the limited conditions and knowledge of the subject. All of these aspects are suggested to overcome further research in the future. Future studies can build on this research and study attributes such as management structures, leadership skills, interdepartmental dynamics as those factors could have in some way affected tourist satisfaction. Prior research showed that a variety of factors such as innovation, geographical location of research, learning, entrepreneurial and employee orientations could affect the hotel performance. There is a significant relationship between the tourist culture and service quality where expectation for diverse services is influenced by the cultural profile of hotels. Thus, future research could include a cultural feature in the framework. Nevertheless, this present research has helped to resolve some of the discrepancies in measuring tourist satisfaction and has highlighted the nature of the relationship between customer satisfaction and customer engagement particularly in Jaipur as a tourist destination. Several suggestions have been made for future research. First, the above research model can be applied to other hospitality areas such as lodging and/or food-service operations. New findings can be compared with the outcomes suggested in this research to examine any differences between different industries. Second, future research can also research particular hotels. From studying specific hotels, perception and service innovation can be studied. Finally, the current research model can also be connected with other important concepts in the marketing field, such as culture. Therefore, the relationship between customer engagement, customer satisfaction, and culture can be developed and may be supported more efficiently.

References

Ahuvia, A. C. (2005), "Beyond the Extended Self: Loved Objects and Consumers' Identity Narratives," Journal of Consumer Research, 32 (1), 171–84.

Anderson, Benedict (1983), Imagined Community. London: Verso.

Anderson, Eugene W. (1998), "Customer Satisfaction and Word-of-Mouth," Journal of Service Research, 1 (1), 5–17.

Bagozzi, Richard P., Youjae Yi, and Lynn W. Phillips (1991), "Assessing Construct Validity in Organizational Research," Administrative Science Quarterly, 36 (3), 421–58.

Bakker, Arnold B., Jari J. Hakanen, Evangelia Demerouti, and Despoina Xanthopoulou (2007), "Job Resources Boost Work Engagement, Particularly When Job Demands Are High, "Journal of Educational Psychology, 99 (2), 274–84.

Ball, A. D. and L. H. Tasaki (1992), "The Role and Measurement of Attachment in Consumer Behavior," Journal of Consumer Psychology, 1 (2), 155–72.

Costello, Anna B. and Jason W. Osborne (2005), "Best Practices in Exploratory Factor Analysis:Four Recommendations for Getting the Most from Your Analysis," Practical Assessment, Research and Evaluation, 10 (7), 1–9.

Cova, Bernard (1997), "Community and Consumption: Towards a Definition of the Linking Value of Product or Services," European Journal of Marketing, 31, 297–316.

Csikszentmihalyi, Mihaly (1990), Flow: The Psychology of Optimal Experience (1st ed.). New York: Harper & Row.

Dabholkar, Pratibha (1990), "How to Improve Perceived Service Quality by Improving Customer Participation," in Development in Marketing Science, B.J. Dunlap (Ed.). Cullowhee, NC: Academy of Marketing Science.

Dabholkar, Pratibha A. and Richard P. Bagozzi (2002), "An Attitudinal Model of Technology-Based Self-Service: Moderating Effects of Consumer Traits and Situational Factors," Journal of the Academy of Marketing Science, 30 (3), 184–201

Etgar, Michael (2008), "A Descriptive Model of the Consumer Co-Production Process," Journal of the Academy of Marketing Science, 36 (1), 97–108.

Falk, P. and C. Campbell (1997), The Shopping Experience. London: Sage.

Fang, Eric R. (2004), "Creating Customer Value through Customer Participation in B2B Markets: A Value Creation and Value Sharing Perspective," Dissertation, University of Missouri-Columbia.

Holbrook, Morris B. (2006), "Rosepekiceciveci Versus Ccv," in The Service-Dominant Logic of Marketing: Dialog, Debate and Directions, Robert F. Lusch and Stephen L. Vargo, Eds. N.Y.: M.E. Sharpe.

Holbrook, Morris B. (1999), "Introduction to Consumer Value," in Consumer Value: A Framework for Analysis and Research, Morris B. Holbrook, Ed. London: Routledge.

Kozinets, R. V. (2001), "Utopian Enterprise: Articulating the Meanings of Star Trek's Culture of Consumption," Journal of Consumer Research, 28 (1), 67–88.

Kozinets, R. V. (1997), "I Want to Believe: A Netnography of the X-Philes' Subculture of Consumption "Advances in Consumer Research, 24, 470–75.

Luschen, G. R. F. and G. H. Sage (1981), Handbook of Social Science of Sport. Champaign, IL: Stipes Publishing Company.

Mahler, David Q. (2000), "An American Century of Retailing," Chain Store Age, April, S44.

Mano, Haim and Richard L. Oliver (1993), "Assessing the Dimensionality and Structure of the Consumption Experience: Evaluation, Feeling, and Satisfaction," Journal of Consumer Research, 20 (3), 451–66.

Margolin, V. (2002), The Politics of the Artificial: Essays on Design and Design Studies. Chicago: University of Chicago Press.

Nix, G., R.M. Ryan, J.B. Maly, and E.L. Deci (1999), "Revitalization through Self-Regulation: The Effects of Autonomous Versus Controlled Motivation on Happiness and Vitality," Journal of Experimental Social Psychology, 35, 266–84.

Nkwocha, Innocent, Yeqing Bao, William C. Johnson, and Herbert V. Brotspies (2005), "Moderating Role of Product Involvement in Brand Extensions," Journal of Marketing Theory and Practice, 13 (3).

Oliver, R. L. (2006), "Co-Producers and Co-Participants in the Satisfaction Process: Mutually Satisfying Consumption.," in The Service Dominant Logic of Marketing: Dialog, Debate and Directions R.F. Lusch and S.L. Vargo, Eds. Armonk, NY: M.E. Sharpe.

Olsen, Svein Ottar (2007), "Repurchase Loyalty: The Role of Involvement and Satisfaction,"

Psychology & Marketing, 24 (4), 315.

Ortiz, Mandy H. (2008), "Three Essaays on Consumer Devotion," The University of Alabama.

Patton, Michael Quinn (2002), Qualitative Research and Evaluation Methods. Thousand Oaks: Sage.

Prahalad, Coimbatore K. and Venkat Ramaswamy (2004), "Co-Creation Experiences: The Next Practice in Value Creation," Journal of Interactive Marketing, 18 (3), 5–14.

Prahalad, Coimbatore Krishnarao and Venkatram Ramaswamy (2003), "The New Frontier of Experience Innovation," MIT Sloan Management Review, 44 (4), 12–18.

Prahalad, Coimbatore K. and Venkatram Ramaswamy (2002), "The Co-Creation Connection," Strategy and Business, 27 (2), 50–61.

Rogers, C.R. (1951), Client-Centered Therapy. New York: Houghton Mifflin.

Sheth, Jagdish N., Bruce I. Newman, and Barbara L. Gross (1991), "Why We Buy What We Buy: A Theory of Consumption Values," Journal of Business Research, 22, 159–70.

Thompson, Craig J., William B. Locander, and Howard R. Pollio (1989), "Putting Consumer Experience Back into Consumer Research: The Philosophy and Method of Existential-Phenomenology," Journal of Consumer Research, 16 (September), 133–46.

Trent, Ashley (2008), "Get the Party Started," in Marketing News.

Unger, L. S. and J. B. Kernan (1983), "On the Meaning of Leisure: An Investigation of Some Determinants of the Subjective Experience," Journal of Consumer Research, 9 (March), 381–92.

Vargo, Stephen L. and Robert F. Lusch (2004), "Evolving to a New Dominant Logic for Marketing," Journal of Marketing, 69 (January), 1–17.

Vargo, Stephen L. and Robert F. Lusch (2008), "Service-Dominant Logic: Continuing the Evolution," Journal of the Academy of Marketing Science, 36 (1), 1–10.

Antecedents and Consequences of Financial Capability and Financial Inclusion for Women Empowerment in Rajasthan: A Scale Development and Validation

Neha Somani* & Avantika Singh*

Abstract

The Eleventh (2007–12) and Twelfth Five Year Plans (2012–17) in India have aimed at inclusive growth, therein implying equitable growth. Towards this aim, it is imperative to address the problems and needs of those groups who so far remain excluded. Women have been the most underprivileged and discriminated section of society not only in India but all over the world, in various aspects of social and economic life, including in the financial sector. The paper elucidates the relationship of financial literacy, financial capability and financial inclusion with women empowerment through a conceptual framework. In this research, scales for financial capability and women empowerment have been developed. Items for the scales were generated through literature review and empirical observations done through focus group discussions with rural women, SHG** women members and in-depth interviews with experts. This research paper discusses the process of scale development, validity testing and reliability testing of financial capability and women empowerment scales. Using Likert scaling, the scales were tested through survey comprising experts in management and social sciences. The validated scale comprised only those items which had high corrected inter-item to total correlation (CITC) and high discriminator values, i.e., high t-values. After scale validation, a pilot study was conducted among 40 women SHG members in Ajmer district. The reliability coefficients were within the acceptable range. The validity and reliability of the scale has been established. The scale can be used for further data collection with respect to this topic of enquiry.

Keywords: Women empowerment, financial literacy, financial capability, financial inclusion, inclusive growth, validity.

Introduction

The Eleventh (2007–12) and Twelfth Five Year Plans (2012–17) in India have aimed for inclusive growth, therein implying equitable growth, in tune with the philosophy of universalism and democratic principles enshrined in the Constitution of India (Planning Commission, 2008, 2013). For growth to be inclusive, it is imperative to focus on the problems and needs of those social groups who have so far remain excluded, such as the

---

* Central University of Rajasthan
** SHG=Self Help Group

poor, the rural, women, Scheduled Castes, Scheduled Tribes, and other disadvantaged and marginalized people. Out of these, women empowerment has sailed high on the policy agenda in recent years, and numerous policies and programmes towards improving the freedom and socio-economic status of women are being implemented. Concomitantly, financial inclusion of women has gained tremendous attention among development practitioners, policymakers, bankers and scholars, particularly in developing countries. Improving access to financial services is viewed as an effective strategy for development of rural people. Sufficient evidence shows enhanced access to banking and other livelihood services speeds up economic growth and also addresses other problems like income inequality and poverty (HM Treasury, 2007).

This research builds upon the conceptual framework developed by the authors (Somani and Singh, 2016), depicting the relationship between financial inclusion and related terms, namely, financial literacy and financial capability, and the impact of these on women empowerment. This research paper discusses the process of scale development and validity testing of scales to measure financial capability and women empowerment. Subsequently the reliability of the scale has been tested. This research paper is organized as follows. The next section presents the literature review and conceptual framework for the study. Subsequently, the research methodology is discussed, followed by results, discussion and conclusion.

Review of Literature

This section presents an overview of the terms focused on in this research, namely, women empowerment, financial inclusion, financial capability and financial literacy.

Women Empowerment

Rappaport (1987: 122) defined empowerment as "a process by which people, organizations, and communities gain mastery over issues of concern to them". Women's empowerment refers to the proliferation in alternatives available to women so that they may pick those alternatives that they consider important and attain improved consequences for themselves as well as society (Kabeer, 2001). Towards its aim of studying the impact of financial inclusion on women empowerment, the present research reviews the research findings on the impact of credit programmes, micro finance institutions (MFIs) and self-help groups (SHG) participation on women empowerment. Hashemi *et al.* (1996) have analyzed the impact of credit programmes on the various indicators of empowerment, namely, economic empowerment, mobility in the public domain, ability to make large and small purchases, ownership of assets, decision making role, freedom from male domination, ability to make choices, decisions related to visit to natal place, sale of jewelry or land, working outside, political empowerment, and a composite of all these indicators. It has been observed that women's access to credit is an important aspect of the magnitude of their economic contribution, increase in asset holding and an increase in purchasing power, their political and legal awareness, and the value of the composite empowerment index. Islam *et al.* (2012) have shown that empowerment of rural women in developing countries can reduce gender inequality.

Financial Inclusion

According to the Rangarajan Committee (2008: 1), "Financial inclusion may be defined as the process of ensuring access to financial services and timely and adequate credit where needed by vulnerable groups such as weaker sections and low income groups at an affordable cost". Financial services comprise savings, loans, insurance, payments, remittance facilities and financial counselling/ advisory services by the formal financial system. However, "It is important to distinguish between access to – the possibility to use – and actual use of financial services" (World Bank, 2008: 2). Financial inclusion ultimately helps in achieving inclusive and sustainable growth by linking disadvantaged groups to the formal financial system.

Financial Capability

Financial capability refers to an individual's ability to manage and take control of their finances (Taylor, 2011). Over their life cycle, individuals have to handle a number of risks. Those individuals who make wise financial choices and successfully interact with financial service providers are more likely to achieve their financial ends, evade financial and economic risks, improve their household's wellbeing, and support economic growth. Financial capability reflects an individual's knowledge of financial matters, their ability to manage their money and to take control of their finances. Financial capability is conceptually distinct from being poor or deprived. A poor and deprived individual may have high financial capability and vice-versa. Public policies on financial inclusion and consumer protection are also laying emphasis on enhancing financial capability (World Bank, 2014).

Financial Literacy

Financial literacy is often equated with the knowledge and skills to make key financial decisions. Studies tend to measure financial literacy based on questions that test knowledge of financial concepts – such as the value of money (inflation), interest rates, compounding, and risk diversification – that are needed to make key financial choices (Huston, 2010; Lusardi and Mitchell, 2009; Xu and Zia, 2012). The OECD (2005: 4) defines financial literacy as "the process by which financial consumers/investors improve their understanding of financial products, concepts and risks, and through information, instruction and/or objective advice, develop the skills and confidence to become more aware of financial risks and opportunities, to make informed choices, to know where to go for help, and to take other effective actions to improve their financial well-being".

Conceptual Framework

The conceptual framework of the study is presented in figure 1. This framework depicts the inter-relationships of financial literacy, financial capability and financial inclusion, and the causal relationship of financial inclusion with women empowerment. According to the framework financial literacy is related with the dimensions of knowledge of financial concepts, skills to make financial decisions and awareness of financial risks and opportunities. Financial capability includes the dimensions of living within means, budgeting, and monitoring expenses, using information, not overspending, and covering unexpected expenses, saving, not being impulsive and achievement orientation. Financial inclusion includes the availability, access and usage of financial services. This research conceptualises that financial literacy and financial capability are positively associated with financial inclusion, and that financial inclusion leads to women empowerment, which includes economic, legal, sociocultural, political, psychological and interpersonal dimensions. Financial capability and financial inclusion are influenced by social, demographic and economic factors, such as educational attainment, income level, occupation and location.

Figure 1: Conceptual Framework of the Study

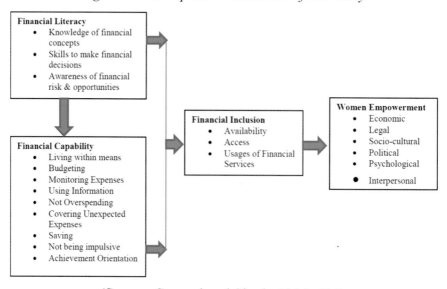

(Source: Somani and Singh, 2016: 496)

Research Methodology

Research Methods

This research is exploratory in nature and employs multiple research methods, namely literature review, focus group discussions (FGDs), in-depth interviews and expert interviews. The literature review covered published works on the themes mentioned in the preceding section. FGDs were conducted with 120 rural women, SHG members in Rajasthan, who participated in the 7th Colloquium on Micro Finance and Livelihoods, organized on January 19–20, 2015 at Jaipur, Rajasthan, by the Centre for Microfinance, Jaipur and the Sir Ratan Tata Trust. The authors of this paper also participated in the Colloquium. These women came from all over Rajasthan, and had been associated with SHGs for at least one year. In-depth interviews were also conducted with 12 key informants from NABARD, Centre for Microfinance, Institute for Development Studies, non-governmental organisations (NGOs), MFIs, and state-government departments dealing with financial inclusion and women empowerment. The focus-group discussions and in-depth interviews enabled the authors to address descriptive questions related to antecedents, obstacles and challenges to financial capability, financial inclusion and women empowerment, and have been published elsewhere (Somani and Singh, 2016).

Based on the information gathered from the literature review, FGDs and in-depth interviews, the authors generated items for financial capability and women empowerment scales. The items were rated by 15 experts (faculty and research scholars) from different departments of Central University of Rajasthan, such as Public Policy Law & Governance, Management, Commerce, Social Work and Economics.

Research Tools

Separate tools were developed to measure the variables under study, namely, financial literacy, financial capability, financial inclusion and women empowerment. The tool for measuring financial literacy section was prepared on the basis of literature review. Questions related to numerical ability, interest calculation and awareness of financial products were included in the tool. The tool for financial inclusion contained questions related to access and usage of financial products. This was a nominal scale with provision for recording responses in the form of yes or no. Yes was represented by 1 and no by 0. The questions were formulated on the basis of insights from the literature review and in-depth interviews with key informants.

For development of scales to measure financial capability and women empowerment, the research tools included note-taking for FGDs, checklists for in-depth interviews with key informants, and structured close-ended questionnaires for interviews with experts. Each research activity, its corresponding research method and tool used for data collection are summarized in table 1. Scale development was done through Likert scaling.

Table 1: Details of the Research Methods and Research Tools Used for Item Generation for Financial Capability and Women Empowerment Scales

S. No.	Purpose	Research Method	Respondent	Tool Used for Data Collection	Output
1.	To collect qualitative data regarding the variables under study	Focus group discussion	Rural women SHG members	Participant observation, note-taking	Generation of items for the scale to measure the variables under study
2.	To collect qualitative data regarding the variables under study	In-depth interview	Key informants such as officers from NABARD, banks, NGOs, government departments, etc.	Checklist	Generation of items for the scale to measure the variables under study
3.	To get experts' opinion about the suitability of items in the scale	Interview	Experts from Central University of Rajasthan	Questionnaire with close-ended questions using Likert scale	Elimination of items with low CITC and low t-values. Preparation of final schedule for survey

Results and Discussion

Validation of Financial Capability and Women Empowerment Scales

The validity testing comprised five steps, namely item generation, deletion of items to eliminate duplication, rating of items by experts, computation of t-values and CITC scores, and elimination of items with low scores. These steps are outlined in figure 2.

In the first step, items related to financial capability and women empowerment were generated from the information gathered through literature review, focus group discussions and key informant interviews. This process resulted in the generation of 240 items. In the second step, the researchers reviewed the items and deleted 107 of them on the basis of duplication or irrelevance. After deletion, a total of 133 items were left, including 73 items on financial capability and 60 on women empowerment. The third step comprised rating of items by 15 experts using Likert scaling, which is a unidimensional scaling method. Each of the 133 items was evaluated by experts individually using a paper-based test in terms of degree of agreement with the construct under study. The rating scale varied from 1 as strongly unfavorable to the concept, 2 as somewhat unfavorable to the concept, 3 as undecided, 4 as somewhat favorable to the concept, and 5 as strongly favorable to the concept. In the fourth step, the data was fed into SPSS v.21. The scale comprised few reversal items, the responses for which were reversed at the time of data entry. The corrected inter-item to total correlations (CITC) and t-values were computed.

Figure 2: Process of Validation of Financial Capability and Women Empowerment Scales

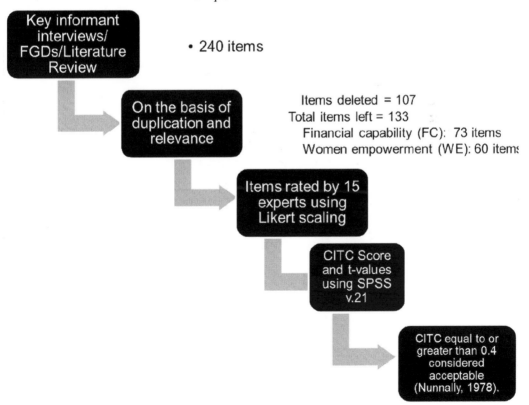

In the last step, the items with CITC equal to or greater than 0.4 were retained in the scale. The items which had high t-values were considered to be better discriminators and were retained in the scale. For each item, the CITC score presents the correlations with each other as well as with the total correlation across all items. Thus, in this process, a new variable is created which is the sum of all individual items for every respondent or expert and this new variable is included in the correlation matrix computation. In social science research, the item-to-total correlation equal to or greater than 0.4 is considered acceptable (Nunnally, 1978). The items with CITC values below 0.4 were highlighted in order to remove from the scale. The CITC scores of items for financial capability are presented in table 2 and that for women empowerment in table 3. The items with low CITC scores are marked in bold text.

Table 2: CITC Score of Financial Capability Scale Items

Item description	CITC Score
A1 I am able to earn sufficiently to fulfill my family's requirements	0.4
A2 I don't have a regular source of income (R)	0.4
A3 I spend money unnecessarily and unwisely (R)	**-0.203**
A4 I try to control expenses or more careful while expending.	0.4
A5 I spend money on items that are beneficial for the entire household.	**0.385**
A6 I spend money on items that help the family improve its living conditions.	**0.048**
A7 When I receive money, I plan how I will use it.	**0.262**
A8 I do not prepare plans and budgets.	**-0.015**
A9 I am never late at paying my bills.	**0.087**
A10 I have to borrow in order to meet major expenses such as rent.	**0.376**
A11 I have to make cutbacks in order to meet major expenses such as rent.	0.444
A12 I spend according to income.	**0.251**
A13 I spend more than income.	0.666
A14 I face shortfall of money for necessities.	0.892
A15 I know the coping strategies to cover shortfalls.	0.664
A16 I have a good idea about my monthly expenses.	**0.273**
A17 I have to borrow money to pay off the debt which I owe.	0.625

Item description	CITC Score
A18 When I run short of money for food, I borrow from family, friends and work colleagues.	0.63
A19 When I run short of money for food, I find extra work/work extra hours.	0.558
A20 I run short of money for food and other necessity items because I have fluctuating/non reliable income.	0.556
A21 I run short of money for food and other necessity items because I have no work/unable to work.	0.41
A22 I run short of money for food and other necessity items because of unexpected events and expenses.	**0.015**
A23 I run short of money for food and other necessity items because of increase in the cost of food and necessity products.	**-0.064**
A24 I get information or advice from my colleagues, friends, family members, etc. when I have an important decision to make related to finance.	0.447
A25 I verify terms and conditions while doing agreement/buying product.	0.599
A26 I personally buy things that are not necessary before I have bought food and paid for other necessity items.	**0.384**
A27 I personally buy things which I know that are not necessary even though I know I can't afford them.	**0.037**
A28 If tomorrow I have to meet any major unexpected expenses, I could cover it full or without borrowing money.	**0.352**
A29 I prefer to buy things on credit rather than wait and save up	**0.294**
A30 I have saving in a secret place or with friends/family.	0.683
A31 When I have money left after the expenditure on food and necessity items, I save for emergency/ uncertainty.	0.432
A32 When I have money left after the expenditure on food and necessity items, I save for planned expenditures.	0.543
A33 I don't think and plan for the future	0.632
A34 I plan for the long-term such as children's education and marriages.	0.589
A35 I plan for emergencies and unexpected events.	0.548
A36 I don't have surplus fund so I don't invest.	0.404
A37 I actively seek new investment opportunities.	**0.387**
A38 I borrow from moneylenders and other informal sources and pay high interest.	0.579

Item description	CITC Score
A39 I have access to loan and borrow from bank/ PACS/ SHGs, etc.	0.419
A40 I have a bank account	0.63
A41 I save regularly and deposit in bank account/ or with SHG.	0.607
A42 I use savings for emergencies, retirement and to build assets.	0.512
A43 I have a habit of regular saving.	0.537
A44 I don't save and have no saving.	0.476
A45 I have insurance cover for at least one family member.	0.418
A46 I have no insurance.	0.456
A47 We have unity in the family and good coordination among the family members.	**0.044**
A48 I have good reputation and support in the society.	**0.227**
A49 I have good relations in the community.	0.52
A50 My friends will support me in times of need.	0.642
A51 We own land and property.	**-0.261**
A52 We own livestock.	**0.313**
A53 We own tractor and other farm equipment	**-0.144**
A54 We own motor vehicles/ two wheelers.	**-0.109**
A55 I lack education and any specialized skills	**0.16**
A56 I am well educated and possess specialized skills.	**-0.179**
A57 I live more for the present than for tomorrow.	**0.341**
A58 I keep provisions for old age.	0.503
A59 I plan for major expenses like marriage, house construction, etc.	0.439
A60 I plan for expected events like children education, etc.	0.599
A61 I plan for unexpected events like flood, diseases, death, etc.	0.703
A62 I find it more satisfying to spend money than to save it for the long term.	**0.195**
A63 I don't waste money/spend impulsively.	0.414
A64 I prefer to buy things on credit rather than wait and save up.	0.464
A65 I only buy products which are appropriate for my family's needs.	0.327
A66 I always work hard to be among the best at what I do.	**0.027**

Item description	CITC Score
A67 I am concerned about my social status among people I know.	**-0.019**
A68 I want other people to respect me.	0.621
A69 At times I learn from my friends that how they are developing, and if I felt that I were not progressing well then I might copy them or ask them how I manage to be where they are.	**-0.101**
A70 At times I learn after experiencing some problems.	**0.329**
A71 If I save and invest regularly, eventually the small amount will add up and I will be secure.	0.747
A72 I make financial decisions for myself.	**0.239**
A73 I make financial decisions for my family.	0.717
AT	1

Source: Field Study

Out of the 73 items in the financial capability scale, 29 items with low CITC score were identified. Out of 60 items in the women empowerment scale, 17 items with low CITC Score were identified.

Table 3: CITC Score of Women Empowerment Scale Items

Item Description	CITC Score
B1 I often visit hospital	**0.049**
B2 I often visit cinema	0.722
B3 I often visit natal places (maternal home)	0.608
B4 I often visit market for shopping	0.562
B5 I visit cooperative society or NGOs or SHGs	0.782
B6 I can move within the village independently	**0.129**
B7 I often visit friends and relatives'	0.778
B8 I often visit the bank	0.669
B9 I can take decision of enrolment of children to school.	0.487
B10 I can make an appointment with the doctor/ go to doctor for my children or for my treatment.	0.502
B11 I can involve with any cooperative society or NGOs or SHGs.	0.424

Item Description	CITC Score
B12 I can decide to visit to father's or other relative's house	**-0.063**
B13 I purchase items for myself like oil, cosmetics, clothes, etc.	0.61
B14 I purchase small items of daily cooking preparation like cooking oil, vegetables, spices, etc.	**-0.028**
B15 I can take decision of purchase or sale of land.	0.882
B16 I can decide vaccination of children.	0.421
B17 I take decision of adoption of family planning.	**0.121**
B18 I can decide about spending of my own money.	**0.076**
B19 I can spend my husband's money	**0.253**
B20 I can decide about marriage of my children.	**0.199**
B21 I can decide about when to have children and number of children to have.	**0.131**
B22 I offer presentation/gifts to relatives on a particular occasion.	0.648
B23 I can borrow or lend money.	0.801
B24 I can take decision about house repairing.	0.852
B25 I exercise control on family income and expenditure.	0.749
B26 I buy household assets (such as a refrigerator or TV)	0.659
B27 I initiate income generating activities independently.	0.526
B28 I can work outside home.	0.637
B29 I provide economic and social support to other relatives.	0.646
B30 I can join women's societies or other societies.	**0.203**
B31 I can talk with unknown persons.	0.48
B32 I can take decision about children's education'.	**0.18**
B33 I seek treatment for a sick family member.	0.408
B34 I adopt family planning methods.	**0.212**
B35 I share opinion with husband about having children.	**0.217**
B36 I cast vote in election independently.	0.608
B37 I possess television/watch/sofa/refrigerator/etc. in my own name.	0.586
B38 I have my own gold ornaments.	0.526

Item Description	CITC Score
B39 I save and invest money.	0.739
B40 I have land in my own name.	0.487
B41 My family members can take away land and jewelry against my will.	**0.387**
B42 My family prevents me to visit my natal home.	**-0.457**
B43 My family prevents me to work outside home.	**0.066**
B44 I have experienced verbal or physical abuse from husband.	**-0.327**
B45 I listen radio.	0.617
B46 I watch television.	0.617
B47 read newspaper.	0.475
B48 I am involved in women's club or society.	0.766
B49 I am involved in women's committee.	0.809
B50 I am involved in NGO activities.	0.797
B51 I am involved in cooperative society.	0.62
B52 I am involved in local government institution.]	0.756
B53 I am able to feed my family with my earnings.	0.73
B54 I am able to educate my children with my earnings.	0.529
B55 I contribute large share of income in my family.	0.637
B56 I take major decisions in the household.	0.515
B57 I help neighbors.	0.411
B58 I resolve local conflicts.	0.497
B59 I protest against actions which badly affect the community.	0.438
B60 I use the loan amount taken by SHG/Bank in fulfilling my own purpose.	0.423
BT	1

Source: Field Study

After computation of CITC scores, the average rating for each item was calculated. Thereafter, the responses for each item were arranged in descending order. The top quarter and bottom quarter of responses for each item were selected, their means were calculated followed by t-test. Table 4 presents the t-values of the items in the financial capability scale and table 5 depicts those in the women empowerment scale. The t-test helps us find evidence of a significant difference between the means of the two groups. Higher t-value means that there is a significant difference between the two means. In other words, the items with higher t-values are better discriminators, and are therefore, retained in the scale. According to the tables 4 and 5, only those items were considered which had high discriminator value (1 or more than 1). These items were marked in bold in these tables. This process resulted in eliminating items with low CITC score (less than 0.4) and low t-values (less than 1). Finally the financial capability scale had 35 items and women empowerment scale had 42 items.

Table 4: t-values of the Items of Financial Capability Scale

Item No.	Upper	Bottom	Difference	Item No.	Upper	Bottom	Difference
A1	4.67	3.33	**1.34**	A38	3.33	4.67	1
A2	5	4.67	0.33	A39	4	5	**1.99**
A3	4	4.33	0.33	A40	5.67	4.67	1
A4	3.33	4.33	**1**	A41	4	5	1
A5	5	4.33	0.67	A42	4	5	1
A6	4.67	4.67	0	A43	4	5	1
A7	4.67	4.67	0	A44	4	5	1
A8	4.33	4	0.33	A45	4	5	1
A9	4.67	4	0.67	A46	4.33	5	0.67
A10	4.67	4	0.67	A47	4.67	4.67	0
A11	4.33	4	0.33	A48	4.67	4	0.67
A12	5	4.67	0.33	A49	4	4.33	0.33
A13	5	4	**1**	A50	5.67	4.67	1
A14	5	4	**1**	A51	4	4	0
A15	5	3.33	**1.67**	A52	4.67	4	0.67
A16	5	5	0	A53	4.67	4	0.67
A17	5	2.33	**2.67**	A54	4.67	4.67	0
A18	5	4	**1**	A55	4.67	4	0.67
A19	5	4	**1**	A56	4	4.33	-0.33
A20	5	3.33	**1.67**	A57	4,67	4.67	0

A21	4.33	3.33	**1**	A58	4.67	4	0.67
A22	4	4	0	A59	5	4.67	0.33
A23	4.33	4	0.33	A60	5	4	**1**
A24	5	4	**1**	A61	5	2.67	**2.33**
A25	5	4	**1**	A62	4.67	4.67	0
A26	4	3.67	0.33	A63	4.67	4	0.67
A27	4	4.33	0.33	A64	4.67	4.33	0.34
A28	4	4.67	0.33	A65	5.33	4.33	**1**
A29	4.67	4.33	0.34	A66	5	4.67	0.33
A30	6.34	4.67	**1.67**	A67	4.33	4.33	0
A31	4	5	**1**	A68	4.67	3.67	**1**
A32	4	5	**1**	A69	3.67	4	-0.33
A33	6.67	5	**1.67**	A70	4.67	4.67	0
A34	3.33	5	**1.67**	A71	5	4	**1**
A35	4	5	**1**	A72	4	4	0
A36	4	5	**1**	A73	5	2.67	**2.33**
A37	6	4.5	1.5				

Source: Field Study

Table 5: t-values of the Items of Women Empowerment Scale

Item No.	Upper	Lower	Difference	Item No.	Upper	Lower	Difference
B1	4.33	3.67	0.66	B31	5	4.67	0.33
B2	4.67	3	**1.67**	B32	4.67	3	**1.67**
B3	4.67	2.67	**2**	B33	5	3.67	**1.33**
B4	5	3.67	**1.33**	B34	4.67	3.33	**1.34**
B5	4.67	2.67	**2**	B35	4.67	3.67	**1**
B6	4.33	4.67	-0.34	B36	5	4.67	0.33
B7	5	3.67	**1.33**	B37	5	3	**2**
B8	5	4	**1**	B38	5	4	**1**
B9	5	4.33	0.67	B39	5	4.67	0.33

B10	5	4	**1**	B40	5	4	**1**
B11	5	4	**1**	B41	2.67	1.67	**1**
B12	5	4.67	0.33	B42	2.33	3.33	**1**
B13	5	4	**1**	B43	2.67	2.67	**1**
B14	4.67	4.33	0.34	B44	2.33	2.33	0
B15	5	3.33	**1.67**	B45	5	4.67	0.33
B16	4.67	3.67	**1**	B46	5	4.67	0.33
B17	4.33	4	0.33	B47	5	4.67	0.33
B18	5	4.67	0.33	B48	5	3.67	**1.33**
B19	4.67	4	0.67	B49	5	2.67	**2.33**
B20	4.67	3.67	**1**	B50	5	3	**2**
B21	4.67	4	0.67	B51	5	3	**2**
B22	5	3.67	**1.33**	B52	5	3.67	**1.33**
B23	5	3	**2**	B53	5	4.33	0.67
B24	5	3.67	**1.33**	B54	4.67	4.33	0.34
B25	5	4.33	0.67	B55	5	4.33	0.67
B26	5	4.33	0.67	B56	5	4.67	0.33
B27	5	4.33	0.67	B57	4.67	4	0.67
B28	5	4.67	0.33	B58	4.33	3.67	0.66
B29	5	4.67	0.33	B59	5	4.33	0.67
B30	4.67	4	0.67	B60	5	4	**1**

Source: Field Study

Pilot Testing

The final scale was then used for conducting pilot survey among 40 women SHG members in Ajmer district of Rajasthan. Data was collected through a schedule comprising five sections, namely, socio-demographic details of respondents, financial literacy, financial inclusion, financial capability and women empowerment. A sample of 40 respondents was identified through multistage random sampling, comprising various stages of sample unit selection. At the first stage, Rajasthan State was selected, followed by Ajmer district, and then four Blocks/Tehsils of Ajmer were randomly selected out of nine Blocks/ Tehsils. Finally, 10 SHG members were selected from each of these four Blocks/Tehsils on the basis of expert/judgment sampling. Due care was taken to ensure representativeness of respondents. Data was collected through schedules administered through personal visits. The respondents under the study comprised 40 female SHG members. The respondents' demographic and socio-economic characteristics are summarized in Table 6.

Table 6: Demographic and Socio-Economic Characteristics of SHG Members in the Pilot Study

S.No.	Characteristic	N	Percentage
1.	**Age group (in years)**		
	20–30	15	37.50%
	31–40	16	40%
	41–50	5	12.50%
	51–60	4	10%
	61 and above	-	-
2.	**Marital Status**		
	Married	40	100%
	Unmarried	-	-
3.	**Education**		
	Illiterate	20	50%
	Literate but not formally educated	2	5%
	No. of years of formal education completed (Up to 5th standard)	18	45%
	Graduate and higher	-	-
4.	**Number of Children**		
	None	-	-
	1	4	10%
	2	15	37.50%
	3	14	35%
	More than 3	7	17.50%
5.	**Occupation**		
	Self employed	6	15%

	Agricultural labourer	18	45%
	Daily wage labourer	12	30%
	Self-Reported Monthly Income (Rs.)		
6.	Up to 1000	-	-
	1001–3000	2	5%
	3001–5000	18	45%
	5001–7000	18	45%
	7001–9000	2	5%
7.	**Number of earning adults in the family**		
	1	5	12.50%
	2	31	77.50%
	3	4	10%
	More than 3	-	
8.	**Period of Affiliation with SHG**		
	Less than 1 year	2	5%
	1–2 years	15	37.50%
	3–5 years	20	50%
	6–8 years	3	7.50%
	8–10 years	-	-
	More than 10 years	-	
9.	**Religion**		
	Hindu	25	62.50%
	Muslim	15	37.50%
	Christian/Jain/Sikh/Other	-	-
10.	**Caste/Category**		
	General	5	12.50%
	OBC	20	50%
	SC	10	25%
	ST	5	12.50%

Source: Pilot Study

Reliability Analysis

In order to purify the scale items further, a quantitative assessment was done at this stage. For this, the reliability of the scale was tested with the help of Cronbach's Alpha which is used as a measure of internal consistency (Chandra and Kumar, 2011). The Cronbach's Alpha estimates the variation in scores of different variables is attributable to chance or random errors (Selltiz et al., 1976). The reliability analysis showed that Cronbach's alpha coefficient of the scale of women empowerment was 0.705 and for the scale of financial capability was 0.862, which is more than the minimum value of 0.60 suggested by researchers. This value indicates the acceptable range of scale reliability (Hair, et al. 2003). The values of Cronbach's Alpha for both scales were well above 0.60, thereby indicating that the survey instrument is reliable.

Conclusion

The present research paper builds upon a framework that conceptualizes the relationship between financial literacy, financial capability, financial inclusion and women empowerment. The paper elucidates the detailed process of scale development, validity testing and reliability testing. The items for the scale were developed through literature review, focus-group discussions and expert testing. Subsequently the scales were validated through computation of CITC scores and t-values. A pilot survey on a sample of 40 women SHG members was carried out in Ajmer district of Rajasthan. Reliability of the scales was established through computation of Cronbach's alpha.

This research has provided a valid and reliable instrument for collecting data related to financial capability and women empowerment. Future researchers can use this instrument for full-fledged data collection. This scale may be used for evaluating the impact of financial inclusion and financial capability programmes on women empowerment. In the post-demonetisation scenario in India, more than ever before, the time is now ripe for public policy initiatives in the areas of digital financial inclusion, particularly the use of debit cards, mobile banking and cashless transactions. The research instrument shared in this research may be used for assessing the impact of digital financial inclusion on women empowerment.

References

Chandra, A. & Kumar, R. (2011). Determinants of individual investor behaviour: An orthogonal linear transformation approach. MPRA. Paper No. 29722, 1–31. Available at: http://mpra.ub.uni-muenchen.de /29722 Accessed October 06, 2015.

Hair, Jr., J.F., Babin, B., Money, A.H., & Samouel, P. (2003). *Essentials of business research methods*. New Jersey: John Wiley & Sons.

Hashemi, S.M., Schuler, S.R., & Riley, A.P. (1996). Rural credit programs and women's empowerment in Bangladesh. *World Development, 24: 4*, 635–653.

Hutson, J. (2010). Measuring financial literacy. *The Journal of Consumer Affairs, 44: 2*, 296–316. doi: 10.1111/j.1745–6606.2010.01170.x

HM Treasury. (2007). *Financial capability: The Government's long-term approach*. Norwich: HMSO.

Islam, N., Ahmed, E., Chew, J., & D'Netto, B. (2012). Determinants of empowerment of rural women in Bangladesh. *World Journal of Management, 4: 2*, 36–56.

Kabeer, N., (2001). Conflicts over credit: Re-evaluating the empowerment potential of loans to women in rural Bangladesh. *World Development, 29: 1*, 63–84.

Lusardi, A., & Mitchell, O.S. (2009). How ordinary consumers make complex economic decisions: financial literacy and retirement readiness. Available at: http://www.dartmouth.edu/~alusardi/Papers/LusardiMitchellOrdinaryConsumers.pdf Accessed: October 22, 2015.

Nunnally, J. C. (1978), *Psychometric theory*. McGraw Hill: New York.

Planning Commission, Government of India. (2008). *Eleventh Five Year Plan (2007–12): Inclusive growth. Volume I*. New Delhi: Oxford.

Planning Commission, Government of India. (2013). *Twelfth Five Year Plan (2012–17): Faster, more inclusive and sustainable growth. Volume I*. New Delhi: Sage.

OECD. (2005). *Recommendations on principles and good practices for financial inclusion and awareness*. OECD. Available at: http://www.oecd.org/finance/financial-education/35108560.pdf Accessed January 20, 2017.

OECD. (2014). *All on board: Making inclusive growth happen*. OECD.

Rangrajan Committee. (2008). *Report of the committee on financial inclusion*. Available at: https://www.nabard.org/pdf/Full_Report.pdf Accessed: October 22, 2015.

Rappaport, J., (1987). Terms of empowerment/exemplars of prevention: Towards a theory for community psychology. *American Journal of Community Psychology, 15: 2,* 121–148.

Selltiz, C., Wrightsman, L.S., & Cook, W. (1976). *Research methods in social relations.* New York: Holt, Rinehart and Winston.

Somani, N., & Singh, A. (2016) Determinants and outcomes of financial capability and financial inclusion for women empowerment in Rajasthan: A conceptual framework and qualitative study. In R. Kasilingam, B. Rajeswari, & R.C. Sivasuramanian (Eds.). *Intelligence, innovation and inclusion: Best practices for global excellence* (pp. 492–501). Chennai: Vijay Nicole.

Taylor, M. (2011). Measuring financial capability and its determinants using survey data. *Social Indicators Research, 102: 2,* 297–314.

World Bank. (2008). *Finance for all? Policies and pitfalls in expanding access.* Washington, D.C.: The World Bank.

World Bank. (2013). *Making sense of financial capability surveys around the world: A review of existing financial capability and literacy measurement instruments.* Washington, D.C.: The World Bank.

World Bank. (2014). *Enhancing financial capability and inclusion in Morocco: A demand side assessment.* Washington, D.C.: The World Bank.

Xu. L., & Zia, B. (2012). *Financial literacy around the world: An overview of the evidence with practical suggestions for the way forward.* Policy Research Working Paper 6107. Washington, D.C.: The World Bank.

Appraising Banking Correspondents Model as an Indicator of Financial Inclusion

Shobhit Goel*

Abstract

The banking sector is an integral part of the broader financial system and constitutes a key provider of finance to business. A well-functioning banking system provides incentives for savings and efficiently channels them to productive investments. It facilitates the exchange of goods and services and supports and promotes a more efficient allocation of resources in the economy. In general, a healthy, robust and stable banking sector plays a crucial role in supporting economic activity, promoting economic growth and ensuring financial stability. Realizing the tremendous need to bring formal banking to the masses, the Government of India with ample support from the nation's banking regulator the Reserve Bank of India (RBI) has undertaken various measures from time to time for financial inclusion (FI).

The drive to cover the un-banked Indian population, has led to initiatives such as the "Lead Bank Scheme", "No Frills Account" (NFA) and more lately promotion of financial inclusion through "Business Correspondent" (BC) model. With the aid of technology-enabled branchless banking initiatives, this drive has been successful in regards to extending access to millions of the Indian population. However, empirical evidence suggests that while the BC model has been highly successful in some places, it has remained underutilized at many other centres. Since the BC model is inclusive of various diverse sources and backgrounds such a behavior is quite expected. The main two drivers of the BC model vis-à-vis company based BCs and individual BCs both have their own strengths and shortcomings. While the company based BCs have been able to provide better access by opening centres at various points throughout the length and breadth of the country with distant locations and diverse regional and climatic conditions it is the individual BC who has proved by way of his performance that limited resources are no bottlenecks in better utilization of its centres.

The paper has taken into account a case study of the performances of both the above discussed types of BC centres, two individual BC centres and two company based BC centres around the city of Lucknow to examine the reasons for underutilization of company based BCs and also recommends ways to improve their performance in better achievement of the goal of financial inclusion. While the difficulties faced by low

---

* Business School Amity University, Lucknow

income households in accessing banking services presents a case for the acceptance of BC model for expanding the reach of banking services, it is important to note that the measures of FI success should not be focused on providing access alone but also to simultaneously educate the masses about various aspects of financial services which can be rendered through these initiatives if the term financial inclusion is to have its true and fullest expression.

Keywords: Financial Inclusion, poorest of the poor, Business Correspondent, Government, case study.

Introduction

Inclusive growth i.e. a broad based growth, shared growth, and pro-poor growth is possible only through proper mechanisms which channelize all the available resources from top to bottom. Financial inclusion is an innovative concept which makes alternative techniques to promote the banking habits of the people especially the rural people in a country like India which is largely rural in nature in terms of area and number of people. Financial inclusion is aimed at providing banking and financial services to all people in a fair, transparent and equitable manner at affordable cost. Households with low income often lack access to bank account and have to spend time and money for multiple visits to avail the banking services, be it opening a savings bank account or availing a loan, these families find it more difficult to save and to plan financially for the future.

In recent years, India has witnessed a high rate of economic growth, which has resulted in greater personal wealth for many Indians. However, a vast section of the society is still financially excluded, meaning it does not have access to formal financial institutions. In light of recent research that shows a strong correlation between financial exclusion and poverty and inequality, the Indian government has made financial inclusion an integral part of its planning strategy. But how do you spread a banking network to a huge number of settlements at an affordable cost? In India, an effort has been made to achieve financial inclusion by using information and communication technology through a Business Correspondent model.

Financial inclusion as defined by the Reserve Band of India (RBI) is the process of ensuring access to appropriate financial products and services needed by all sections of the society in general and vulnerable groups such as weaker sections and low income groups in particular, at an affordable cost, in a fair and transparent manner, by regulated, mainstream institutional players

India has more than 6.3 lac villages. Apart from the villages in States like Kerala, Mizoram etc., most of the villages have good percentage of illiteracy with the unsuspecting villagers being vulnerable to local money lenders. Shivering tales of how the money lenders have exploited such villagers for generations are rampant throughout the country.

To bring about a change and to take formal and systemic banking to the masses the Government and the RBI have from time to time come out with various measures to propagate financial inclusion which have been tabulated later in this paper.

Since the inception of the BC model, a large number of organizations are now working as BCs/BFs for banks and, while these agencies are experiencing business growth in terms of client outreach and transaction volumes, many are struggling to remain financially viable.

Review of Literature

A study conducted by the Skoch Development Foundation revealed that, at the end of two years, the gap between costs and what banks pay their BCs is between Rs. 26.25 to Rs. 73.45 per account. Nonetheless, even though the current model seems to be unviable for most BCs, a large majority of BCs continue to believe that this model has the potential to thrive in the long run by expanding the existing client base and adding value added services.

However, little knowledge on the cost and revenue patterns of the various BC models (specifically at the agent or customer service provider level) is available in the public domain. Beyond a certain threshold, the traditional commercial bank branch could prove to be too expensive and too far removed from the local community to be an effective channel for financial services to every single household. Such constraints can be overcome by working through the BCs and BFs. This model also provides the opportunity for many existing institutions (such as the non-profit MFIs, cooperative credit societies, and self-help promoting institutions (SHPIs)) to get linked to mainstream commercial banks to offer savings and other financial services (Bindu Ananth & Asha Krishnakumar, 2010).

BC is a better alternative than Bank Branches: Normally a rural bank branch can serve 3,000 to 4,000 families in 12 to 15 villages within a radius of around 15 kilometers. A Bank branch may typically require more than 5 years to break even in unbanked area, while a private sector and foreign bank with IT connectivity may require more time. The BC option potentially enables banks to reach out at much lower cost (Yeshu Bansal &N. Srinivasan, 2009).

Rationale of the Study

In addition, while BC agents serve as a crucial element in the success of the BC model, little is known about how the behavior of agents is affected by different incentive mechanisms employed in different models. Lastly, there is a dearth of information about the reasons behind dormancy of accounts, low transactions in client accounts and client drop-out – issues that critically affect the viability of the BC model in the long run. Hence, our study undertook a two- step analysis. First, we looked at the crucial aspects of cost and revenue pattern of agents/customer service providers of BCs. Second, we focused on issues related to agent and client behavior in order to critically assess the feasibility of the BC model.

Research Design and Methodology

The study is empirical in nature though it draws heavily on first hand data. The primary data is collected through structural questionnaires personally administered by the researcher.

The data has been collected by the participant approach and by interacting with the participants like officials of NGOs, Bankers and SHG members, experts in the field and by referring to relevant documents and literature.

Reasons of Financial Exclusion

Let us now briefly glance through the reasons for the hitherto financial exclusion of the masses.

  (i) Geographical Location –
- remoteness of residence
- hilly & sparsely populated areas with poor infrastructure & difficult physical access
- distance from bank branch
- branch timings

 (ii) Economic Factors –
- low income
- low assets

(iii) Social Factors –
- ease of availability of informal credit
- culture

- ☐ Gender
- ☐ (iv) Financial illiteracy-
- ☐ illiteracy
- ☐ lack of awareness

(v) Documentation Process –
- ☐ Cumbersome
- ☐ KYC – documentary proof of identity/address

(vi) In-efficiency of the financial Institutions –
- ☐ high cost of operations
- ☐ less volume & more number of clients
- ☐ unsuitable products
- ☐ language
- ☐ staff attitude
- ☐ poor functioning and financial health of some financial institutions (such as financial Cooperatives) which limit the effectiveness of their outreach figures.
- ☐ Primary Agricultural Cooperative Societies (PACS), which restrict their membership to persons with land ownership are also not effective in offering savings services.

Consequences of Financial Exclusion

After hovering at a moderate 3.5 percent pace from the 1950s through the 1980s, India's economic growth rate accelerated to 6.5 percent between 1990 and 2010. However, the growth has not been shared equally. Income inequality, as measured by the Gini Coefficient, increased from 32.9 in 1993 to 36.2 in 2004 and much of the population of the country remains financially excluded. For example, according to 2008 data from India's National Sample Survey Office, 45.9 million farmer households, of the total 89.3 million farmer households, did not have access to formal credit. As of June 2007, the bank-to-population ratio was a dismal 1:16,000. Out of 600,000 settlements in the country, only 30,000 had a bank branch.

Recent studies have shown a strong link between the degree of financial exclusion and rates of poverty and inequality: the higher the financial exclusion, the higher the inequality and poverty. Hence, in India, financial inclusion has been made an integral part of poverty alleviation strategies, and the Eleventh Five Year Plan envisioned financial inclusion as a key objective.

TABLE 1: Composite Index of Financial Inclusion

Country	Composite Index of Financial Inclusion Percentage of adults (aged 15+) with accounts at a formal financial institution in 2012	Poverty Percentage of Population below national poverty line	Unemployment Percentage of labor force	Gini Index
India	35.2	22%(2015)	4.4(2005)	33,4(2005)
Bangladesh	39.6	22%(2015)	5.0(2009)	32.1(2010)
Brazil	55.9	10%(2013)	8.3(2009)	54.7(2009)
China	63.8	2.8(2004)	4.3(2009)	42.5(2005)
Indonesia	19.6	12.5(2011)	7.1(2010)	34.0(2005)
Korean Republic	93.0	----------	3.7(2010)	31.6(1998)
Malaysia	66.2	3.8(2009)	3.7(2009)	46.2(2009)
Philippines	26.6	25.2(2012)	7.4(2010)	43.0(2009)
Sri Lanka	68.5	8.9(2010)	4.9(2010)	40.3(2007)
Thailand	72.7	13.2 (2011)	1.2(2009)	40.0(2009)

Source: World Bank, 2015 http://povertydata.worldbank.org/poverty/region/LAC | Retrieved May 12, 2015

The consequences can be pointed below as follows:

- Affects individuals and economy alike
- The households, micro and small enterprises dealing entirely in cash are susceptible to irregular cash flows would be affected
- Limits options for providing for old age security
- Recourse to informal lenders
- Exposed to higher interest rates charged by informal lender
- Highest risk as loans are often secured against the borrower's property
- Banking with informal sources does not provide interest benefit and tax advantages and are far less secure
- In the most severe forms, it could ultimately lead to social exclusion.

Major Benefits of financial Inclusion

- ☐ For the customer can avail a variety of financial products provided by institutions regulated and supervised by credible regulators.
- ☐ The regulator benefits from the audit trail which is available as transactions are conducted transparently in supervised environment.
- ☐ The economy benefits, as greater financial resources become transparently available for efficient intermediation and allocation, for uses that have the highest returns.
- ☐ It strengthens the financial deepening and leads to financial development in a country, which would in-turn accelerate economic growth of the country.

Major Government and the Regulator initiatives

The government and the regulator, in this case the RBI have taken several measures from time to time to bring about financial inclusion in the country. These include

- ☐ Nationalization of banks
- ☐ Prescription of priority sector targets
- ☐ Lending to weaker sections at concessional rates
- ☐ Initiation of the lead bank scheme
- ☐ Regional Rural Banks (RRBs),
- ☐ Urban Co-operative Banks (UCBs)
- ☐ Primary Agricultural Credit Societies (PACS)
- ☐ Self-Help Groups (SHGs)
- ☐ The Financial Inclusion Technology Fund (FITF)
- ☐ Formation of 1 lac Customer Service Centres (CSCs) in 6 lac villages
- ☐ Simplification of the KYC Norms
- ☐ Pilot Project of SLBC for 100% Financial Inclusion
- ☐ Use of appropriate technology viz., smart card/mobile technology to extend banking services
- ☐ Formulation of an Incentive Scheme for quicker adoption of Electronic Benefit
- ☐ Financial Literacy and Credit Counseling
- ☐ Targeting of villages where population is more than 2000 people for 100% Financial Inclusion now is being extended to villages with population 2000.
- ☐ Lead Bank Scheme: This scheme was introduced in 1969 whereby a particular district was assigned by RBI to a particular public sector bank. This lead bank is responsible for promoting banking services and financial literacy in that district in-coordination with other banks.

☐ No frills account: This scheme was introduced in 2005 whereby banks were instructed to open accounts with very low balance or zero balance.

☐ Business Correspondents: This scheme was introduced in 2006 to extend banking facility to unbanked regions and has been discussed in details subsequently in this paper.

☐ Mandatory 25% rural branches: This scheme has been introduced from this year whereby of the total no. of bank branch licenses to be granted to bank's 25% have to be in rural areas.

Business Correspondents (BC) Model

A BC is an entity that acts as a teller for the bank and carries out a full range of transactions on behalf of the bank. BCs are paid commissions by banks for the services they render. Initially, only non-governmental organizations (NGOs), micro-finance institutions, registered nonbanking financial companies, and post offices were allowed to function as BCs. However, now the guidelines have been expanded to include individuals, local grocery shops, and for-profit companies. The objective of establishing the BC role was to reach all villages with populations greater than 2,000 by March 2012, and then to reach the rest of the villages in a phased manner over three to five years.

For banks, some of the advantages of using BCs are:

☐ Greater reach. By using BCs, banks can reach out to areas that lack formal financial services at a much faster rate and lower cost than they can by building brick-and-mortar branches. The BC model also enables banks to offer financial services to new customers beyond their bank networks.

☐ Doorstep banking. The use of BCs enables banks to provide banking services, including loan disbursement and recovery, at convenient locations or even door-to-door.

☐ Better loan performance. Since local stakeholders like NGOs, post offices, etc., are involved in the process, they know the customers at a personal level. The personal connection enhances the customers' accountability to the BC, which in turn improves loan performance and repayment rates.

☐ Quick expansion. Scaling up of the model is possible in a short span of time.

Eligible Criteria for Selection for BCs

As per RBI guidelines the following are eligible for selection as Business correspondents.

- Societies registered under Mutually Aided Cooperative Societies (MACS) Act or the Cooperative Societies Acts of States.
- Section 25 Companies.
- NGOs/MFIs set up under the Indian Societies/Trust Act
- Registered NBFCs not accepting Public Deposits.
- Post Offices
- Individual kirana/medical/fair price shop owners/Public Call Office (PCO) operators/Agents of Small Savings Schemes and Insurance Companies/ Petrol Pumps owners/Retired Teachers
- Authorized Functionaries of well-run Self-Help Groups (SHGs) linked to Banks.
- PACs and CSCs

The Reserve Bank of India's guidelines regarding BCs allows flexibility to banks regarding the use of technology for financial inclusion. This has resulted in innovations to provide inexpensive and efficient technological solutions. Today a vast array of technology, including hand-held mobile devices, Internet, and mini-ATMs and kiosks, is available.

Some of the information and communication technology based solutions being used by BCs are

1. Smart Card Solution (Biometric):

  ☐ Each customer is provided with a Smart Card, which works as electronic pass book.
  ☐ Contains details of the account holder
  ☐ Used to authenticate the account holder through biometrics
  ☐ BCs are provided with PoS (Point of Service) terminal which are equipped with wireless connectivity, printer, biometric scanner and voice enunciation in local language.

2. Mobile Based Solution (Biometric):

  ☐ The difference from smart card is that biometric of the customers are stored on the NFC enabled mobile phone provided to BC.
  ☐ Customers are issued a plastic photo identity card which carries a unique number, which is linked to the account of the customer
  ☐ When this number is dialed on mobile, it prompts for biometric authentication
  ☐ A customer biometric is verified with one stored on Mobile phone and the one scanned at the time of transaction at PoS terminal with BC

3. Mobile -2- Mobile Based (non-Biometric) Solution:

- ☐ The customers should have an account and must possess a mobile with SMS facility available.
- ☐ Customer would call a toll free no. of the bank and would get routed to an Interactive Voice Response system (IVR) in the language preferred.
- ☐ A call would originate to the registered mobile no. and the customer would ask to choose a PIN, which is a secure PIN for carrying out financial transaction and the PIN would be an interactive PIN and would not store in the handset.
- ☐ Once PIN is obtained, the customer can call the toll free number and provide his/her PIN and choose the financial services.
- ☐ In case of cash withdrawal, the customer would be prompt to enter the amount of withdrawal.
- ☐ The customer would get an SMS with the Transaction ID and the One Time Password (OTP). With this, the customer can approach the BC. On entering the Transaction ID, the system verifies whether it is a valid transaction and then prompts for the OTP, on entering the OTP the system display the complete transaction to the BC and the BC pays the requisite money to the customer.

However, in India there are challenges relating to electricity and Internet connectivity in remote areas. As a result, mobile phone technology has emerged as the most effective and prevalent solution. Most of the banks use General Packet Radio Service (GPRS) enabled mobile-based online applications. Portable printing devices are synchronized with mobile handsets. Data are transferred to the bank's intermediary server in real time. Internet security features include a default GPRS security check, an HTTPS-enabled database, and log-in password security check. Each of the BC's customers is given a biometric smartcard, which makes identification easier and more secure. With the use of mobile technology, banks can reach vast geographic areas from a remote location.

Financial Inclusion Through Business Correspondent Model

India's financial inclusion initiative has made exceptional progress since 2010 as can be seen from the chart below. (Source: RBI report on financial inclusion and financial literacy April 2013). The number of business correspondents which were 34174 as on 31st March, 2010 increased to 168380 as on 30th December, 2012. Moreover 17950 urban BC centers existed as compared to just 447 such centers earlier. The Reserve Bank continued with its efforts to ensure extension of banking facilities to all unbanked villages. For this, about 490,000 unbanked villages with population less than 2,000 were identified and allotted to banks for coverage under the ongoing Phase-II of the roadmap. At end- March 2015, as reported by State Level Bankers Committees (SLBCs), 390,387 villages were covered by 14,207 branches, 357,856 business correspondents (BCs) and 18,324 other modes, such as automated teller machines (ATMs) and mobile vans. In view of the ongoing implementation of PMJDY, banks were advised to complete Phase- II coverage by August 14, 2015

The use of the BC model has the potential to change the lives of millions of people in the remotest parts of the country. For poor and vulnerable people, who could not think of going to the bank, banking has come to them. Increases in the number of bank accounts and the volume of loans and deposits in areas that use the BC model could indicate there is now far greater awareness of banking services. Frauds and diversions of government payments are declining as people get their social security and pension payments through bank accounts, at their doorsteps.

Table 2: Financial Inclusion Plan-Summary Progress of All Banks Including RRBs

Particulars	Year ended March 2010	Year ended March 2014	Year ended March 2015	Progress April 2014 – March 2015
Banking Outlets in Villages – Branches	33,378	46,126	49,571	3,445
Banking Outlets in Villages – Branchless mode	34,316	337,678	504,142	166,464
Banking Outlets in Villages –Total	67,694	383,804	553,713	169,909
Urban Locations covered through BCs	447	60,730	96,847	36,117
Basic Savings Bank Deposit A/c through branches (No. in million)	60.2	126.0	210.3	84.3
Basic Savings Bank Deposit A/c through branches (Amt. in ₹ billion)	44.3	273.3	365.0	91.7
Basic Savings Bank Deposit A/c through BCs (No. in million)	13.3	116.9	187.8	70.9
Basic Savings Bank Deposit A/c through BCs (Amt. in ₹ billion)	10.7	39.0	74.6	35.6
BSBDAs Total (No. in million)	73.5	243.0	398.1	155.1
BSBDAs Total (Amt. in ₹ billion)	55	312.3	439.5	127.3
OD facility availed in BSBDAs (No. in million)	0.2	5.9	7.6	1.7

OD facility availed in BSBDAs (Amt. in ₹ billion)	0.1	16.0	19.9	3.9
KCCs (No. in million)	24.3	39.9	42.5	2.6
KCCs (Amt. in ₹ billion)	1,240.1	3,684.5	4,382.3	697.8
GCC (No. in million)	1.4	7.4	9.2	1.8
GCC (Amt. in ₹ billion)	35.1	1,096.9	1,301.6	204.7
ICT A/Cs BC Transaction (No. in million)*	26.5	328.6	477.0	477.0
ICT A/Cs BC Transactions (Amt. in ₹ billion)*	6.9	524.4	859.8	859.8

Source: RBI report on financial inclusion and financial literacy April 2015

The BC model is being used effectively for overall community development and social empowerment. With the assistance of self-help groups funded through transactions handled by BCs, new businesses are being setup. More and more people are benefiting from credit linkages facilitated by BCs and are becoming more self-reliant. With the help of credit, today they are able to afford education for their children, which is changing their lives forever.

There are however, several challenges being faced by the BC model such as

- Accounting, frauds, and misappropriations.
- Viability issues. Despite an increasing level of awareness about the value of banking services, the majority of no-frills accounts opened by BCs are inactive. This has raised concerns that the model may not be viable. As a result, there is a shortage of funding for building the capacity of BCs. In some cases, BCs have lost money, forcing them to close. In addition, expanding into unbanked areas involves costs that banks have to absorb. If banks are not able to recover the cost for small transactions, their ability to provide credit is limited.
- Regulatory concerns. Current regulations require BCs to complete accounting and settle cash with bank branches within 24 hours of a transaction, which may not be possible due to the huge distances involved.

Case Study

A study was undertaken to compare the performances of two of the more popular BCs vis a vis individual BCs as against company BCs

The below table shows data collected from two villages. The first two are from major national level company BCs and the latter two are individual BCs

Table 3: Case Study

Name of village	Popula-tion (Ap-prox.)	Distance from nearest Bank branch	Villagers having Bank accounts	BC accounts as on 31st Mar, 2011	BC accounts as on 31st Mar, 2012	Average customers per day	%age of customers covered
Paharpur	4000	7 km	108	0	1252	45	31%
Ghaila	2200	10 km	52	0	550	22	25%
Mampur Bana	4500	3 km	451	0	2300	55	51%
Ajgana	3000	4 km	150	0	1800	40	60%

From the above chart we can see that the percentage of customers covered through BC channel is just 25% at Ghaila which is a company BC while it is at a respectable 60% at village Ajgana, District Barabanki which is an individual BC.

Infact both Mampur Bana and Ajgana have covered more than 50% of the village population which includes the accounts of both male and female villagers who apart from normal banking needs get government payment to their accounts under the various scheme s like MNREGA, Jaccha Bachha, Vidhwa pension etc.

Findings

The major reasons for the success of individual BCs in perpetrating financial inclusion as compared to company BCs are –

1. Higher business higher revenues: The individual BCs are the small entrepreneurs who have got into the business with a motive of profit as compared to salaried employees handling company BC units. They know that more the number of customers greater the number of transactions and hence greater their earnings as the revenue model is based on number of transactions. Hence they make efforts to open as many accounts as possible by meeting the gram pradhans, village gatherings etc. and educate the villagers about the benefits of transacting with them.

2. No time constraints. : The individual BCs work late hours and even on holidays and Sundays while employed BCs have a typical 10 to 5 routine.

3. Have more freedom of expression: The individual BCs hold meetings in the

villages where often they serve snacks, etc to attract villagers. Those employees handling company BCs have no such facility and their suggestions are often ignored by their bosses.

Conclusion

Banks and BCs need to give more attention to the financial viability of the channel. Currently, a lot of focus is on the number of accounts opened and achieving the financial inclusion targets. Banks need to scale up their efforts substantially towards educating the clientele in their respective vernacular languages regarding the benefits of banking habit. Banks are able to

achieve their financial inclusion mandate and at the same time earn revenues from the BC operations because of higher account activity. Customers get access to a secure banking system and formal financial products without the need to go to a bank branch. The use of the BC model has the potential to change the lives of millions of people in the remotest parts of the country. For poor and vulnerable people, who could not think of going to the bank, banking has come to them. Increases in the number of bank accounts and the volume of loans and deposits in areas that use the BC model could indicate there is now far greater awareness of banking services. BCs at the village level need to be strengthened to take up feasible and financially viable business of financial inclusion.

Financial inclusion is more than a policy imperative; it represents huge opportunities for banks. Making financially excluded people financially capable and providing them with customized feasible products would be the road ahead for financial inclusion. Business Correspondent Network Managing MFIs and banks should continue to look at leveraging the business correspondent model in the best possible ways to deliver impact and value to consumers and there by expediting the process of financial inclusion leading to inclusive growth.

Suggestions for Improvement in Performance of Company BC

1. The person employed to work at the BC unit should be from the village itself and should have good standing and reputation among the villagers.
2. His salary should have a fixed as well as a variable component. The variable part should be linked to the no. of accounts opened as well as the daily no. of transactions and the business proposals sourced in a month.
3. There should be regular meetings of this employee with company bosses to decide on holding meetings and other marketing initiatives, etc. in the village.

Some other suggestions applicable for all types of BCs:

1. Should have good relationships with the linked Bank branch.
2. Should cover adjacent villages that don't have the facility of BCs.

References

1. Financial Inclusion | A Road India needs to Travel by HT Media Ltd., Retrieved from http://rbidocs.rbi.org.in/rdocs/Speeches/PDFs/FICHI121011S.pdf. Accessed on August 30, 2013.

2. http://expertscolumn.com/content/minimum-balance-account-ie-no-frills-account, Accessed on August 05, 2013

3. http://rbidocs.rbi.org.in/rdocs/Publications/PDFs/STR020311_F.pdf. Accessed on August 27, 2013

4. http://www.scribd.com/doc/29443419/Research-Paper-on-Financial-Inclusion. Accessed on May 30, 2013

5. http://www.undp.org.in/content/pub/PovertyReduction/Scoping-Paper-on-Financial-Inclusion.pdf, Accessed on May 28, 2013

6. Joshi Deepali pants. (2010): The Financial Inclusion Imperative and Sustainable Approaches. India: Cambridge University Press

7. Joshi, Deepalipant (2013), financial inclusion and financial literacy, Reserve Bank of India

8. Kishore, Anupam (2012), Business Correspondent model boosts financial inclusion in India http://www.minneapolisfed.org/publications_papers. Accessed on August 30, 2013

9. Mohan, R. (2002). Transforming Indian Banking: In Search of a Better Tomorrow, RBI Bulletin

10. Mohan, R. (2004). Financial Sector Reforms in India: Policies and Performance Analysis, RBI Bulletin

11. Mohan, R. (2006). Agricultural Credit in India: Status, Issues and Future Agenda, Economic and Political Weekly (March), pp.1013–23i

12. NCAER (2003). India Market Demographics Report 2002, New Delhi: NCAER

13. Nicosia, (2012), The Banking Sector and Economic Growth. Retrieved from http://www.centralbank.gov.cy/nqcontent.cfm?a_id=12402&lang=en. Accessed on May 30, 2013.

14. Ravichandran K., Khalid A (2009), Financial Inclusion- A path towards India's future economic growth, Retrieved from http://ssrn.com/abstract=1353125. Accessed on August 30, 2013

15. Reserve Bank of India (2004). Report of the Advisory Committee on Flow of Credit to Agriculture and Related Activities from Banking System, RBI, Mumbai

16. Reserve Bank of India (2010). *Report on Trend And Progress of Banking In India* 2009–10 (June), Retrieved from http://rbidocs.rbi.org.in/rdocs/Publications/PDFs/RTP081110FL.pdf, Accessed on January 30, 2013

17. Swamy V, VijayLaxmi (2011), *Role of Financial Inclusion for Inclusive Growth in India – Issues & Challenges*. Retrieved from http://skoch.in/fir/Paper Financial Inclusion Challenges & Opportunities.pdf, Accessed on July 28, 2013

18. World Data Bank Poverty and Inequality Database, Retrieved from http://povertydata.worldbank.org/poverty/region/LAC | May 12, 2015, World Bank accessed on November 27, 2015

Ensuring Delivery excellence in software testing projects by using Software Tester Maturity Index model

Dhruv Kartikey*

Abstract

The ultimate desire to include any process for any methodology or concept is to have more autonomy and predictability. Similarly in the area of software testing, an ideal situation could be imagined as software engineers perform testing operations without depending on any external or internal sources and that, they are completely independent to carry out testing operations and deliver a zero-defect delivery. In order to accomplish zero-defect delivery, Software Tester Maturity Index model is introduced. This will help in taking decisions for aligning the testing process and testers according to the demand across various sprints under an agile framework of software development. This unique method of calculating, Software Tester Maturity Index also contains an analytical framework to support the predictability and quality of deliverables. It shows how the model gives the required information to route the modules for test engineers to ensure quality. At the end experimental results of tests are presented which would enable product line managers to have predictability statistics to ensure software stability.

Keywords: Software Tester Maturity Index, Tester's confidence, software stability.

Introduction

Software testing being the most essential phase of software development emphasizes a lot on the depth of testing and various other strategies associated with it. In initial stages of a software testing project the data regarding effectiveness of testing is very limited. Though retrospective meetings happen to assess improvement points for increasing the effectiveness of testing but as and when the data increases it is very important to quantify them in order to control the uncontrolled grey areas. This comes down to the fact, as to how well equipped are software testing engineers in terms of resources and tools provided to them to perform testing.

Software Tester Maturity Index uses individual bonafide inputs during software testing based on specified parameters, which automatically derives the value based on formula. During software testing at any level it is very important to understand the confidence of the testers in their interaction with the ecosystem that comprises

* EdgeVerve Systems Limited, Infosys Group of Companies

of both software application as well as the team's overall efficiency. Here Tester's confidence has nothing to do with determining their reliability or ability to learn new things. Also this model does not suggest any kind of a parameter for performance appraisal of the testers. Rather this model shall help the software testing managers to identify the grey areas during any software testing project for the smooth conduction of the project. After successive iterations of implementing this model, the grey areas could be better detected. An ideal situation for a software testing engineer shall be a scenario wherein they have least dependency on any kind of internal and external support, and high proficiency in testing skills. This model subsequently helps the product line managers and technology leaders to better equip their teams to perform software testing such that there is no compromise on the quality of the deliverables.

After having described our model of software tester maturity index (Section 1), we evaluate our approach by showing how our model derives not only the index value that shows the depth and quality of software testing performed on a project but also associated risks, by presenting experimental results (Section 2).

Section 1

The model of software tester maturity index, thereafter referred to as MI, is based on six parameters, for which the scale can vary for various testing projects. All these parameters have their own maxima and minima values. These values are keyed in to the formula after a testing assignment by an unbiased consultant/team leader, who are assumed not to manipulate the data. All those parameters that deal with tester and its function alone are a positive parameter and directly proportional to MI. Whereas any parameter that involves parties other than tester shall be a negative indicator therefore inversely proportional to MI.

First parameter (P1) is Proficiency, which is defined by what is required for testing, minus what the tester is equipped with. But this shall again be calibrated on the basis of a set value of maxima and minima. Here Proficiency parameter P1 shall be directly proportional to MI. Its value is independent of other parameters.

$$P1 \propto MI$$

Second Parameter (P2) is SARA, known as Scope and Risk Analysis, which as the name suggest refers to identifying the scope and associated risks. But this shall again be calibrated on the basis of a set value of maxima and minima. Here SARA parameter P2 shall be directly proportional to MI. Its value is less than OR equal to Proficiency parameter (P1). Here the understanding is that Scope and Risk Analysis cannot exceed the value of the Proficiency of the tester.

$$P2 \propto MI$$

Third Parameter (P3) is External Support. This refers to tester taking help from sources outside the designating testing team for the project such as talking to the client and its technical teams, or talking to the developers regarding the understanding of the application flow. But this shall again be calibrated on the basis of a set value of maxima and minima. Its value is independent of other parameters. It shall be inversely proportional to MI.

$$P3 \propto 1/MI$$

Fourth Parameter (P4) is Internal Support. This refers to tester taking help from internal sources such as testing team stakeholders for the project. But this shall again be calibrated on the basis of a set value of maxima and minima. Its value is independent of other parameters. It shall be inversely proportional to MI.

$$P4 \propto 1/MI$$

Fifth Parameter (P5) is Test Execution. This refers to tester performing testing and not the analysis of the test results. But this shall again be calibrated on the basis of a set value of maxima and minima. Its value shall be less than OR equal to SARA parameter (P2). The understanding here is that Test Execution cannot out par the value of scope and risk analysis done for the module under testing. It shall be directly proportional to MI.

$$P5 \propto MI$$

Sixth Parameter (P6) is Risk Review. This refers to the tester's act of validating the test results and to assess the scope and risk coverage planned versus scope and risk coverage achieved. But this shall again be calibrated on the basis of a set value of maxima and minima. Its value shall be less than OR equal to SARA parameter (P2). The understanding here is that Risk Review cannot out par the value of scope and risk analysis done for the module under testing. It shall be directly proportional to MI.

$$P6 \propto MI$$

Finally the value of MI can be derived combining all the above parameters as below:

$$MI = K \text{ efficiency constant} * \{(P1*P2*P5*P6)/(P3*P4)\} ^ {1/6}$$

Here the K efficiency constant shall be a value on a certain scale example 1 to 10 for a tester's efficiency. Where for every tester shall be rated by a lead or independent consultant with certain valued based on the tester's experience in the domain and technical skills. 1 being the lowest and 10 as highest. This scale can again vary for various projects. This paper do not suggest the derivation of value of efficiency constant as this is a point of an individual's perspective towards a tester's quality of deliverables.

Section 2

This section refers to experimental data based on Software Tester maturity index, MI. Here for all the parameters were assumed on a scale of 1 to 5. 1 being the lowest and 5 as highest. For efficiency constant K, we assume the value from 1 to 10. 1 being the lowest and 10 as highest. These calibrations can vary for various projects on the basis if there demand for classification. Here various testers are referred to as Tester 1, Tester 2 and so on, who are testing modules A and B and so on respectively as an indicative.

Refer to table 1.1a, that computes the software tester maturity index, for a sample testing project assuming a group of testers who are novice in the skill sets of software testing or domain or application technology. Here the efficiency constant K contains the value as 1 through out. The readings indicate that Tester 1 though new to testing, but its parameter reading shows a perfect example of a smooth operation from the tester on module A, but since the tester is new to the skill sets of software testing or domain or application technology the magnifying factor i.e. constant K remains 1. Vice versa is the case for Tester 4 operating on module D and so on for other testers 2 and 3 performing testing on modules B and C.

Table 1.1a: Experimental data for testers with efficiency level as novice.

Experiment 1	Proficiency	SARA	External Support	Internal Support	Test Execution	Risk Review	Efficiency constant	Software Tester Maturity index
	P1	P2	P3	P4	P5	P6	K	MI
Tester 1, Module A	5	5	1	1	5	5	1	2.92
Tester 2, Module B	4	3	3	2	2	3	1	1.51
Tester 3, Module C	3	2	5	5	2	1	1	0.88
Tester 4, Module D	1	1	3	4	1	1	1	0.66

Refer to table 1.1b, that computes the software tester maturity index, for a sample testing project assuming a group of testers from all level of skill sets of software testing or domain or application technology therefore the efficiency constant K is having different values. The value of Software Tester Maturity Index varies for different testers. For tester 1, who is new to software testing or domain or application technology, is performing well in Module A which suggests ease of testing in module A with no grey areas identified. Whereas for Tester 4, who is an experienced tester, is facing issues in terms of proficiency and needs a lot of support both from internal and external stakeholders. Though the value of maturity index for tester 4 is higher than that of tester 1 but the credibility of the reading from tester 4 is more than that of tester 1. Therefore the areas for improvement here can be acted upon.

Table 1.1b: Experimental data for testers with all kinds of experience levels (ascending order).

Experiment 2	Proficiency	SARA	External Support	Internal Support	Test Execution	Risk Review	Efficiency constant	Software Tester Maturity index
	P1	P2	P3	P4	P5	P6	K	MI
Tester 1, Module A	5	5	1	1	5	5	1	2.92
Tester 2, Module B	4	3	3	2	2	3	4	6.04
Tester 3, Module C	3	2	5	5	2	1	6	5.28
Tester 4, Module D	1	1	3	4	1	1	10	6.6

Refer to table 1.1c, that computes the software tester maturity index, for a sample testing project assuming a group of testers from all level of skill sets of software testing or domain or application technology therefore the efficiency constant K is having different values. Here the conditions are opposite to what is showed in table 1.1b. The value of Software Tester Maturity Index varies for different testers. For tester 1, who is an experienced tester fetches an maturity index reading that shows not only the ease of testing operation in module A but also the credibility of the index as higher than that of other testers. Whereas for Tester 4 operating on module D, with a low expertise level is struggling with all the parameters and thus on a lower rating.

Table 1.1c: Experimental data for testers with all kinds of experience levels (Descending order).

Experiment 3	Proficiency	SARA	External Support	Internal Support	Test Execution	Risk Review	Efficiency constant	Software Tester Maturity index
	P1	P2	P3	P4	P5	P6	K	MI
Tester 1, Module A	5	5	1	1	5	5	10	29.2
Tester 2, Module B	4	3	3	2	2	3	7	10.57
Tester 3, Module C	3	2	5	5	2	1	5	4.4
Tester 4, Module D	1	1	3	4	1	1	1	0.66

Refer to table 1.1d, that computes the software tester maturity index, for a sample testing project assuming a group of testers who are experienced in the skill sets of software testing or domain or application technology. Here the efficiency constant K contains the value as 10 through out. Here since the efficiency levels of all the testers are same throughout therefore the effectiveness of the maturity index is high for all the testers. And thus different readings of the testers suggest different level of ease of testing operation across the modules. The grey areas therefore could also be acted upon by the leads and technical managers.

Table 1.1d: Experimental data for testers with high level of efficiency

Experiment 4	Proficiency	SARA	External Support	Internal Support	Test Execution	Risk Review	Efficiency constant	Software Tester Maturity index
	P1	P2	P3	P4	P5	P6	K	MI
Tester 1, Module A	5	5	1	1	5	5	10	29.2
Tester 2, Module B	4	3	3	2	2	3	10	15.1
Tester 3, Module C	3	2	5	5	2	1	10	8.8
Tester 4, Module D	1	1	3	4	1	1	10	6.6

Conclusion and future work

In this paper we introduced the concept of Software Tester Maturity Index that computes the data after every testing operation and suggests the area of improvements for the testers. Here the assumption is made that the values for all the seven parameters are not manipulated to affect the computed maturity index value.

In future work, more and more effectiveness of the parameters shall be brought in, and also will explore other dimension of testing operation and the testers, so that the reading form Software Tester Maturity Index is more credible and indicative in nature.

References

Paolo Arcaini, Angelo Gargantini and Paolo Vavassori, "Automatic Detection and Removal of Conformance Faults in Feature Models", *IEEE International Conference on Software Testing, Verification and Validation (ICST),2016*

Robert Feldt, Simon Poulding and David Clark, "Test Set Diameter: Quantifying the Diversity of Sets of Test Cases", *IEEE International Conference on Software Testing, Verification and Validation (ICST),2016*

Araújo, C.A., Delamaro, M.E., Maldonado, J.C., "Correlating automatic static analysis and mutation testing: towards incremental strategies", *29th Brazilian Symposium on Software Engineering, 2015*

Camargo, K.G., Ferrari, F.C. & Fabbri, S.C.," Characterising the state of the practice in software testing through a TMMi-based process", *CBSOFT 2013 Journal of Software Engineering Research and Development ISSN: 2195–1721*

Silva Ouriques, J.F., Cartaxo, E.G. & Lima Machado, P.D, *"Revealing influence of model structure and test case profile on the prioritization of test cases in the context of model-based testing", CBSOFT 2013 Journal of Software Engineering Research and Development ISSN: 2195–1721*

Emelie Engström,Kai Petersen, "Mapping software testing practice with software testing research — SERP-test taxonomy", *IEEE Eighth International Conference on Software Testing, Verification and Validation Workshops (ICSTW),2015*

Bertolino A., "Software Testing Research and Practice", *Lecture Notes in Computer Science, vol 2589. Springer, Berlin, Heidelberg,2003*

Measurement and Dynamics of Cognitive and Structural Social Capital during Microfinance Intermediary Processes: A Study of Community based Organizations

Harbhan Singh* & Anoop Kumar Atria*

Abstract

This paper has attempted to quantify, measure and analyze the inter-dynamics between the social capital formation among microfinance beneficiaries and intermediary processes of microfinance. Social capital is a network based resource which is derived through cognitive and structural forms and in this paper they are quantified through statistical techniques. We approached more than 500 microfinance clients in Andhra Pradesh, Tamil Nadu and Kerala with convenience sampling but somehow only 300 clients responded. We have surveyed them and asked about their demographics, economic, financial and social dimensions through structured questionnaires. Moreover, we have applied multivariate statistical techniques on the data collected through questionnaires and found significant relationship between microfinance intermediary processes, cognitive and structural social capital formation among the microfinance beneficiaries. A major limitation of this research is that the rural areas of Andhra Pradesh, Tamil Nadu and Kerala are not included due to assorted reasons. Other limitations include multiple lending which seems to be more decisive and defaulters are not included in the study. The present study focuses upon the social and financial processes which are participated in the development of entrepreneurship of the microfinance beneficiaries. The study is useful for MFIs for designing new products and services for lower income group. It is expected that the study will add significant knowledge in the area of social capital and microfinance intermediary processes and it will be helpful for the scholars to find out enhanced and substantial measures of social capital measurement.

Keywords: Social Capital Formation, Cognitive Social Capital, Structural Social Capital, Microfinance Intermediary Processes, Community based Organizations (CBOs).

Introduction

In the consideration of major development barriers poverty and unemployment take place before all problems. The roots of poverty are widespread in the world in which Sub-Saharan Africa, South Asia, East Asia and Pacific regions are the most deprived in terms of poverty and unemployment. World Bank, UNDP, UNO

---

* S.P.C. Government College, Ajmer

and other prominent International Organizations with the collaborations with local governments are still striving to overcome these problems.

Broad improvements in human welfare will not occur unless poor people receive wider access to affordable, better quality services in health, education, water, sanitation, and electricity. Without such improvements in services, freedom from illness and freedom from illiteracy-two of the most important ways poor people can escape poverty.[1]

Economic growth is essential for poverty reduction, but even very rapid growth in developing countries will not be sufficient enough to reduce extreme poverty below 3 percent globally by 2030, without complementary policies to assist the poor. In all countries but even more so in developing economies, economic growth is more effective in fostering poverty reduction and broad-based prosperity if the pattern of growth becomes more labor intensive and if poor people's work becomes more productive. Consequently, labor productivity, the sectoral composition of growth and its impact on job creation matter for poverty alleviation.[2]

Poor people live without fundamental freedoms of action and choice that the better-off take for granted. Poverty has many dimensions. In addition to low income (living on less than $1 a day), illiteracy, ill health, gender inequality, and environmental degradation are all aspects of being poor. This is reflected in the Millennium Development Goals (MGDs), the international community's unprecedented agreement on the goals for reducing poverty.

Humans are social organisms and they tend to group themselves for basic needs. The question here is the ability to be able to earn enough to be able to survive in the community. The concept of social capital is not new to this world but the writings in this context are relatively new. Alexis-Charles-Henri Clérel de Tocqueville (1835 and 1840) wrote about the Democracy in America. After that L.J. Hanifan (1916) wrote regarding local support for rural schools. The relevant history has good examples of collective action and social cohesion toward critical issues. A famous example is given below:

"In 1848 the French revolutionary movement demanded the right to work for the proletariat. The rebels maintained that society was in debt to the poor and that the time had come to repay this debt. However, the liberal state ideology did not approve of the idea of society's debt to the poor. It did not want to burden the financial system with the poverty issue. However, those in power could not ignore the demands of the masses for redistribution of society's wealth and welfare. The rebellion forced the ruling class to search for new ways to manage the poverty problem peacefully. Social scientists such as Auguste Comte demanded the even more drastic alternative of a "philanthropic" or "positive" poverty policy, based not on rights but on morals. He also coined the term "collective good", which could be achieved through a "Social Contract". The state would recognize the poor as rights-bearing citizens, but these poor citizens would have to recognize that their citizenship involved both rights and obligations."

Here, the discussion over poverty and unemployment was necessary because poverty consumes cognitive resources. "So if you want to understand the poor, imagine yourself with your mind elsewhere. You did not sleep much the night before. You find it hard to think clearly. Self-control feels like a challenge. You are distracted and easily perturbed. And this happens every day. On top of the other material challenges poverty brings, it also brings a mental one…Under these conditions, we all would have (and have!) failed"

The decision making and prosperity of an individual is affected by the particular area they inhabit. Here is an example of sugarcane farmers of Tamil Nadu, India, as evidence for the aforesaid statement:

"Sugarcane farmers in Tamil Nadu, India, receive most of their income once a year during the harvest. Immediately before receiving their income, the same farmers exhibit higher financial stress and lower cognitive scores, relative to the postharvest period. This cannot be explained by a change in nutrition, physical exhaustion, biological stress, or a practice effect on the cognitive test."

The above example signifies the importance of the cognitive state of mind and its role in the income generating activity. This particular aspect has another aspect-cognitive parameters are directly proportionate to financial decision making. Cognitive parameters may be affected by trust, solidarity, social cohesion, inclusion, collective action, cooperation, reciprocity and so forth. The core of Social Capital doesn't exist through single individuals, and without adequate and acceptable cognitive states of mind among at least two individuals, social capital will be absent.

"A number of constraints associated with poverty may be difficult to observe and could extend beyond material deprivation: a preoccupation with daily hassles and their associated depletion of cognitive resources required for important decisions; low self-image and its blunting of aspirations; and norms that may require investments in social capital to the detriment of private opportunities."

The present research reveals the process of poverty alleviation through microfinance and how cognitive and structural social capital originates and reacts with microfinance.

Literature Review

Social Capital and Microfinance Tradeoff

"Relationships matter"-a simple definition of Social Capital given by John Field signifies its importance in this dynamic world. Relationships and associations in an organization or group or community cater to a common place for resource sharing, decision making, economic exchange, collective action and so on. When people associate together for a common goal, they tend to interact with each other. At this point of interaction, social capital building starts in proportion to their degree of interaction. Networks provide a basis for social interactions, cohesion and other intermediary processes because they enable people to cooperate and interact with each other for gaining mutual benefits.

"Microfinance is a financial approach to support the poor by giving them small loans at cheaper rates and without collaterals. Microfinance sector has navigated a long journey from micro savings to micro credit and then to micro enterprises and now entered the field of micro insurance, micro remittance and micro pension to the poor people. This steady and evolutionary augmentation process has given a great opportunity to the rural poor in India to attain rational economic, social and cultural empowerment, tend to improved living standard and quality of life for participating households. The successful spread of microfinance is due to the assumption that local social networks, between people who know and trust each other, are able to reduce the failures of financial markets in developing countries. In this sense, information sharing and collective action among social network members produce mutual benefits. Social networks are therefore considered as a resource or 'capital' for microfinance programs. In microfinance group lending methodologies similar aspects of social capital emerge, and the 'social collateral', i.e. the formed group, is generally considered as the social capital element upon which successful microfinance programs are built."[3]

"....in credit transactions social sanction and collateral assets are alternative means of reassuring the lender. Wealthy persons do not need social sanction, whereas the poor do. Similarly, the economies of scale which collective action facilitates are more likely to be otherwise unreachable by the poor: hence the membership of ROSCAs. Bates argues that it is the wealthy who are most tempted to exit from the obligations of kin groups. Finally, if the main cost of membership is time, the poor have an advantage since they face lower costs. There is, however, an offsetting tendency. The creation of clubs and authorities will generally require some leadership and leadership is much more likely to come from agents in higher income groups. They will be more respected, and so face lower costs of initiating collective action, and since initiative will tend to produce both leadership and income, the two will be correlated. If the clubs and authorities necessary for the creation of norms and rules are initiated predominantly by higher income groups, they will both tend to address the problems faced by higher income groups and tend to attract membership from higher income groups."

The above discussion shows the bondages and bridges between social capital and microfinance. It is observed during various studies at international and national levels that social capital enhances capabilities, efficiency, cooperation, solidarity, resource sharing, trust and collective action while the microfinance processes are taking place. Henceforth, the assimilation of social capital and microfinance can be helpful in poverty and unemployment reduction.

Relationship between Social Capital and CBOs of Microfinance

A CBO is an organisation or group of individuals that provides social services at the local level. It is a non-profit organisation (if recognized) whose activities are based primarily on volunteer efforts. This means that CBOs depend heavily on voluntary contributions for labour, material and financial support.

A community-based organization is a locally controlled and consumer-oriented agency that fosters self-reliance and self-sufficiency in the overall advancement of human welfare and reflects the values of the community in which it resides. Some community-based organizations focus on a particular geographic area, working to provide services and support to the residents of a particular neighbourhood.

All such organizations, institutions or congregation of people, which have local area/village-based presence, maturity and structural arrangements. These are owned and managed by members. They are formal, legal entity or informal registered organizations maintaining separate books of accounts, systems & ways of working. They have group identity- membership. They should not be affiliated to any religious, political or separatist's parties/groups.

Over the last ten-fifteen years, microfinance programmes have come to be well thought-out as one of the most powerful instruments for alleviating poverty. The successful stretch of microfinance is due to the assumption that local social associations, between people who know and trust each other, are able to diminish the failures of financial markets in developing countries. In this intellect, information sharing and collective action among social network members produce mutual benefits. Social associations are therefore considered as a reserve or 'capital' for microfinance programmes.

"The core ideology of social capital is that social networks are crucial and important asset. Networks provide a basis for social interactions, cohesion and other intermediary processes because they enable people to cooperate and interact with each other for gaining mutual benefits."[4]

"The successful spread of microfinance is due to the assumption that local social networks, between people who know and trust each other, are able to reduce the failures of financial markets in developing countries. In this sense, information sharing and collective action among social network members produce mutual benefits. Social networks are therefore considered as a resource or 'capital' for microfinance programmes."[5]

In most countries there are ethnically or traditionally defined groups that are un-served or underserved by existing formal financial institutions. There are cases in which a certain group within a community cannot or will not take part in a financial services project due to a religious, ethnic, or other social influence. It is essential to recognize these restrictions while identifying community based organizations or groups, henceforth, products and services can be customized according to the groups.

Building and maintaining a level of trust when different ethnic or religious groups are involved can make providing microfinance services more complex. Societies diverge in their stock of "social capital – those features of social organization such as networks, norms, and trust that facilitate coordination and cooperation for mutual benefit" (Putnam, 1993).

These structures depend on traditions of collaboration and a certain level of trust between members of society. In societies with high social capital, where systems and structures have been developed to build trust and foster social and economic transactions beyond the family and group, it will be easier and less costly to build sustainable systems for financial intermediation (Bennett 1997).

When identifying a target market, microfinance intermediaries must ensure that they are able to communicate with their clients clearly. If serious language barriers exist, it may make financial services to certain clients too costly. In addition, legal or financial jargon, even when in the client's language, may create a communication barrier. Microfinance Intermediaries must ensure that communication with clients is appropriate to their level of understanding, particularly if clients are anxious to access financial services and do not fully understand the implications and responsibilities of doing so.

Providing effective financial services to low-income individuals, therefore, often requires social intermediation – "the process of creating social capital as a support to sustainable financial intermediation with poor and disadvantaged groups or individuals" (Bennett, 1997). Generally Microfinance Intermediaries provide some form of social intermediation, particularly when they work with groups. In some cases social intermediation is carried out by other organizations working with Microfinance Intermediaries.

"In addition to the more immediate bonds, affiliations, and networks that people develop in association with others on a more specific basis, humans also develop and sustain a much broader range of understandings, organizational arrangements, governing practices, policies, and the like. As with smaller (e.g., dyads and triads) groupings, more encompassing social arrangements, procedures, or "structures" do not exist as "givens" or objective states, but also are problematic in their initial formulation and continuity. Consequently, the emergence, direction, and continuity of all existing modes of organization are contingent on people acting in ways that affirm these earlier forms and patterns of association."[6]

"In microfinance group lending methodologies similar aspects of social capital emerge, and the 'social collateral', i.e. the formed group, is generally considered as the social capital element upon which successful microfinance programs are built."[7]

In group lending processes, loans are offered to microfinance clients by using a group guarantee for the repayment of every member's loan. Group lending processes can, in turn, be divided into lending to Community Based Organizations (CBOs) or Solidarity Group Lending (SGL), where the solidarity group is largely considered as a guarantee mechanism. An important set of microfinance techniques is based on solidarity group lending schemes.

Lending to CBOs (village banking, self-help groups, or ROSCAs) involves providing loans to larger groups (from twenty to 100 people). The group manages and mobilizes the acquired fund and then provides loans to its members. Members are normally asked to save money, to remain to the group and, depending on the adaptation of the method, the group chooses a president, a credit committee to determine loan delivery, and a treasurer.

"Group lending schemes rely on social capital to defeat information asymmetries that cause financial market failures. Institutions (formal and informal) can help disseminate adequate, accurate information that allow market players to make appropriate, efficient decisions. Group-based lending schemes are a case in point. These schemes…work because members have better information about each other than banks do."[8]

Putnam's (1993) definition of social capital refers to "features of social organisation, such as networks, norms, and trust that facilitate coordination and cooperation for mutual benefit. Social capital enhances the benefits of investment in physical and human capital." As per this definition, social capital is considered as the totality of horizontal associations whose crucial elements include cooperation and mutual benefits, and democratic involvement in rules and norms.

Figure 1: Horizontal and Vertical Structures in CBO

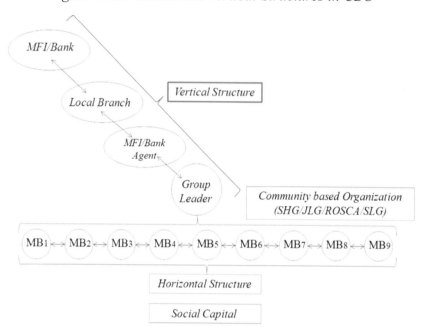

MB-Microfiance Beneficiary. Source: Researchers' Illustration

Social capital encompasses a broader set of relationships, and do not deny the possibility of negative outcomes for some of the actors involved and "a given form of social capital that is valuable in facilitating certain actions may be useless or even harmful for others" (Coleman, 1988).

Woolcock (2002) raised new issues of "bonding" and "bridging" social capital. The bonding social capital exists between relatives, neighbours, close friends etc. while the bridging social capital exists among the associates, colleagues etc., further more in vertical relationship of social capital, the capacity to leverage resources, is called linking social capital. These three types of capital serve different outcomes for the common efforts when they are in different compositions or proportions.

Horizontal Social Networks in CBOs of Microfinance

In community based organizations, trust, solidarity, collective action, norms, etc. are the important ingredients of social capital. Ito (2003) stated, "the group mechanism is associated with social capital mainly as a result of its horizontal social structure".

The social structure of group provides its members access to facilities and increased income due to the dynamics of the elements of social capital.

Furthermore, Ito (1998) stated, "peer pressure itself can be viewed as an element of social capital inasmuch as it is embedded within the horizontal structure of the ROSCA membership. In group lending microfinance programs participation is promoted by an external agent, the NGOs for example. Under the joint liability arrangements the borrower takes over the lender's responsibilities for selecting other borrowers, monitoring their repayment behaviour and taking action, if necessary, to enforce repayment."

Henceforth, peer monitoring is a flourishing way to exploiting social capital so as to reduce financial market imperfections in developing countries.

Vertical Relationships in CBOs of Microfinance

According to Woolcock (1999), success of microfinance depends on different types of social relationships or interactions that are mobilized by group lending microfinance programmes. He stated, "Repayment and cost efficacy in microfinance depend on relations among borrowers (horizontal relationships), relations between borrowers and the field agent (mainly vertical relationships), relations among staff members. Mobilizing and maintaining those relations are the key institutional linkage that shape how group-based microfinance programs work."

Microfinance plays a significant role in growth and poverty alleviation by using social relationships as collateral. However, providing proper access to financial services is neither the only goal of microfinance intermediaries nor the only impact or outcome they produce. In the real sense, this role is bi-faceted; on the one side, social capital is a resource for the microfinance programmes, which can improve access to credit by the poor and on the another side, microfinance can favour the construction of new social capital. Microfinance and social capital are linked in this causal relationship (Fisher and Sriram, 2002) and should be taken into consideration in the design, implementation, and monitoring, or rather in all the phases of the microfinance programme.

Measurement of Social Capital

There is considerable debate and controversy over the issue of measurement of social capital. The problem in measuring social capital is that it doesn't exist in quantifiable manner and it has many sources and dimensions. Measurement of social capital caused problems in separation from sources and consequences (Adam & Ronceic, 2003). For example trust, which is a common component of social capital. Some authors treat trust as equivalent to social capital (Fukuyama, 1995, 1997), some assume trust as the source of social capital (Putnam, 1993), some evaluate trust as a significant form of social capital (Coleman, 1988). World Banks' Social Capital Assessment Tool which is based on the framework proposed by Bain and Hicks (1998) and developed by Krishna and Shrader (1999), explains the methodologies, interview guide and score formation, is globally acceptable tool for social capital measurement. Moreover, the World Bank also provide sources of social capital, given below:

"In order to apply the concept of social capital at a practical and operational level, it can be broken down into five key dimensions:

1. Groups and Networks-collections of individuals that promote and protect personal relationships which improve welfare.

2. Trust and Solidarity-elements of interpersonal behavior which fosters greater cohesion and more robust collective action.

3. Collective Action and Cooperation-ability of people to work together toward resolving communal issues.

4. Social Cohesion and Inclusion-mitigates the risk of conflict and promotes equitable access to benefits of development by enhancing participation of the marginalized.

5. Information and Communication-breaks down negative social capital and also enables positive social capital by improving access to information. These dimensions capture both the structural and cognitive forms of social capital."[9]

Bain and Hicks (1998) proposed a framework for measuring social capital which has been used in Social Capital Assessment Tool (SCAT) made by Krishna and Shrader[10] (1999). Bain and Hicks (1998) divide the social capital at two levels viz. macro level and micro level. Macro level includes rule of law, level of decentralization, level of participation in policy processes, legal framework and policy regime. The micro level of social capital includes cognitive and structural social capital.

Figure 2: Framework for Measuring Social Capital

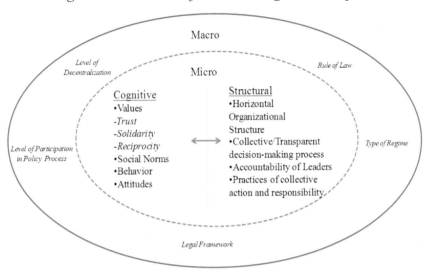

Source: Bain, K., & Hicks, N. (1998). Building social capital and reaching out to
excluded groups: the challenge of partnerships. World Bank.

Cognitive social capital envisage with values, trust, solidarity, reciprocity, social
norms, behavior, and attitudes. Structural social capital includes horizontal
organization structure, collective and transparent decision making process,
accountability of leaders, and practices of collective action and responsibility.

Research Gap

Review of literature leads to the following research gaps:

1. Social Capital variables have not been correlated with the Microfinance
   variables at micro level.
2. Structural and cognitive social capital were not measured separately with
   respect to poverty alleviation forces.

Research Objectives and Hypothesis

The objectives of this study are as follows:

1. To study dynamics between cognitive, structural social capital and
   microfinance in community based organizations.
2. To examine quantum of cognitive and structural social capital generated
   during the microfinance intermediary processes and progression.

The hypothesis under study is:

H_o: Microfinance intermediary processes have no significant relationship with cognitive and structural social capital.

H_a: Microfinance intermediary processes have significant relationship with cognitive and structural social capital.

Research Methodology

Research Design

Proposed Research involves empirical investigation of micro nature which comprises social capital measurement of CBOs through microfinance. The proposed research characterized by the prior formulation of specific research questions and hypotheses testing is presented here. Thus, the information needed is clearly defined. As a result, this research is pre-planned and structured. It is typically based on predetermined representative samples and specifies the methods for selecting the sources of information and for collecting data from those sources.

Sample Design

- Population-Community Based Organizations in Indian Microfinance Industry
- Elements- Microfinance Beneficiaries which are framing significant part of CBOs
- Sampling Unit – Microfinance Beneficiaries of CBOs of selected regions of India
- Sampling Techniques- For the proposed study, Judgment at first stage and Convenience Sampling at second stage has taken.

At the first stage, Microfinance Poverty Penetration Index (MPPI)[11] is taken to select states and regions of India. Microfinance India-State of the Sector Report 2010 envisages with MPPI of top five states as given below:

Table 1: MPPI of Top Five States of India

Name of state	MPPI	Weights
Andhra Pradesh	6.35	0.423
Tamil Nadu	2.77	0.184

Kerala	2.49	0.166
Karnataka	1.74	0.116
West Bengal	1.65	0.11

Source: State of the Sector Report-Microfinance, 2010

The top three states viz. Andhra Pradesh, Tamil Nadu and Kerala are representing more than 50 % of MPPI. Hence, there are three states which are showing appropriate microfinance density and penetration among poor people.

At the second level, due to Cost and Time constraints, Convenience sampling has employed for microfinance beneficiaries and CBOs.

Sample Size – the sample size within the time, cost, and distance constraints, is three hundred.

Table 2: Sample Size and Distribution

State	*Sample Size*
Andhra Pradesh	100
Tamil Nadu	100
Kerala	100
Total Sample Size	**300**

Sources of Data and Information

Primary as well as Secondary data sources are used to generate evidence to supplement the research design.

The Primary source of data included the respondents i.e. Microfinance Beneficiaries which are framing significant part of CBOs. The researcher has made it possible through all of the primary source data collection technique viz. observation, interview and structured questionnaires from the respondents as per the convenience.

Secondary sources are comprised of Annual Reports of MFIs, Annual Reports of NABARD, Publications of CGAP, World Bank's Social Capital Initiative, Social Capital and Microfinance Journals, Government of India's Policy Documents, Planning Commission's Reports etc.

Analysis Tools

We have applied Multiple Regression Analysis to find out the magnitudes of Structural and Cognitive Social Capital.

Results & Discussion

Table 3: Demographics

Sr. No.	Variables	Categories	Percentage
1	Type of Area	1-Urban	65.3
		2-Rural	34.7
2	Number of Households	1-0-5	47.7
		2-5-10	35.3
		10 and above	17
3	Place of Interaction	1-Community office	14.7
		2-Group Leaders' House	22.7
		3-Any members' House	42.3
		4 Any Other	20.3
4	Occupation	1-On-farm	39.7
		2-Off-farm	60.3
5	Education Status	1-Illiterate	39
		2-Up to 10th Std.	50.3
		3-Graduate & above	10.7
6	Availability of Basic Amenities	1-Yes	67.3
		2-No	32.7
7	Meeting Frequency in a Year	1- One Time	12
		2-Two Times	56
		3-Three Times	32
8	Economic Status	1-Below Poverty Line	41
		2-Above Poverty Line	45
		3-Well to do	14

Relationship between Cognitive, Structural Social Capital and Microfinance Intermediary Processes

The relationship between Cognitive and Structural Social Capital and Microfinance is measured by their respective components. Cognitive Social Capital envisage with Trust and Solidarity, Social Cohesion and Inclusion, and Reciprocity, whereas Structural Social Capital is made of Collective Action and Cooperation, Information and Communication, Bridging and Bonding Social Capital, and Groups and Networks. Microfinance Intermediary Processes includes dimensions like Micro Credit and Savings, and Microfinance Repayment Patterns.

The difference and magnitude in the means of scores of Cognitive Social Capital (Score_CSC), Structural Social Capital (Score_SSC) and Microfinance Intermediary Processes (Score_MF) are measured through Multiple Linear Regression with suitable assumptions of Linearity, and Multicollinearity.

Table 4: Variables Entered/Removed[a]

Model	Variables Entered	Variables Removed	Method
1	Score_SSC, Score_CSC[b]	.	Enter

a. Dependent Variable: Score_MF. b. All requested variables entered.

There is only one model with Microfinance (Score_MF) as dependent variable and Cognitive Social Capital (Score_CSC), Structural Social Capital (Score_SSC) as independent variables and during the fitting regression line no variable was removed and the method was Enter.

Table 5: Model Summary[b]

Model	R	R Square	Adjusted R Square	Std. Error of the Estimate
1	.500[a]	.250	.245	.218

a. Predictors: (Constant), Score_SSC, Score_CSC. b. Dependent Variable: Score_MF

The above Table 5 of Model Summary is providing the information such as R, R^2, adjusted R^2, and the standard error of the estimate while fitting the regression line between Cognitive Social Capital (Score_CSC), Structural Social Capital (Score_SSC) and Microfinance (Score_MF). As illustrated in the table, 25% of the total variance in the Microfinance (Score_MF) is explained by the regression model. Here, R explains the correlation between the observed and expected values of

Cognitive Social Capital (Score_CSC) and Structural Social Capital (Score_SSC). The standard error of the estimate measures the dispersion of the Cognitive Social Capital (Score_CSC) and Structural Social Capital (Score_SSC) around its means which is 0.218. This is the standard deviation of the error term and the square root of the Mean Square for the Residuals in the ANOVA table given below:

Table 6: ANOVA[a]

Model		Sum of Squares	df	Mean Square	F	Sig.
1	Regression	4.729	2	2.364	49.558	.000[b]
	Residual	14.170	297	.048		
	Total	18.899	299			

a. Dependent Variable: Score_MF. b. Predictors: (Constant), Score_SSC, Score_CSC

The ANOVA is given in the Table 6 and the significance value is 0.000 which is less than critical value of 0.05, therefore the Microfinance (Score_MF) has significant different mean than Cognitive Social Capital (Score_CSC) and Structural Social Capital (Score_SSC), and have linear relationship. The Sum of Squares associated with the three sources of variance, Total, Regression and Residual. The Total variance is divided into the variance which is possibly explained by the Cognitive Social Capital (Score_CSC) and Structural Social Capital (Score_SSC) (Regression) i.e. 4.729 and the variance which is not explained by the Cognitive Social Capital (Score_CSC) and Structural Social Capital (Score_SSC) (Residual) i.e. 14.170.

Table 7: Coefficients[a]

Model		Unstandardized Coefficients		Standardized Coefficients	t	Sig.
	B	Std. Error	Beta			
1	(Constant)	1.609	.181		8.883	.000
	Score_CSC	.493	.054	.966	9.130	.000
	Score_SSC	1.008	.102	1.049	9.920	.000

The beta value in the unstandardized column for Constant is high than the Cognitive Social Capital (Score_CSC) and Structural Social Capital (Score_SSC) that means the Constant makes the strong unique contribution to explaining the dependent variable. The t value is statistically significant being less than 0.05. The coefficient of the Cognitive Social Capital (Score_CSC) and Structural Social Capital (Score_SSC) represents the change in the mean response for one unit of change in Microfinance (Score_MF), while the other terms in the model are held constant. The sign of the coefficients indicate the direction of the relationship between the term and the constant. The relationship between Cognitive Social Capital (Score_CSC), Structural Social Capital (Score_SSC) and Microfinance (Score_MF) can be expressed in the equation form as:

$$m=1.609+0.493\hat{c}+1.008\hat{s}$$

Where, in the above equation, **m**=Microfiance, ŝ= Structural Social Capital, ĉ= Cognitive Social Capital, when Microfinance (**m**) is measured on five point Likert Scale.

Table 8: Coefficients[a]

Model		95.0% Confidence Interval for B		Correlations		
		Lower Bound	Upper Bound	Zero-order	Partial	Part
1	(Constant)	1.252	1.965			
	Score_CSC	-.600	-.387	-.042	-.468	-.459
	Score_SSC	.808	1.208	.199	.499	.498

Coefficients[a]

Model		Collinearity Statistics	
		Tolerance	VIF
1	(Constant)		
	Score_CSC	.226	4.431
	Score_SSC	.226	4.431

a. Dependent Variable: Score_MF

The variance inflation factor (VIF) indicates the quantum of variance of a coefficient is inflated due to the correlations among the predictors in the model. Furthermore, the Tolerance value is presenting the variability of the Cognitive Social Capital (Score_CSC) and Structural Social Capital (Score_SSC). If this value is very small (less than 0.10), it indicates that the multiple correlation with other variables is high, suggesting the possibility of Multicollinearity.

In Table 8, in the tolerance column is not less than 0.10 i.e. 1.00 which is indicating that the multiple correlation with other variables is low or absent and the VIF is 1.000 for the variables which showing absence of multicollinearity (correlation among predictors). The Part Correlation Coefficient is representing the magnitude of the total variance in the Microfinance (Score_MF) which is uniquely explained by the Cognitive Social Capital (Score_CSC) and Structural Social Capital (Score_SSC), here, the value is 4.431 for both type of Social Capital.

Figure 1: Normal Residual Plot and Scatter Plot of Score_MF

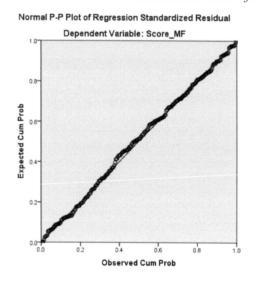

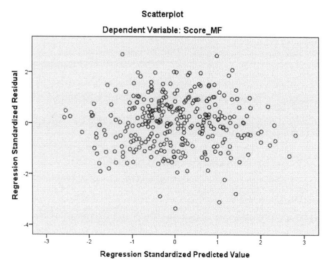

The above mentioned "Normal P-P Plot of Regression Standardized Residual" ensures normality in the Score_SoCap and the dotted points of dependent variable are following the straight line.

The above scatter-plot of standardized residuals against predicted values is a random pattern concentrated around the approximate line of zero standard residual value. The above scatter-plot depicts no clear relationship between the residuals and the predicted values which is steady with the assumption of linearity.

Limitations

Researchers tried to explore new concepts, test various existing models, and develop new models on a continuous basis. But they are restricted in some forms, as there are lots of constraints. Some of the limitations for the study can be enumerated as below:

1. There were more than 550 questionnaires distributed in Andhra Pradesh, Tamil Nadu and Kerala but only 300 questionnaires (approx 54%) were received on time. The distance was significantly large from the place of research.
2. The present study envisage with the psychological variables and inferences on which statistical assumptions (assumptions of regression analysis) have been imposed carefully.

Conclusion

The present study is done in the urban areas of Andhra Pradesh, Tamil Nadu and Kerala. The Community Based Organizations (CBOs, JLGs, SHGs, ROSCAs) were mostly made of female members although some of the groups were found with greater numbers of male members. The size of households in a CBO is generally found between 0 and 5. Members of CBOs tend to meet at any members' house with no rigidity. The employed members of the CBOs are mostly engaged in off-farm activities. The education status of members were not adequate, only 60% (approx) people were literate. There are 32% (approx) members who didn't have basic amenities. Members of CBOs tend to meet at least two times in a year. The economic status of members was not so satisfactory. The microfinance services are predominantly availed by the members who were below poverty line and just above the poverty line. The present study shows a significant relationship of social capital with various demographics such as type of area, number of members, place of interaction, occupation, education status, meeting frequency in a year, and economic status of the members.

Cognitive and structural social capital, both are created during the microfinance intermediary processes. The regression equation clearly indicates the positive magnitude of these two forms of social capital. Moreover, the amount of structural social capital dominates over the amount of cognitive social capital. It means that horizontal organization structure, collective decision making, collective action and cooperation and leadership are more valuable than trust, solidarity, reciprocity, social norms, attitudes and behavior but these two forms of social capital are not separate and they show a collaborative effect in CBOs.

Furthermore, microfinance intermediary processes enable the beneficiaries to enhance the level of trust, reciprocity, collective action, cooperation, social cohesion, inclusion, information and communication. In addition they show an increased tendency to save, mutual understanding of credit, regular loan repayment, systematic procedure for loan repayment, priority of loan repayment over household expenses, and less peer pressure. To summarise, cognitive and structural social capital originate and participate in microfinance intermediary processes significantly.

References

Bain, K., & Hicks, N. (1998). Building social capital and reaching out to excluded groups: the challenge of partnerships. World Bank.

Baker, W. E. (1990). Market networks and corporate behavior. American journal of sociology, 589–625.

Bourdieu, P. (1986). 'The Forms of Capital.' Pp. 241–58 in Handbook of theory and research for the sociology of education, edited by John G Richardson. New York: Greenwood Press.

Bourdieu, P. (2011). The forms of capital.(1986). Cultural theory: An anthology, 81–93.

Burt, R.S.; Hogarth, R.M.; Michaud, C. (2000): The Social Capital of French and American Managers. In: Organization Science (11): 123–147.

Burt, Ronald. (2001). 'Structural Holes Versus Network Closure as Social Capital.' Pp. 31–56 in Social capital : theory and research, edited by Ronald Burt. New York: Aldine de Gruyter.

Collier, Paul. (2002). 'Social capital and poverty: a microeconomic perspective.' Pp. 19 – 41 in The Role of Social Capital in Development, edited by Thierry Van Bastelaer. Melbourne: Cambridge University Press.

Fine, Ben. 2001. Social capital versus social theory : political economy and social science at the turn of the millenium. London: Routledge.

Krishna, Anirudh. 2001. 'Moving from the Stock of Social Capital to the Flow of Benefits: The Role of Agency.' World Development 29: 925–943.

Lin, N. (2001): Social Capital: A Theory of Social Structure and Action. Cambridge: Cambridge University Press.

Narayan, Deepa, and Lant Pritchett. 1999. "Social capital: Evidence and implications." Pp. 269–296 in Social Capital: A multifaceted perspective, edited by Ismail Serageldin. Washington, DC: World Bank.

Woolcock, M. (1998): Social Capital and Economic Development: Toward a Theoretical Synthesis and Policy Framework. In: Theory and Society 27(2): 151–208.

Woolcock, Michael, and Deepa Narayan. (2000). "Social capital: Implications for development theory, research, and policy." The World Bank Research Observer 15: 225–249.

Notes

1 Kenneth Kaoma Mwenda, Gerry Nkombo Muuka, (2004),"Towards best practices for micro finance institutional engagement in African rural areas: Selected cases and agenda for action", International Journal of Social Economics, Vol. 31 Iss: 1 pp. 143 – 158

2 World Bank Group. (2015). "Global Monitoring Report 2014/2015: Ending Poverty and Sharing Prosperity". Washington, DC: World Bank.

3 Prasad, S., & Singh, H. (2014). Impact Analysis of Social Capital Upon Poverty Alleviation and Standard of Living of Community Based Organizations In Microfinance. *International Journal of Research in Management & Social Science*, 1.

4 Prasad, S., & Singh, H. (2014). Impact Analysis of Social Capital upon Poverty Alleviation and Standard of Living of Community based Organizations in Microfinance. *International Journal of Research In Management & Social Science*, 1.

5 Foschi, L. (2008). Microfinance and social capital. *The Handbook of Social Capital*, 467–490.

6 Miall, C. E., Pawluch, D., & Shaffir, W. (Eds.). (2005). *Doing ethnography: Studying everyday life*. Canadian Scholars' Press.

7 Prasad, S., & Singh, H. (2014). Impact Analysis of Social Capital upon Poverty Alleviation and Standard of Living of Community based Organizations in Microfinance. *International Journal of Research in Management & Social Science*, 1.

8 Dasgupta, P., & Serageldin, I. (Eds.). (2001). *Social capital: a multifaceted perspective*. World Bank Publications.

9 Web.worldbank.org,. (2015). *Social Capital – Sources of Social Capital*. Retrieved 7 April 2015, from http://web.worldbank.org/WBSITE/EXTERNAL/TOPICS/EXTSOCIALDEVELOPMENT/EXTTSOCIALCAPITAL/0,,contentMDK:20185225~menuPK:418213~pagePK:148956~piPK:216618~theSitePK:401015,00.html

10 Krishna, A., & Shrader, E. (1999, June). Social capital assessment tool. In*conference on social capital and poverty reduction, World Bank, Washington, DC* (Vol. 22, p. 24).

11 Intensity of Penetration of Microfinance among Poor (MPPI) was derived by dividing the share of the state in microfinance clients by share of the state in population of poor. Since the microfinance clients are in the numerator, a value of more than 1 indicates that clients acquired were more than proportional to the population. Higher the score is above 1, better the performance. Lower the score from 1 the poorer is the performance in the state.

An Empirical Study of Infrastructure Investment of Indian Life Insurers in Globalized Economy

Manish Dadhich*

Abstract

The Government of India has taken a number of steps to encourage infrastructure investment in order to create a conducive and an advanced business environment. The first articulation of a strategy for infrastructure development as part of the reform program is to be found in the 8th five year plan which was published at the end of 1992. The gigantic task of financing infrastructure investment during the 12th five year plan would require a shift from the traditional mode of bank financing towards other modes. Investment policies and regulatory guidelines for insurance companies, pension funds, banks and other financial institutions need to be sufficiently flexible for these entities to choose an appropriate risk-return profile within fiduciary constraints. While facing the challenge of infrastructure financing, the problem is not of inadequacy of financial savings but lack of financial intermediation capabilities of mobilizing and channeling domestic financial savings into infrastructure in such a manner that does not create risks associated with the traditional bank financing mode. The present paper outlines the portfolio management with special reference to infrastructure investment of life insurers of India and to analyze the current pattern or deviation with the help of some statistical tool i.e. Chi-square, ANOVA etc. Moreover, the study also delves into the way forward for better mix of infrastructure investment.

Keywords: Portfolio management, Gross domestic product, Life fund, Infrastructure investment, Mandatory investment regulations.

Introduction

For economic development, investment is necessary and investments are usually made out of savings. Insurance companies are major instruments for the mobilization of savings of people particularly from the middle and lower income groups. These savings are channeled into investment for economic growth. Insurance serves a number of valuable economic functions that is largely distinct from other types of financial intermediaries. Apart from providing protection, an insurer can affect the economic growth in the form of financial intermediary (Curak, et al., 2009)[1]. The

---

* Sir Padampat Singhania University, Udaipur

[1] Curak, M., Loncar, S., & Poposki, K. (2009). Insurance Sector Development and Economic Growth in Transition Countries. *International Research Journal of Finance and Economics*, No. 34, 29–41.

273

rapid growth of life insurance premium not only increases the role of a life insurer as risk provider, but also increases its importance as institutional investor (Lee, et al., 2013)[2]. India is one of the fastest growing economies in the world today. To sustain this economic growth there must have matching infrastructure.

For better infrastructure investment, there is need to anticipate future requirements and capacity otherwise the infrastructure becomes inadequate in a few years leading to the same gap as before. Government's commitment to improve and expand infrastructure in the country is reflected in the investment in infrastructure during 12th plan. The total investment in infrastructure during the 12th plan is projected at Rs. 5574663 crore as compared to Rs. 2424277 crore during 11th plan. The first articulation of a strategy for infrastructure development as part of the reform program is to be found in the 8th Five Year Plan which was published at the end of 1992. In India, the notion of infrastructure was first discussed extensively by the Rangarajan Commission in 2010 while examining the statistical system of India. Infrastructure has been used as an umbrella term for many activities. Due to various descriptions, it becomes difficult to analyze infrastructure statistics in a comparable way and draw meaningful conclusions. Presently, there are six broad sectors of infrastructure viz. Transport, Energy, Communication, Drinking Water Supply and Sanitation, Irrigation and Storage are covered under infrastructure.

Infrastructure and Economic Growth

Infrastructure is one of the most important factors that drive economic growth of a country. Good infrastructure is the basic requirement for any production process to work efficiently. Infrastructure itself may not be a part of the production process, but is important for associated services. It is an important input to the production process and raises the productivity of other sectors. Infrastructure connects goods to the markets, workers to industry, people to services and the poor in rural areas to urban growth centers. Infrastructure lowers costs, enlarges markets and facilitates trade. Thus, infrastructure provides services that support economic growth by increasing the productivity of labor and capital thereby reducing the costs of production and raising profitability, production, income and employment.

Duggal et al (1999) found that a country's development is strongly linked to its infrastructure strength and its ability to expand trade, cope with population growth, reduce poverty and produce inclusive growth. The World Bank in its World Devel-

---

[2] Lee, C. T., Chien-Chiang., & Chang, Chien, H. (2013). Does Insurance Activity Promote Economic Growth? Further Evidence Based on Bootstrap Panel Granger Causality Test. *The European Journal of Finance*. Vol. 2, No.1, p.1–24.

opment Report 1994 pointed out that productivity growth is higher in countries with an adequate and efficient supply of infrastructure services. The report also points out that "infrastructure capacity grows step by step with economic output – a one percent increase in the stock of infrastructure is associated with one percent increase in gross domestic product (GDP) across all countries"[3].

Over two decades, India has implemented wide-ranging reforms that opened up the economy. More recently, activity has slowed down reflecting not only the weak global environment but also the emergence of strains created by the pressure that rapid economic growth has put on energy, natural resources, infrastructure and skills. Lack of high quality infrastructure has been an impediment in India's economic growth. To revive the economy a number of efforts are being undertaken, of which investment in infrastructure is one.

Review of Literature

Lee, et al (2013) investigated the causal relationship between the insurance activities and GDP, using a data set of 10 OECD countries. It was found that there was a significant and positive relationship between the overall insurance growth and economic growth for 5 countries out of 10 OECD countries. A. Sharma (2013) concluded the gigantic task of financing infrastructure investment during the 12th Plan would require shift away from the traditional mode of bank financing towards other modes.

Investment policies and regulatory guidelines for insurance companies, pension funds, mutual funds, banks and other financial institutions need to be sufficiently flexible for these entities to choose an appropriate risk-return profile within fiduciary constraints[4]. Sahoo & Das (2009) found that infrastructure stocks, labour force and total investment played an important role in the economic growth of India. More importantly, it found that the infrastructure development in India has a more significant positive contribution to economic growth for both private and public investments. Further, the causality analysis shows that there is a unidirectional causality from infrastructure development to output growth[5]. Parekh & Banerjee (2010) concluded that the Indian economy is developing and the contribution of insurance in GDP has increased in the recent past[6].

---

[3] Duggal, V.G., Saltzman, C., & Klein, L. R. (1999).Infrastructure and Productivity: A Nonlinear Approach. *Journal of Econometrics*. No. 92, p.47–74.

[4] Sharma, A. (2013). Infrastructure Investment: A Trillion Dollar Question. CIRC Working Paper No. 06. New Delhi: *CUTS Institute for Regulation and Competition*, p.15.

[5] Sahoo, P., & Das, K. R. (2009). Infrastructure Development and Economic Growth in India, *Journal of the Asia Pacific Economy*. Vol.1, p. 355.

[6] Parekh, A., & Banerjee, C. (2010). Indian Insurance Sector- Stepping into the Next Decade of Growth, Retrieved from http://mycii.in/ pdf.

Objectives of the Study

In light of the above literature review, the objectives of the present study are as follows:

a. To study the future outlook of infrastructure investment and economic growth of India.
b. To examine and explain the trends of investment patterns of selected companies.
c. To signify and recommend the contribution of life insurers to infrastructure reforms.

Research Methodology

a. **Collection of data:** The study is based on secondary data. The required data collected from published annual reports of life insurers, Journals of Insurance Institutions of India, Guideline of IRDA, website of planning commission and Nitiayog.
b. **Tools of analysis:** The collected data recorded, analyzed and interpreted in a significant manner with the help of SPSS 21 and excel sheet. The statistical tools used for the study included Chi-square, ANOVA[7].
c. **Sampling Area:** This study is based on empirical research. The corner stone is the analysis of pattern of infrastructure investment of following life insurance companies of India.

  (a) Public Sector:

    – Life Insurance Corporation of India

  (b) Private Sector:

    – SBI Life Insurance Company Limited
    – ICICI Prudential Life Insurance Company Limited
    – Max Life Insurance Company Limited
    – Bajaj Alliance Insurance Company Limited

a. **Period of study:** The data was collected during the period April 2008 to March 2015.

Hypothesis

H_{o1}: There is no significant difference among pattern of infrastructure investment of

---

[7] Sharma, R. K. (2008). Business Research Methods, National Publishing House, New Delhi. p.62.

the selected life insurers of India.

H_{02}: There is no significant difference in infrastructure investment in between the life insurers and in between the years.

Need of Infrastructure Investment

Development of infrastructure is important for sustainable and inclusive economic growth of India. It also helps in developing export orientation, attracting more foreign investment. The strategy for the 12th Plan encourages private sector participation in infrastructure directly as well as through various forms of Public Private Partnerships (PPPs). Infrastructure investments increased from about 5% of GDP during the 10th plan period to 7.2% during the Eleventh Plan period. During the 12th Plan period infrastructure investment is projected to increase to 8.2% with 9% in the last year, 2016–17. Almost 50% of the total infrastructure investment is expected to be financed by private sources during the 12th Plan as against 36% during the 11th Plan period (Planning Commission 2013). It is expected that private investment will not only expand capacity, but also improve the quality of service and reduce cost and time overruns in implementation of infrastructure projects.

Magnitude of Infrastructure Investment during the 12th Plan

The investment projection for 12th plan period stands at Rs. 5574663 crore as compared to Rs. 2424277 crore during 11th plan period. The sub sector with the highest investment of 1502 thousand crore is electricity, followed by 944 thousand crore in telecommunications, 914 thousand crore in roads and bridges, 519 thousand crore in railways and 504 thousand crore in irrigation.

Table 1: Projected Investment in Infrastructure-12th Plan
(Rs Crore at Current Prices)

Particular	Total 11th Plan	12th Plan Projections					Total 12th Plan
		2012–13	2013–14	2014–15	2015–16	2016–17	
Roads & bridges	453121	150466	164490	180415	198166	221000	914536
Railways	201237	64713	78570	96884	121699	157355	519221
MRTS(Mass rapid transport)	41669	13555	17148	22298	29836	41322	124158

Airport	36311	7691	10716	15233	21959	32116	87714
Ports	44536	18661	25537	35260	49066	69256	197781
Electricity	728494	228405	259273	294274	333470	386244	1501666
Non-conventional energy	89220	31199	42590	58125	79075	107637	318626
Oil & gas pipelines	62534	12211	16604	23833	36440	59845	148933
Telecommuni-cations	384962	105949	136090	176489	230557	294814	943899
Irrigation	243497	77113	87386	99178	112506	128186	504371
Water supply & sanitation	120774	36569	42605	49728	58084	68333	255319
Storage	17921	4480	6444	9599	14716	23202	58441
Total	2424277	751012	887454	1061316	1285573	1589308	5574663

Source: Twelfth five year plan (2012–2017), Volume1, Planning Commission

Further, the plan adopted a strategy of encouraging higher private investment in infrastructure, directly and through public private partnerships (PPPs). The share of private investment in infrastructure was projected to rise substantially from 37 per cent in 11th plan to about 48 per cent in the 12th plan.

Table 2: Projection of Infrastructure Investment and Financing during 2012–2017

Particular	Amount (Rs. Crores)	% of total
Total Infrastructure Investment	**5,574,663**	**100%**
Govt. (Central/State) Budget and Internal generation	**1,973,732**	**35%**
Private -Internal Accruals/Equity	**825,291**	**15%**
Borrowing		
Govt. PSU	**917,092**	**16%**
Private	**1,858,549**	**33%**
Total	**2,775,641**	**50%**

Availability of Borrowing		
Domestic Bank Credit	**1,164,646**	**21%**
NBFCs	**618,462**	**11%**
Pension/Insurance funds	**150,248**	**3%**
External Commercial Borrowings (ECBs	**331,834**	**6%**
Likely Total Debt Resources	**2,265,171**	**41%**
Gap between Estimates and Likely requirement	**510,470**	**9%**

Source: Report of Planning Commission 2013

Table 2 delineates acquisition of fund for infrastructure reforms and core financing instrument are Government sector, private participation, banks, NBFCs and insurance companies for the year 20012–17. The Government's agenda reveals a highly ambitious plan for Indian infrastructure and aims at making it 'Better than the Best'. This proactive approach includes projects to develop freight corridors supported by better train linkages (Diamond Quadrilateral Project) and modernize port and airports (Sagar Mala Project). It also includes projects to build an optical-fiber network up to the village level, ensure a basic level of infrastructure to all and to conduct a national and state highway construction programs.[8]

During the 12th plan period, the top spending areas for infrastructure investment will remain electricity, roads, bridges, telecom, renewable energy, oil and gas pipeline projects and railways.

Pattern of Investment of Life Insurance Companies

According to IRDA (Investment) Regulations, 2000 a life insurer can have three major lines of business – Life, Pension and General Annuity and Unit Linked Life Insurance. The premium collected from these classes of business is to be invested in the respective Funds. Life insurers in India typically manage or invest their fund with various portfolios in the economy which are classified as:

a. **Life Funds (Traditional Fund)**

The life fund consists of five different avenue of fund where life insurers are required to invest mandatory as guided by IRDA.

---

[8] Report of Infrastructure Statistics 2012, Vol. I, Issue III, p. 2.

    – Central Government Securities
    – State Government Securities or other Approved Securities
    – **Housing and Infrastructure Investments**
    – Approved Investments
    – Other than Approved Investments

b. **Pension & General Annuity Funds**

    – Central Government Securities
    – State Government Securities or other Approved Securities
    – Approved Investments

b. **Unit Linked Insurance Plan (ULIP) Funds**

    – Approved Investments
    – Other than Approved Investments

Infrastructure Investment of Life Insurers of India

Insurance business related investments are made in accordance with the Insurance Act, 1938, the IRDA (Investment) Regulations, 2000, and various other circulars/ notifications issued by the IRDA in this context from time to time. Without prejudice to Section 27 or Section 27A of the Act, Every Life insurance firm should invest, and at all times keep invested, its Controlled Fund (CF) (i.e. Shareholders' and Policyholders' fund excluding the funds relating to pension and general annuity business and unit linked life insurance business) in the following manner:

Table 3: Mandatory Life Business Investment Regulation by IRDA

S.N.	Type of Investment	Limit in percentage
(i)	Central Government Securities	Not less than 25%
(ii)	Government Securities or other approved securities (including (I) above)	Not less than 50%
(iii)	**Infrastructure and Social Sector Investment**	**Not less than 15%**
(iv)	Other Approved Investment to be governed by Exposure/Prudential Norms specified in Regulation 5	Not exceeding 20%
(v)	Other than in Approved Investments to be governed by Exposure/Prudential Norms specified in Regulation 5	Not exceeding 15%

Source: Notification of IRDA Investment Regulation, 2000

In this section, different tools are used to analyze the portfolio of only infrastructure investment of life insurers and comparing the actual investment percentage with required investment guideline. This study focuses on the analysis of the infrastructure investment pattern of five major life insurers of India viz. LIC of India, SBI Life Insurance Company Limited, ICICI Prudential Life Insurance Company Limited, Max Life Insurance Company Limited and Bajaj Alliance Life Insurance Company limited. Moreover, the study attempt to find whether there is deviation between the guidelines of insurance authority (IRDA) and investment practices of the insurers[9].

Table 4: Infrastructure Investment of Life Insurers of India (in crore)

Life Insurers	2008	2009	2010	2011	2012	2013	2014	2015
LIC of India	59715	62065	65755	80491	84532	102000	133305	147066
SBI Life	652	663	775	746	1104	1398	2371	3365
ICICI Pru.	452	526	688	1080	1686	2418	2630	3500
Max life Ins.	429	504	765	1131	1779	2152	2494	2832
Bajaj Alliance	404	510	1045	1081	1614	2024	2767	3200

Source: Annual reports of respective life insurers

As regards insurance companies, it is noteworthy that the investment guidelines of insurance companies specified by IRDA require them to invest not less than 15 percent of their investments in infrastructure and social sectors.

Table 5: Infrastructure Investment of Life Insurers: Percent-wise

Year wise	LIC of India		SBI life ins.		ICICI Pru. ins		Max life ins.		Bajaj Alliance	
	Exp.	Obs.	Exp.	Obs.	Exp.	Obs.	Exp.	Obs.	Exp.	Obs.
2007–08	15	11.41	15	19.32	15	16.52	15	23.97	15	15.89
2008–09	15	10.23	15	18.19	15	16.91	15	20.32	15	17.31
2009–10	15	09.40	15	16.14	15	15.90	15	21.93	15	22.80
2010–11	15	10.08	15	15.82	15	16.45	15	23.17	15	18.58

---

[9] Insurance Regulatory and Development Authority, *Annual Report-2014–15, Government of India*, Page 131.

2011–12	15	09.24	15	18.01	15	18.82	15	24.60	15	19.79
2012–13	15	09.82	15	16.74	15	19.57	15	21.79	15	18.46
2013–14	15	11.28	15	19.65	15	16.99	15	18.98	15	19.95
2014–15	15	10.81	15	19.78	15	18.19	15	16.66	15	18.23
Chi-square value	12.174		05.824		03.898		**25.359**		09.975	

Source: Compiled by the researcher

Tabulated value of Chi-square $\chi^2_{\ 7}(0.05) = 14.067$

Data Analysis and Interpretation

Chi-square test is applied to test whether the differences between the expected and observed value of investment are significant or not. If the calculated value of chi square is greater that table value of chi square, then it can be inferred that there is significant difference. Moreover, there is no significant difference between expected and observed value of investment if the calculated value is less than table value.

$$\chi^2 = \sum_{i=1}^{k} (O_i - E_i)^2 / E_i$$

It can be observed from the table 5 that the calculated values of Chi-square have compared with the table value. Looking at the figure of calculated value of Chi square, it can be inferred that there is no significant difference between expected and observed value of infrastructure investment of all life insurers except the Max life insurance in which calculated value (25.359 > 14.067) is more than tabulated value.

Table 6: Descriptive Statistics of Infrastructure Investment of Life Insurers

	N	Mean	Std. Deviation	Std. Error	95% Confidence Interval for Mean	
					Lower Bound	Upper Bound
LIC of India	8	10.2838	0.81659	.28871	9.6011	10.9664
SBI life insurance	8	17.9563	1.57905	.55828	16.6361	19.2764
ICICI Prudential	8	17.4188	1.29183	.45673	16.3388	18.4987

Max life	8	21.4275	2.66981	.94392	19.1955	23.6595
Bajaj Allianz	8	18.8763	2.05055	.72498	17.1620	20.5905
Total	40	17.1925	4.13309	.65350	15.8707	18.5143

The table 6 outlines information on number of cases, mean, standard deviation and confidence interval of the life insurers' investments.

Table 7: Test of Homogeneity of Variances

Levene Statistic	df1	df2	Sig.
2.200	4	35	.089

The table 7 delineates test of homogeneity of variances along with Levene's test which is used to examine the equality of variance. Since the value is 2.200 and its associated significance value is 0.089 which is greater than 0.05 so it can be interpreted that the variances are equal for all the five life insurers.

Table 8: ANOVA of Infrastructure Investments of the Life Insurers

	Sum of Squares	df	Mean Square	F	Sig.
Between Groups	553.085	4	138.271	42.778	**.000**
Within Groups	113.132	35	3.232		
Total	666.216	39			

Source: Output of SPSS

In the above ANOVA table 8, F-value is the ratio between-groups mean square and within-group mean square. It is clear from above table that there is significant difference in infrastructure investment of the selected life insurers because F-value is 42.778 and its associated significance is 0.000 which is smaller than the p-value 0.05percent. Thus, Null Hypothesis can be rejected and interpret that there is significance difference in mean percentage of infrastructure investment of all life insurers across the years.

Recommendations

In India life insurers provide vital but limited funds for the infrastructure sector due to a number of factors:

First, both insurance penetration (ratio of premium to GDP in a year) and insurance density (ratio of premium to total population) have grown since 2000 but still is much lower as compared to 9% of GDP in USA and 11% of GDP in France. So there is need for robust penetration and density of insurance.

Second, IRDA's mandatory investment regulation 2000 restricts the limit of infrastructure investment up to 15% only, so there is need for flexible portfolio of investment.

Third, public insurance firms are inherently risk averse. They invest more than required in government securities. Public sector LIC invest around 60% against the minimum prescribed requirement of 50% and invests mostly in the paper of publicly listed infrastructure companies to meet the statutory requirements.

Fourth, rapid growth of private insurance business has been driven by unit linked insurance policies and prevailing norms do not permit to investment in infrastructure (Sinha & Sidharth, 2014)[10].

The total investments of life insurance companies grew from Rs. 6,042 Billion in March 2007 to Rs. 15,813 Billion in March 2012 which is more than a two and half fold growth. As at the end of March 2012, about 7% of total investments of life insurance companies were deployed in housing and infrastructure sector. Moreover, the announcements made in Union Budget 2014–15 to establish 100 smart cities, robust manufacturing contribution to GDP, enhance industrialization, create new employment opportunities and further success of 'Make in India', it is expected to bring some reforms in infrastructure projects through the execution of the following tasks:

  i. Better planning and coordination across governmental institutions.
  ii. Project execution and monitoring discipline.
  iii. Greater participation from the private players.

Life Insurance companies are appropriate to fund infrastructure projects due to their long term liabilities. According to preliminary estimates published by the Reserve Bank of India; contribution of insurance funds to financial savings was 16.2 per cent in 2011–12, viz., 2.4 per cent of the GDP at current market prices. Development of the insurance sector is thus necessary to contribute in infrastructure investment and economic transformation.

---

[10] Sinha, S. & Sidharth, S. (2014). Long Term Financing of Infrastructure. *Working paper of IIM*, Ahmedabad, p.9.

Conclusion

The colossal task of financing infrastructure investment during the 12th plan would require a shift away from the traditional mode of bank financing towards other modes. Investment policies and regulatory guidelines for insurance companies need to be sufficiently flexible in order to invest larger amounts of long term funds for infrastructure-projects. The paper also shows that there is significance difference in mean percentage of infrastructure investment of all selected life insurers across the years.

Insurance and pension fund combined account for close to 32% of household savings in financial assets which is second to bank deposits. However, because of certain mandatory investment norms followed by insurance companies and various pension funds, very little of this money finds its way to infrastructure projects. At a time when the economy, and the nation, need long term funds to lay the foundation for future growth, insurance and pension sector provide the right balance in terms of volume as well in terms of tenor.

Insurance funds may be permitted to deposit part of their long-term funds with banks for infrastructure financing. Project evaluation and fund management skills at insurance companies need to be encouraged to develop specialized appraisal skills in the infrastructure projects.

The Government should look at launching some more infrastructure finance projects and should examine the possibility of infrastructure bonds carrying some sort of an explicit guarantee. This will immediately improve the rating of the projects and allow investment by insurance companies and pension funds.

The regulators should examine the possibility of allowing insurance companies to access the credit default swap markets to hedge their exposure to paper floated by the infrastructure projects. In a nutshell, improving investment demand seems to constitute the central pillar of the suite of solutions needed by the economy. Infrastructure reforms are indeed a paper tiger and are slowly showing its prowess, if implemented in its true spirit considering social implications as a successful model, it will help India to take a giant leap and stand into the league among the developed countries of the world.

References

Sahoo, S. & Saxena, K.K. (1999). Infrastructure and Economic Development: Some Empirical Evidence. *The Indian Economic Journal*. No.47, p.39–57.

Shah, A. (1992). Dynamics of Public Infrastructure and Private Sector Profitability. *Review of Economics and Statistics*. No.74 (1), 28–36.

Solow, R. (1956). A Contribution to the Theory of Economic Growth. *Quarterly Journal of Economics*. No.70, 65–94.

Kumar, N., & Dadhich, M. (2016). an Analytical Study of Life Insurance Facilities Provided by Life Insurance Companies. *SAARJ Journal on Banking & Insurance Research*. Vol.5, Issue 1, p.82–92.

Verma, A. & Bala, R. (2013). The Relationship between Life Insurance and Economic Growth: Evidence from India. *Global Journal of Management and Business Studies*. Vol. 3, No.4, p. 413–422.

Public Healthcare Workforce Absenteeism in India

Anurag Saxena*

Abstract

High prevalence of absenteeism among public healthcare service providers in Low and Middle Income Countries (LMICs) has been a long acknowledged problem. The high rate of absenteeism implies significant share of public healthcare budget is wasted and can have a significant negative impact on meeting health goals as specified in terms of Sustainable Development Goals, National healthcare policies etc. Though the issue of absenteeism among healthcare workforce is very critical in the context of LMICs, however, in existing literature, relatively less attention has been paid to studying absenteeism in LMICs. This research explores the causes of absenteeism among doctors working in primary health care centers in India. For understanding the causes of absenteeism 25 semi-structured interviews are carried out with doctors and district officers, and typology of factors influencing the rate of absenteeism is developed. Results of the study highlight that the causes of absenteeism can be broadly divided into two categories, namely, organizational factors and individual/personal factors.

Keywords: Public health, health workforce, absenteeism, India.

Introduction

For any healthcare system, timely availability of finance; infrastructure such as hospitals, dispensaries, furniture; healthcare workforce such as doctors, nurses, compounders; and other consumables such as medicines contribute to its proper functioning. However, of all these resources it is the healthcare workforce which has been said to be the most critical and at the same time most complex to obtain (European Union, 2008; Simoens & Hurst, 2006; WHO, 2007). Highlighting the importance of healthcare workforce, WHO (2006) stated that workers in a healthcare system acts as gatekeepers and navigators for useful or waste application of other resources available to it. Along similar lines, a number of studies and documents noted the important role played by the workforce in healthcare systems (Satpathy & Venkatesh, 2006; Sundararaman, 2007).

In a healthcare system, once a trained workforce is hired and posted at different dispensaries/hospitals, they are required to be present at their place of posting and

* Indian Institute of Public Health Gandhinagar

provide services to the people in need of care. However, it is not always so. High prevalence of absenteeism among public healthcare service providers in Low and Middle Income Countries (LMICs) has been a long acknowledged problem (WHO, 2006). In most of the LMICs, healthcare provider's salary constitutes more than 60% of the public healthcare expenditure. Hence, a high rate of absenteeism implies significant share of public healthcare budget is wasted. A high level of prevalence of absenteeism also results in reducing the effective availability of the workforce in the concerned healthcare system, thereby, it can have a significant negative impact on meeting health goals as specified in terms of Sustainable Development Goals, National healthcare policies etc.

Though the issue of absenteeism among healthcare workforce is very critical in the context of LMICs, however, in existing literature, relatively less attention has been paid to studying absenteeism in LMICs (Belita, Mbindyo, & English, 2013). This research work explores the causes of absenteeism among doctors working in primary healthcare centers in India. As per Indian Constitution, health is primarily a state government subject where state governments are responsible for maintaining appropriate health service delivery mechanism. This research work focuses on causes of absenteeism among doctors working in primary healthcare centers (dispensary) of one of the state government Department of Indian System of Medicine and Homeopathy (ISM&H). For the purpose of this study, absenteeism has been conceptualized as public healthcare workers being absent from work, when he/she is scheduled to be at work – unauthorized absence from work (Beil-Hildebrand, 1996).

Literature Review

Some large-scale studies have tried to gauge the extent of absenteeism among public healthcare service providers. Banerjee, Deaton, & Duflo (2004) carried out a study in Udaipur district of Rajasthan state for knowing the health status of the population, pattern of healthcare usage, and public healthcare facilities in the region. In the study 143 public healthcare facilities consisting of subcentres, PHCs, and CHCs were identified and doctors, nurses, other medical and non-medical persons posted there were monitored for a period of about one year. At the end of the study, it was found that during the period of observation rate of absenteeism among healthcare workforce in subcentres and aid post was about 45%, and for PHCs and CHCs absenteeism rate was around 46%.

In a large scale study by Chaudhury, Hammer, Kremer, Muralidharan, & Rogers (2006) rate of absenteeism among health workers in PHCs in India has been pegged at around 40%. In the study, 20 states in India were covered and a total of 1,350 centers were observed for a period of about 7 months. These studies indicate that absenteeism is quite common among public healthcare workforce in India. Moreover, if the presence of doctors in public healthcare facilities is erratic or infrequent then it is likely that given an option most often patients may choose not to go to public healthcare facilities. Thereby undermining the objective of the public healthcare system.

Method

For understanding, the causes of absenteeism 25 semi-structured interviews are carried out with doctors and district officers, and typology of factors influencing the rate of absenteeism is developed. Before starting the study, a meeting was held with the Director of the concerned Department. During the meeting, the scope and objective of the study were explained to the Director and an approval for undertaking the data collection was requested. The request was approved by the Director. Before conducting semi-structured interviews, informed consent was also obtained from the participants. All of the participants used to be contacted by telephone first to inform them about the objective of the study and a request to participate in the study. The contacted persons those who agreed to participate in the study choose time and place of their convenience and the researcher used to travel to the agreed location. During the interviews, contacted doctor's estimate of the prevalence of absenteeism among doctors working in primary healthcare centers of the Department was sought. Along with it, information was also collected on the reasons for which contacted doctors chose to be absent, and their observation about causes of absenteeism amongst fellow doctors.

Results

From discussions with doctors and District officers, it emerged that mostly doctors are available at their dispensary until 2 – 3 pm, however, most of them chose to leave dispensary after 2–3 pm. An attempt to create a typology of factors that have an influence on the absenteeism among doctors highlighted that these causes can be broadly divided into two categories, namely, organizational factors and individual/personal factors.

Organizational factors having an impact on the prevalent rate of absenteeism amongst doctors are those factors that are related to the characteristics and working culture of the organization. Analysis of the data highlight that the major factor that has a maximum impact on the absenteeism is the dispensary location. Most of the doctors contacted for this study emphasized that mostly the healthcare centers managed by the department are in remote areas where means of transport are irregular and doctors have to travel a long distance from their place of residence. Due to the long distance between dispensary and doctor's residence, doctors chose to leave their dispensary early so as to reach home on time – before it gets dark. Intermittent availability of means of transportation at the places where healthcare centers are situated also add to the anxiety among doctors to leave the facility bit earlier.

The doctors and district officers under consideration for this study were from the state government Department of Indian System of Medicine and Homeopathy (ISM&H). Doctors from these systems of medicines, generally do not cater to emergency cases, hence, mostly the patients coming to them are not facing immediate life-threatening situation. Realizing that their decision to leave dispensary bit early will not have any health consequences for the patients also makes it easier for doctors to choose to leave the dispensary early. During the course of the study, it was also observed that post 2–3 pm, hardly any patient come to the dispensary even when the doctor was there. Some doctors also pointed out that as most people in the area adjoining the dispensary are marginal workers, hence for any non-emergency case they prefer to see the doctor mainly during the morning hours – before leaving for their own job. So post-lunch break not many patients come to the center. It was also shared by the doctors that they have a 3 hour break between morning and evening OPD shifts. Sitting alone during the break and after the break waiting for patients make doctors feel bored, due to which they choose to leave early.

Another major reason that was quoted by most of the doctors was poor infrastructure at their dispensary in terms of lack of drinking water and clean toilet facilities (normally village panchayat common toilet facility is used by the doctors). Lack of these facilities has a negative impact on the willingness of the doctors to stay for long at their center and motivate them to leave early. During summer when the average temperature is high (in excess of 40 degree Centigrade), lack of air cooler and drinking water facility at the dispensary also make doctors reluctant to go to their dispensary. Lack of clean toilet facilities was stated by the female doctors as a major contributing factor in their decision to either leave early or not to come to work.

Another factor that influences absenteeism among doctors is the district officer's expectation from them. District officers are aware of the limitations faced by doctors at their workplace, hence, expect them to be on time at their dispensary in the morning and expect them to be there at least until lunch break. Also, in the studied department there is a lack of performance incentives (monetary/non-monetary) or corrective actions. The punishment action that is followed in the department is punishment posting – as a punishment doctors are posted in areas further from their place of residence. District officer's expectation, lack of performance incentives, and corrective action resulted in an atmosphere that is not motivating doctors to walk the extra mile required for delivering excellence in public healthcare services.

The personal/individual factors that were stated by the respondents as having an impact on absenteeism are related to perceived societal roles and responsibility, and health issues to the individual and in the family. Among perceived societal roles and responsibilities respondents shared things such as the need for attending a family function, making preparation for a religious activity scheduled on a working day. In the category of health issues, doctors responded that at time if someone in their immediate family is severely ill then there is always some chance of an emergency or need of an extra hand to take care of the family member. In such a situation, they chose not to go their dispensary.

Discussion

This research work aims to understand the causes of absenteeism among doctors working in primary healthcare facilities in Indian Public healthcare system and focuses on the doctors working in primary healthcare centers (dispensary) of the state government Department of Indian System of Medicine and Homeopathy (ISM&H). The results of this study highlight that two broad categories of factors have an impact on doctor's decision to remain absent from their place of work. These are organizational level and individual level factors. Organizational level factors highlighted by the study are facility location, working conditions, management expectation, lack of performance incentives, and corrective actions. Personal factors are societal and family duties.

Results of this study highlight a need to improve dispensary level infrastructure. The absence of required infrastructure support has a negative impact on doctor's morale where the magnitude of impact varies across gender. The results also highlight a need for ensuring meaningful engaged of doctors at the workplace. It will help in reducing the monotony that many times doctors posted in remote areas face while performing their duty. It will help in motivating the doctors and will ensure better availability of doctors at the place of their posting. The results of this study also highlight a need to put measures that can motivate doctors and help them in performing their job in a better way.

Conclusion

The results of the study provide insight into the factors that need to be focused on to reduce the level of absenteeism among doctors working in Indian public healthcare system. The results also highlight the need to improve governance in Indian public healthcare system. Overall the study contributes to building evidence on causes of absenteeism amongst LMICs.

References

Banerjee, A., Deaton, A., & Duflo, E. (2004). Health Care Delivery in Rural Rajasthan. *Economic and Political Weekly*, *39*(9), 944–949.

Beil-Hildebrand, M. (1996). Nurse absence—the causes and the consequences. *Journal of Nursing Management*, *4*, 11–17.

Belita, A., Mbindyo, P., & English, M. (2013). Absenteeism amongst health workers – developing a typology to support empiric work in low-income countries and characterizing reported associations. *Human Resources for Health*, *11*(34).

Chaudhury, N., Hammer, J., Kremer, M., Muralidharan, K., & Rogers, F. H. (2006). Missing in Action: Teacher and Health Worker Absence in Developing Countries. *Journal of Economic Perspectives*, *20*(1), 91–116.

European Union. (2008). *Green paper on the European workforce for health*. Retrieved from http://ec.europa.eu/health/ph_systems/docs/workforce_gp_en.pdf

Satpathy, S. K., & Venkatesh, S. (2006). Human Resources for Health in India's National Rural Health Mission: Dimension and Challenges. *Regional Health Forum*, *10*(1), 29–37.

Simoens, S., & Hurst, J. (2006). *The Supply of Physician Services in OECD Countries. OECD HEALTH WORKING PAPERS NO. 21*. Retrieved from http://www.oecd.org/health/health-systems/35987490.pdf

Sundararaman, T. (2007). Community health-workers: scaling up programmes. *The Lancet*, *369*(9579), 2058–2059.

WHO. (2006). *The World Health Report 2006 – working together for health*. Geneva.

WHO. (2007). *Not Enough Here...Too Many There...Health Workforce in India*. World Health Organization, Country Office for India.

Organizational Behavior and Women Employees in Corporate India: Milestones, Issues and Challenges

Sriram Soundararajan* & Upasana Singh**

Abstract

In the past 50 years difficult journey, Indian women, have come a long way. Indian women are now occupying the senior seats and leadership positions once filled by males and have silently begun challenging the conventional male ideas that had shaped the policies earlier. There was a study which compared performance of women on the board of Fortune 500 Companies, and found women to have positive effects that improve corporate performance. Catalyst (2007). What the study revealed and found was that when comparing the worst and best quartile of female representation, this had significant effects on the corporate performance. The study's resultant effects were 1. Return on Equity increased by 53%, 2. Profit Margin by 42%, and 3. Return on Invested Capital by 66%. One interesting area that the study further found was that a minimum of three women on the board gave the best results. A McKinsey (2007) study also confirms this relationship. The McKinsey study's main findings pointed out that companies with the highest gender diversity teams, as compared to the industry average, see a much higher Return on Equity (10%), a higher operating result (48%), and a stronger stock price growth (70%). It further added that having at least one woman on the board decreases bankruptcy by a full 20% (Wilson & Atlantar, 2009). Interestingly, as a result, companies with more women on their boards see better corporate governance and ethical behavior (Franke, 1997). But what remains a fact is that, even after decades of progress toward making women equal partners with men in the economy and society, the gap between them remains large. There is also a considerably significant body of research that shows for women, the subtle gender bias that persists in organizations and in society disrupts the learning cycle at the heart of becoming a leader. There were also prescriptions from the research that companies can take in order to rectify the situation. Indian corporate organizations today have some very high profile and talented women leaders since the days of male chauvinism, but are they doing enough is the question. What are the issues and challenges of women executives in India? This Case traces the careers of top Indian women executives and their journey so far.

Keywords: Organizational behavior, Corporate Women, Gender equality, Women leaders.

---

* IBS Business School Hyderabad
** JK Lakshmipat University, Jaipur

As you become more successful, the gender barriers disappear. The credibility challenges you have during your growing up years starts disappearing when you start demonstrating success. – Kiran Majumdar Shaw

For women, I would like to say—you have expertise, passion and love for work — so give something—whether it is in the profit or the non-profit sector. I feel it is a wonderful thing to spend that time and energy and balance families. – Meher Pudumjee

Plan better, be organized. I chose to be a working wife and mother. Why should I compromise on either? – Chanda kochhar

Kiran Mazumdar Shaw counts among the top women entrepreneurs in the country. Mazumdar Shaw joined Biocon Biochemicals Limited, Ireland as a trainee manager. She started the Indian arm of the company in the same year, soon after joining them. A garage space was rented by her in Bangalore and with an initial investment of Rs. 10,000 she commenced her entrepreneurial journey. The banks would not trust her initially and loans were a problem since biotechnology was a new field and women entrepreneurs back then were rare. There were some banks that would even ask her father to be guarantor. Recruiting and convincing people to join her startup were also an uphill task for her. A retired garage mechanic was her first employee. There were also problems related to Uninterrupted power, superior quality water, sterile labs, imported research equipment, and workers with advanced scientific skills. Despite all these hardships, she still did not give up and continued to work hard.

Her venture succeeded within the first year, after starting as an industrial enzyme manufacturer and commenced exporting to USA and Europe, started churning profits. With these earnings, they had enough money to buy a 20-acre property. Her main focus was on discovery of novel enzymes and novel techniques for development of solid substrate fermentation technology through research and development and that took the company's operations to a new dimension. In the year 1987, Narayan Vaghul **of ICICI ventures supported creation of a venture capital fund of USD 250,000.** and in 1989, BIOCON became the first Indian biotech company to receive US funding for proprietary technology studies. In the year 2004, Biocon went for an IPO which was oversubscribed 33 times. Infosys head honcho Narayan Murthy had advised her to follow this strategy. BIOCON also became the second Indian company to cross the 1 billion mark on the first day of listing. The capital raised through this IPO helped her in creation of affordable innovation and focus on cost-effective techniques and low-cost alternatives for drugs too.

Mazumdar Shaw, apart from making Biocon a great success story, has been involved with several philanthropic activities. A CSR wing called Bio coin Foundation that focuses on health, education and infrastructure in rural areas was started, while also supporting the Arogya Raksha Yojana and Mazumdar Shaw Cancer Centre in Bangalore. This has been Quite a remarkable journey for an entrepreneur who began her journey as a trainee and is now the 92nd **Most Powerful Woman in the World.**

Meher Pudumjee has been brought up in a family where education has been given the strongest value. Her parents always believed that if you educate someone, it's the best gift you can give them. Apart from values that her parents instilled in her at a young age, they also taught Pudumjee the freedom to make choices. There was never any obligation for her to join the family business, either while growing up or when she went to study engineering at the Imperial College London. By the time she graduated, her courtship with her fiancé (Pheroz Pudumjee, now her husband) was well under way and that pulled her back to India in 1990. That was also the first time she showed interest in joining Thermax, where she started as a trainee, along with 100 other engineering graduates that year. She had a dream to turn Thermax into a global provider of boilers and chillers, and the lady has been constantly chasing her dream. The company under her guidance has already made its presence in South East Asia, Middle East, Africa, Russia, India, the UK and the US.

In the business world, Pudumjee is rated a good listener. Naushad Forbes, director, Forbes Marshall, a competitor of Thermax in steam engineering and a personal friend, says, "Meher never tells people what to do; but always asks." Deep Anand, chairman, Degremont, a competitor of Thermax in the waste management space, admits that he has appointed Pudumjee on his board because "as a young corporate leader, I see her as a great role model for my daughter who will take over the business. Meher will never take the soft option." And Gautam Thapar, chairman, Crompton Greaves, says he values Pudumjee as an independent director on his board because "she doesn't shy away from asking questions directly until satisfied and often looks at the softer aspects of what we do."

Neelam Dhawan has had her fair share of failures before she acquired her glorious success. In fact, companies like Hindustan Lever Ltd. (now Hindustan Unilever Ltd.) and Asian Paints did not hire her as the HR people of these companies thought she did not have the spark in her. It was largely a stereotypical bias of the 80s and 90s that a woman cannot handle the role of the successful marketer. But Neelam Dhawan was not among the quitters, who accept failure too quickly. She was among the rare species, who are stronger than most of their contemporaries, including males. She was determined to venture into the unchartered territory of the IT industry of that time, that too in the role of a marketer, where no Indian lady had ever claimed any noticeable achievement. But, she successfully created history and became an inspiration for thousands of young ladies, who quit midway getting disheartened. the employers of her main field FMCG had closed doors for her and it led to her entry into IT and software industry in the field of marketing. Neelam Dhawan had a privileged childhood, where her parents never discriminated between girls and boys. She earned a graduate's degree in Economics from St. Stephen's College, New Delhi in 1980, followed by an MBA in marketing management in 1982 from FMS New Delhi. She was extremely dejected, when she was rejected by the FMCG giants such as Hindustan Unilever and Asian Paints but she had an undaunted conviction that she's made for marketing and her qualification at FMS New Delhi was a call of destiny. Her decision to join HCL was just to continue her marketing career and learn new insights. Surprisingly, she joined HCL as a trainee executive and continued working there for the next 14 years. Her career flourished with the growth of HCL until it became a brand name in the IT industry. She joined IBM as Vice President soon after her HCL stint and was a member of the company board of directors. HP was her next destination, where she was Vice President of customer solutions group, In HP, she was responsible for strategic growth of Alliances and partnerships. She joined Microsoft Corporation India Pvt Ltd in 2005 as head of Sales & Marketing Operations. She has been the Managing Director at Hewlett-Packard India Pvt Ltd. since July 1, 2008, with a portfolio that includes software engineering, research and IT services. She has been a Member of Supervisory Board of Koninklijke Philips Electronics NV since April 2012. Ms. Dhawan serves as a Director at HP India Pvt Ltd

Chanda Kochhar as boss of the country's largest private-sector lender, has to contend with the current bane of India's banking system: Bad Loans. The bank reported a double-digit increase in consolidated assets to $135 billion in 2015, but net earnings didn't rise as much, due to huge provisions for bad debts. ICICI Bank launched its Express Home Loan service offering mortgages online with approval in 8 hours. Among Kochhar's pet projects, was mobile banking, accounting for one-fifth of all transactions by retail customers, worth an estimated $12 billion in the year ended March 2016. Her bid to retain female staff, she launched iWork@home, which allows employees to work from home for a year and in addition, executives can take children under the age of 3 on business trips, with a caregiver, at the bank's expense.

It was in the year 1984 that Ms. Kochhar began her career, with the erstwhile ICICI Limited and was elevated to the Board of Directors of ICICI Bank in 2001. Ms.Kochar was instrumental in establishing ICICI Bank during the 1990s, and subsequently headed the infrastructure finance and corporate banking business in ICICI Limited. The year 2000, saw her take on the challenge of building the nascent retail business, with strong focus on technology, innovation, process reengineering and expansion of distribution and scale. The Bank achieved a leadership position in this business. She successfully led the Bank's corporate and international banking businesses, in 2006–2007, a period of heightened activity and global expansion by Indian companies. From 2007 to 2009, she was the Joint Managing Director & Chief Financial Officer during a critical period of rapid change in the global financial landscape. She was elevated as the Managing Director & CEO of ICICI Bank in 2009 and is responsible for the Bank's diverse operations in India and overseas. She also chairs the boards of the Bank's principal subsidiaries, which include India's leading private sector life and general insurance companies.

New initiatives for woman employees in Corporate India

There are many Indian organizations that have implemented pro women HR policies. This list includes some not so aggressive, but low key organizations that have progressive HR Policies. Ajuba Solutions India Pvt Ltd, (Ajuba is a premier provider of revenue cycle outsourcing services to healthcare systems, hospitals, academic medical centers, durable medical equipment suppliers, and billing and receivables management); provides the Top 5 HR Policies that worked for their women-force:

- Women's Forum Shakti: This forum connects all women employees and encourages them to come up with problems that they face at work and suggest ideas to improve the work environment. The core team drives many initiatives for the women employees at Ajuba.
- Gynecologist on Call: A qualified Gynecologist has been engaged especially for women employees at the health center of Ajuba called "Svasth Center". The Gynecologist provides consultation as well as counseling regarding contraception, pregnancy, diet and fitness for all women employees.
- Women's Lounge: A special lounge has been created in all the three facilities of Ajuba that offers a space to pregnant or unwell women employees for resting and relaxing.
- Flexi work hours: Taking into consideration the needs of employees who are also working mothers, Ajuba helps the women employees transition slowly back to work after their maternity leave by flexi work hours depending on their work and personal preferences.
- Programs focused on women: Ajuba conducts special programs for women employees consistently, to contribute to their holistic development. Some of the recent programs include self-defense program and breast and cervical cancer awareness programs. Each of these programs is developed exceptionally with utmost quality.

The Tata's are also right at the forefront of progressive women oriented initiatives. Tata Sons is rolling out a set of woman-centric policies that include paid maternity leave of seven months, 18 months of half pay-half working day post-maternity support, flexibility to choose work hours, secure performance ratings during the maternity leave and flexible work duration. Once you complete five years at work, you could avail of a one-year leave at half pay if you are a care-giver at home. Tata Sons has tailored interventions at various life stages of women — child birth, early childhood care, flexible working, cares for elderly and child.

The most vulnerable phase in a women's career is the period soon after maternity — almost 48% of women drop out at this stage," said Saundarya Rajesh, founder president of AVTAR Career Creators. "If a company were to manage the retention and performance of women in this career stage, almost 50% of the battle is won. Add to this a good measure of skill-building to ensure that attitudinal growth also happens — you have a perfect recipe for a gender balanced organization." TCS offered extended maternity leave, flexibility on the kind of roles one would like to opt for and even long leave during their kids' Class X or XII exams. The appointment of a Woman Chief in SBI has raised the expectations of the women employees at SBI and they look forward to fairer HR policies. In the words of Arundathi, "I think women employees have special problems and I will definitely try to be more sensitive to that," Bhattacharya said at her maiden interaction with reporters after taking over the reins of the country's biggest bank.SBI has decided to do away the cap of two transfers during a career to a location where the spouse is located, as there is a need to let couples work and stay together due to which we need to do away with the provision,". The woman MD of SBI has further said that as the head of the bank's investment banking arm SBI Caps, she had made a provision of a sabbatical of up to 6 years for women on first-come-first- served basis, with a cap of 5 per cent of employees going on such long unpaid leaves at a given time.

The Co-founder and Chief Business Officer of Shop Clues Radhika Agarwal said, "We have a holistic employee wellness policy. We have a corporate tie up with premium gyms and fitness studios to encourage our employees to lead a fit life. We arrange for regular health camps, nutrition talks, dental check-ups & self-defense workshop for female employees. Over the last one year, we have managed to attract top talent from different industries thanks to its employee-friendly work environment. Progressive Human Resource Policies such as flexi-timing, liberal leave policies, ample reward and recognition opportunities have played an important role in the high retention rates."

Accenture, a big name in the IT and KPO space gives 22 weeks of paid maternity leave, and eight weeks of fully paid adoption leave for primary caregivers of an adopted child. A big name like Google offers new mothers up to 20 weeks of paid maternity leave and seven weeks as adoption leave. It also reimburses up to Rs.10, 000 in expenses related to adoption. Vodafone has 16 weeks of paid maternity leave and one working week of paternity leave, but no adoption policy.

Challenges

Work Life Balance

Chitra Pandeya (51), like with most women, had to choose between family and career. But unlike many who chose family over career, she has held her own on both fronts. "Aditya Puri did not let me go; instead, he offered me a sabbatical where I had to work for four hours a day and the rest of the time, I could be with my daughter," said Pandeya. "I used to think when I climb to the top and look back to find my daughter stuck in step 1 that would not be a pleasant experience.

One of the early birds of HDFC Bank, in the early stages of its formation, was Ashima Bhat, 44, chose to stick around for more than two decades, riding the glorious wave that lifted the bank to the most valuable in India. "I was there even to decide the carpeting of the first branch," says Bhat. "As a part of the startup, I ended up doing so much more than what was in my job description. This made my work extremely exciting and challenging."

Gender Inequality

The subtle gender bias that persists in organizations, as revealed by significant body of research shows for women, disrupts the learning cycle at the heart of becoming a leader. This research further also points to some steps that companies can take in order to rectify the situation. The context must support a woman's motivation to lead and also increase the likelihood that others will recognize and encourage her efforts and It's not enough to identify and instill the "right" skills and competencies as if in a social vacuum.

Some of the Gender inequality related problems are stated below.

1. Mental harassment: Mental harassment is an age old convention that women are less capable and inefficient in working as compared to men. This attitude which considers women unfit for certain jobs holds back women, in spite of the constitutional provisions in India. Gender bias creates obstacles in their recruitment, and in addition to this, the same attitude governs injustice of unequal salaries for the same job. The true equality has not been achieved even after 61 years of independence. It puts strain on women to greater extent as compared to men, working in such conditions inevitably thus making them less eager in their career.

2. Sexual harassment: Sexual Harassment today, has become a serious problem for almost all working women, who are prone to it, irrespective of their status, personal characteristics and the types of their employment. Sexual harassment happens in public transport, at working places, educational institutions and hospitals, at home and even in police stations when they go to file complaints. It is shameful that the law protectors are violating and outraging the modesty of women.

3. Discrimination at Workplace: Indian women still face blatant discrimination at their workplaces, where they are often deprived of promotions and growth opportunities. But this doesn't apply to all workingwomen. It is shocking to find that a majority of working women continue to be denied their right to equal pay, under the Equal Remuneration Act, 1976 and are underpaid in comparison to their male colleagues. This is also usually the case in factories and labor-oriented industries.

4. Lack of Safety of Working Women: The orthodox mindset in the Indian society makes it difficult for a working woman, while travelling, to balance her domestic environment with the professional life. In some families, it may not be acceptable to work after six o'clock. There are some families that do accept these working hours and may experience considerable anxiety every day about a woman's safety while traveling. So many issues affect a working woman because she is closely protected or watched by her family and the society.

5. Lack of Family Support: Another issue that working women suffers from, is the lack of family support. Family restrictions don't support women to leave the household work and go to office. They also resist for women working till late in office which also hampers the performance of the women and this in turn affects their promotion. Workplace Adjustment and adjusting to the workplace culture, whether in a new company or not, can be intensely stressful. Preparing oneself to adapt to the various aspects of workplace culture such as communication patterns of the boss as well as the co-workers, can be a lesson of life. The issue of maladjustments to workplace cultures may lead to subtle conflicts with colleagues or even with superiors and in many cases office politics or gossips can be major stress inducers.

6. Other reasons include factors like age, level of education, marital status, number of children, personal income and number of jobs currently had where you work for pay and Work situation characteristics like job tenure, size of employing organization, hours worked per week.

Conclusion

The current ground reality in India is that even after decades of progress toward making women equal partners with men in the economy and society, the gap between them remains large. There is a general acknowledgement that gender parity in economic outcomes (such as participation in the workforce or presence in leadership positions); is not necessarily a normative ideal, as it involves human beings making personal choices about the lives they lead; we also recognize that men can be disadvantaged relative to women in some instances. The way forward for corporate entities in India is to follow a strategy that would focus on the large economic opportunity which would be a result of improving parity between men and women.

References

Bhakta, P. (2015, October 14). How Women Bankers like Chitra Pandeya, Anu Aggarwal, Ashima Bhat, Smita Bhagat could Well Become Top Executives in the Industry. Retrieved from http://economictimes.indiatimes.com/industry/ banking/finance/banking/how-women-bankers-like-chitra-pandeya-anu-aggarwal-ashima-bhat-smita-bhagat-could-well-become-top-executives-in-the-industry/ articleshow/49345275.cms

Bharati A., Arab R.O., and Masoumi S.S. (2015) Challenges and Problems Faced by Women Workers in India. Retrieved from http://www.nevillewadia.com/images/ Cronicle2015/Azadeh-Barati15.pdf

Chanda Kochhar, CEO-Managing director, ICICI Bank (2016). Retrieved from http://www.forbes.com/profile/chanda-kochhar/

Ibarra H., Ely R.J. and Kolb, D.M. (2013, September). Women Rising: The Unseen Barriers. Retreived from https://hbr.org/2013/09/women-rising-the-unseen-barriers

Meher Pudumjee, Pitching it Right (2007, December 21) Retrieved from http:// www.livemint.com/Home-Page/usgqVJu9VmbSgrowxnaj2I/Meher-Pudumjee--Pitching-it-right.html

Prerna R. (2013, January 20) Meher Pudumjee: Standing Tall. Retrieved from http://www.business-standard.com/article/specials/meher-pudumjee-standing-tall-111012300067_1.html#

Sharma A. (2011, August 10).Neelam Dhawan: Strong Indian Women Entrepreneur. Retrieved from https://www.boldsky.com/insync/life/2011/neelam-dhawan-indian-women-entrepreneur-100811.html

The Success Story of Kiran Mazumdar Shaw (2015) Retrieved from https://www.chaturideas.com/ic/The_Success_Story_of_Kiran_Mazumdar_Shaw#sthash.q5SjGiuw.dpufhttp://www.azquotes.com/quote/1067151http://prabook.com/web/person-view.html?profileId=725848

Woetzel J., Madgavkar A., Ellingrud K., Labaye E., Devillard S., Kutcher E., Manyika J., Dobbs R., and Krishnan M.(2015, September). How Advancing Women's Equality can Add $12 Trillion to Global Growth. Retrieved from http://www.mckinsey.com/global-themes/employment-and-growth/how-advancing-womens-equality-can-add-12-trillion-to-global-growth